THE
GREAT
LOCKDOWN

THE GREAT LOCKDOWN

LESSONS LEARNED DURING THE PANDEMIC FROM ORGANIZATIONS AROUND THE WORLD

SHIVAJI DAS
AROOP ZUTSHI
JANESH JANARDHANAN

WILEY

Library of Congress Cataloging-in-Publication Data
Names: Das, Shivaji, author. | Zutshi, Aroop, author. | Janardhanan, Janesh, author. | Frigstad, David B., author.
Title: The great lockdown : lessons learned during the pandemic from organizations around the world / Shivaji Das, Aroop Zutshi, and Janesh Janardhanan, with input from David Frigstad (Chairman, Frost & Sullivan).
Description: Hoboken, New Jersey : Wiley, [2022] | Includes index.
Identifiers: LCCN 2021033424 (print) | LCCN 2021033425 (ebook) | ISBN 9781119810421 (hardback) | ISBN 9781119810445 (adobe pdf) | ISBN 9781119810438 (epub)
Subjects: LCSH: COVID-19 Pandemic, 2020—Economic aspects. | COVID-19 Pandemic, 2020—Social aspects. | Quarantine—Economic aspects—21st century. | Economic history—21st century. | Organizational change.
Classification: LCC HC59.3 .D378 2022 (print) | LCC HC59.3 (ebook) | DDC 330.9/052—dc23
LC record available at https://lccn.loc.gov/2021033424
LC ebook record available at https://lccn.loc.gov/2021033425

SKY10030294_100721

Contents

Acknowledgments

Writing a book of such a scope seemed daunting at the beginning. There were 15 contributing organizations from around the world to coordinate with, their leadership teams, legal teams, corporate communications teams, all the way to their boards in some cases. We are very thankful to all the contributors for their time, patience, and consideration, but we are also extremely grateful to all whose names that have not appeared as contributors, but without whose support, this book would not have been possible: Anisha Jain of IndiGrid; Karen Pantinas, Michaela Mendes, and Thomas Merchant of Globalization Partners; Graeme McMillan of Fonterra; Anup Tiwari of SOS Children's Villages; Ceci Yen, and Audrey Chan of GOGOX; Anirban Mukhopadhyay of Abacus Pharma; and Arnd Einhorn and Katrin Meusinger of A. Lange & Söhne.

We are deeply indebted to Mr. David Frigstad, chairman of Frost & Sullivan, for his invaluable support and feedback at various stages of the book. We are also thankful to our colleagues at Frost & Sullivan, who provided important input toward this book.

We are immensely grateful to the team at Wiley for their incredible support throughout the journey of this book, from conceptualization to its final form. In particular, we would like to thank Brian Neill, content acquisitions editor, for his round-the-clock support and very timely interventions; Kelly Talbot, editor, for his sharp pen and his attention to every detail; and Mr. Jesse Wiley for having the confidence in us in developing this work.

Writing a book during the pandemic presented its own unique challenges, given that everyone's lives, including ours, were filled with many ups and downs. Some of us had to deal with personal losses while the whole world was grappling with grief and uncertainty. On that note, very special thanks from us to our partners, parents, children, extended families, and friends for constantly assuring us by providing a sense of normalcy while giving us the strength and confidence to pursue our initiative.

A final note of thanks from us goes to all the healthcare professionals, vaccine researchers, frontline staff, and volunteers in governmental and not-for-profit organizations around the world who have been directly or indirectly involved in managing the COVID-19 pandemic. Your courage, perseverance, and sacrifices are what have given us and everyone in the world courage and hope in continuing with our daily lives.

CHAPTER 1

Introduction

By Shivaji Das, Aroop Zutshi, and Janesh Janardhanan
With input from David Frigstad (Chairman, Frost & Sullivan)

OVID-19 has had an unprecedented impact on businesses and daily life. The virus forced the whole world to go into lockdown. As of May 8, 2021,[1] more than 3.2 million lives have been lost. The equivalent of 255 million full-time jobs were lost in 2020 alone.[2] Industries such as aviation and tourism saw massive declines. Countries, provinces, cities, and even neighborhoods imposed strict controls on movement outside their "borders." Airport terminals were closed, while schools and exhibition venues were converted into treatment and isolation centers. Political upheavals followed, and governments even toppled because of their supposed ineffective handling of the situation. People's behavior changed as they began washing groceries in soapy water and wearing masks when leaving their homes. Suicide rates increased in some societies.

In this context, organizations – for-profit and nonprofit – faced unforeseen challenges. Factories were shut down, supply chains were disrupted, receivables went unpaid, facilities had to be quickly transformed for alternate purposes, and employees fell sick, died, or struggled to turn up at work. Yet the impact was different for various industries. In response, enormous government support schemes were rolled out in major economies. With such support and through quick adaptation to the new conditions, most economies began to see better performance in the second half of 2020. As vaccinations gradually rolled out, the general expectation was that

---

[1]Johns Hopkins Coronavirus Resource Center. Accessed 8 May 2021. https://coronavirus.jhu.edu/map.html
[2]International Labour Organization. ILO Monitor: COVID-19 and the world of work. Seventh edition. 25 January 2021. https://www.ilo.org/wcmsp5/groups/public/@dgreports/@dcomm/documents/briefingnote/wcms:767028.pdf

2022 would witness a global GDP recovery to pre-pandemic levels, despite the devastating COVID-19 second waves in large economies such as India.

This book is an attempt to document the journey of a diverse group of organizations during this tumultuous period that began in early 2020. We selected organizations that come from industries that were most affected by the COVID-19 crisis such as Bangalore International Airport (airport), beCurio (travel), and Tapsi (ride-hailing). We featured organizations such as Terumo, Abacus Pharma (both in healthcare), and SAP (information and communications technology), from sectors that largely benefited from the crisis. We have also included not-for-profit organization such as SOS Children's Villages. These organizations come from all over the world: Uganda, Iran, New Zealand, Hong Kong, India, the US, and Norway, to name a few. We have also ensured that the featured organizations span the range from small and medium enterprises to large global conglomerates, and from young organizations to those with centuries of history. The contributing authors are all chief executive officers or senior leaders in their respective organizations, thereby providing a perspective on the different aspects of economic impact and strategy implementation in order to survive and rebound: human resources, sales, customer experience, finance, operations, technology, and so on.

While the long-term effects as well as any statistical evaluation of the impact of COVID-19 across organizations of different categories will be possible only a few years down the line, through our book we have sought to reveal the early findings of what helped these organizations survive and even excel during the present crisis. This might seem to present the book as a historical account of the business victors, given that many other organizations have disappeared over the last year. A point to note, however, is that the socioeconomic fallout of COVID-19 is far from over, and therefore one of the factors influencing our curatorial choices was to ensure that the showcased organizations have at least made it through the complete unfurling of the current crisis.

Before the Great Lockdown

The years 2010–2019 made for an eventful decade. Some of the world's largest economies saw leadership changes that had significant geopolitical consequences. Xi Jinping came to power in China in the early 2010s.

India elected Narendra Modi as prime minister in 2014, and political outsider Donald Trump won the US presidential election in 2016.

The decade saw the Occupy Wall Street protests in 2011, the Eurozone debt crisis, volatile oil prices, Brexit, the emergence of Black Lives Matter in 2013, skirmishes in the South China Sea, the European refugee crisis, rising trade tensions, natural disasters, and the #MeToo movement in 2017.

The world was also more interconnected than ever before. Global trade reached new highs. Approximately 4.5 billion passengers took a scheduled flight in 2019 – the highest number in history. Digital technologies touched businesses and personal lives in significant ways. E-commerce, m-commerce, streaming, and mobile payments were becoming hugely popular worldwide. Automation, artificial intelligence (AI), and robotics took center stage in multiple industries.

In 2018, Apple became the first company with a trillion-dollar market capitalization, quickly followed by Amazon, Microsoft, and Alphabet. Electric cars and solar-powered homes promised a new, sustainable future.

As 2019 drew to a close, the world looked forward to welcoming a new year and a new decade. The global economic prospects looked strong. There were big challenges to be tackled – climate change, income inequality, hunger, water, sanitation, peace – that needed the united attention of the entire world. While new technologies promised to address some of these challenges, the world had its work cut out for the next decade.

But there was troubling news coming out of China. On December 31, 2019, China alerted the World Health Organization (WHO) of 27 cases of viral pneumonia in Wuhan. On January 11, 2020, China reported its first death from the virus. By the third week of January, reports started emerging from Japan, South Korea, Thailand, and the US about cases of the virus. Fears of a scenario like the SARS epidemic of 2002–3 or the swine flu of 2009–10 took hold.

The Unfolding of the COVID-19 Crisis

The seriousness of the "novel coronavirus" became obvious when on January 23, 2020, China decided to completely isolate Wuhan, a city of 11 million people, from the rest of the country. Although only 17 people had died from the virus at this stage, the rising number of international cases showed how quickly the situation was getting out of control.

The WHO declared the disease a global health emergency on January 30.

By February 2, 360 people had died, including the first death outside of China – in the Philippines. On February 7, Chinese doctor Li Wenliang, who had tried to raise the alarm about the disease, died of it. On February 11, the WHO named the virus "Severe Acute Respiratory Syndrome Corona Virus 2 (SARS-CoV-2)" and the disease it caused as "Corona Virus Disease (COVID-19)."

The number of cases began rising sharply around the world even as travel to and from China was halted. By the end of February, deaths were reported in France, Italy, Iran, and the US. The situation was especially serious in Italy and Iran as cases and deaths surged. On March 11, the WHO declared the COVID-19 outbreak a global pandemic. By the end of March, the US led the world in the number of confirmed cases at more than 81,000, with over a thousand deaths. By the end of April, the global deaths surpassed 200,000, with confirmed cases touching 3 million and affecting over 170 countries worldwide.

Hospitals around the world struggled with shortages of isolation wards, beds, ventilators, and personal protective equipment (PPE), and there was no clear line of treatment for COVID-19. Countries had to figure out ways to "flatten the curve," which meant reducing the number of community transmissions in such a way as not to overwhelm hospitals and ICU capacities. Unprecedented times called for unprecedented measures, and countries turned to lockdowns, partial or complete.

By March 20, 2020, countries such as Italy, Saudi Arabia, Denmark, Ireland, Poland, Iran, Spain, the Netherlands, the Philippines, Brazil, Canada, France, Switzerland, Belgium, Malaysia, Argentina, Portugal, and the US had announced either a national or region-specific lockdown. On March 24 India announced a 21-day lockdown for its 1.3 billion people – the longest during the pandemic. By the end of March, over 100 countries had implemented a nationwide or partial lockdown.[3]

Lockdowns severely disrupted economic activity. For the hundreds of millions of people who depend on daily wages, this meant having no income – and consequently no food. Some governments sprang into action with relief and support programs. In many cases, it fell far short of what would be needed for those most impacted.

---

[3]Coronavirus: The world in lockdown in maps and charts, BBC News, 7 April 2020. https://www.bbc.com/news/world-52103747

The economic disparities and the digital divide in society became even more pronounced during the COVID-19 lockdowns. Millions of logistics and gig economy workers put themselves in harm's way to deliver food and other essentials. While families with computers and good Internet connections switched to online schooling, others who didn't have the means to do so were forced to suspend or stop education.

The COVID-19 pandemic also witnessed something of a healthcare miracle. A vaccine for the disease was developed in less than 12 months – the fastest ever in the history of mankind.

The impact of the COVID-19 lockdowns varied greatly across industries and geographies. While many industries saw a sharp decline as people had to stay at home, others saw a sharp increase in users and, consequently, revenues. An estimate in 2020 by growth advisory firm Frost & Sullivan of the relative impact of COVID-19 on specific industries is presented in Figure 1.1.

In hindsight, it is incredible how, at least in some industries, the advancements in Internet infrastructure over the past 10–20 years enabled the world to switch gears, go online, and resume activities during the lockdown. Many in professional services could conduct their operations remotely. The work-from-home economy flourished as hundreds of millions of people leveraged Internet-enabled tools to collaborate, stay online, and, in many cases, achieve higher productivity levels when compared to physically going to their offices. In addition, business models needed to be rethought as concepts like the gig economy witnessed exponential growth during the pandemic for most sectors. The market capitalization of Internet collaboration companies such as Zoom shot past those of aircraft manufacturers such as Airbus – signifying how important Internet collaboration was in 2020 compared to how the market valued the prospects of air travel. Manufacturers and their supply chains adjusted quickly as well.

However, some industries such as airlines and tourism continued to suffer. Government support programs in the developed economies ensured that many companies stayed afloat. Yet global real GDP declined by 3.3% in 2020 – with some major economies such as the UK witnessing a GDP decline of 9.9%, India 8%, Germany 4.9%, Japan 4.8%, and the US 3.5%.[4] To cope with such disruption, organizations had to adapt fast.

....

[4]Real GDP Growth. 2021. International Monetary Fund. Accessed 08 May 2021. https://www .imf.org/external/datamapper/NGDP_RPCH@WEO/OEMDC/ADVEC/WEOWORLD

COVID-19 IMPACT ON KEY INDUSTRIES, 2020

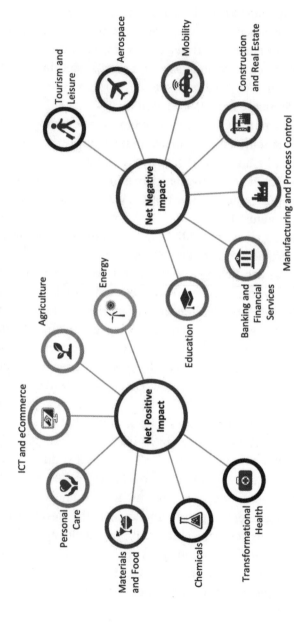

FIGURE 1.1 Relative impact of COVID-19 on specific industries. *Source: Frost & Sullivan.*

A mix of strategies was deployed by organizations, large and small, to restart operations, protect jobs, serve customers, and prepare for a long period of uncertainty. Some businesses such as Burger King made the hitherto unthinkable decision of running a campaign asking customers to visit competitors so that the whole restaurant sector would have some reprieve. Some organizations even saw this as an opportunity to gain a permanent competitive edge. "Survive and rebound" became the mantra of the times.

By the third quarter of 2020, the global economy began reversing its downward trend, led by large economies such as the US and China. A baseline forecast of the overall economic impact of the pandemic is shown in Figure 1.2.

As shown in Figure 1.2, the baseline estimate forecasted that growth would accelerate to 5.7% in 2021, driven by the strong release of demand by mid-2021, extended fiscal support measures, steady deployment of vaccines, and easing restrictions in the second half of the year. The rise is also partially supported by a low GDP base from 2020.

Among the most remarkable insights from the lockdown was the light it shone on practices we had taken for granted prior to the lockdowns. Do we all really need to work from offices? Is so much office and retail space necessary? If we can work remotely, do we need to live in large cities? Why did it take COVID-19 to demonstrate the convenience of e-commerce? Do we honestly need to travel for business and have face-to-face meetings as frequently as we did? COVID-19 also put a spotlight

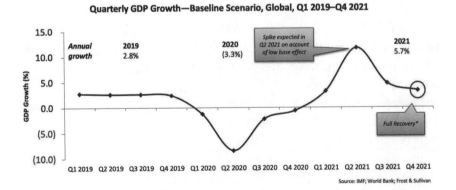

FIGURE 1.2   Overall economic impact of the pandemic. *Source: IMF, World Bank, Frost & Sullivan.*

on other aspects of globalized business we take for granted. Can we truly afford supply chain concentration in a single country or region? What level of inventory is ideal? Should we rethink liquidity thresholds to weather such storms? Can countries afford to depend on other countries for necessities such as masks, gloves, and so on?

The "new normal" during COVID-19 also saw organizations confront a new set of challenges of the virtual world. How can we build a corporate culture without physically meeting the teams? How do we keep employees engaged at home? How do organizations that depend on relationships and face-to-face interactions with clients maintain their engagement virtually? What should organizations do for employee mental health and well-being?

Survival and Rebound Strategies in the Context of COVID-19

This book seeks to reveal strategies that helped many organizations ride through a crisis of such unprecedented magnitude. We hope these strategies can serve as rough templates for organizations to adopt in case there are future disruptions of a similar nature, whether future pandemics, terror attacks, natural disasters, or political strife. Our examination of the overall landscape as well as the deeper insights each contributing author provided into their own organizations suggest that there are certain commonalities in the way businesses successfully strategized and acted to survive and rebound through the pandemic. (See Figure 1.3.)

During the early days of the pandemic, much of the strategy revolved around overcoming the immediate challenges faced by organizations in merely keeping themselves afloat. This called for tactical speed and ingenuity rather than long-term vision as the magnitude of the crisis was still unclear. As most organizations learned how to cope with the economic downfall that followed, some of them used this opportunity to strengthen their position in the market. At different junctures of the pandemic, each of the components listed in the flywheel carried varying degrees of weight. The constituents of each of the strategy flywheel's key components are discussed below.

FIGURE 1.3   Strategy flywheel.

- **Customer Focus:** When lockdowns were first announced, many organizations faced challenges in delivering goods and services to their customers. Call centers and help desks couldn't be manned. Certain industries such as restaurants, tours and travel, and aviation witnessed a near-complete shutdown. Many organizations coped with such disruption by adopting a combination of measures:

  o *Customer protection:* As the virus began spreading exponentially and the science behind transmission was still at a nascent stage, delivering products and services with utmost care became the most important concern for most businesses. This was important not only to save lives but also to limit potential bad press and litigation. Some even went the extra mile to ensure customer safety despite the huge costs involved. Packaging and delivery instructions were redrafted, face-to-face customer services were no longer provisioned for, and social distancing compliance ambassadors were appointed in large public areas such as malls and airports. Bangalore International Airport in India was among the first airports in the world to roll out a contactless passenger journey. In Iran, the ride-hailing company Tapsi instituted new rules to limit the number of passengers allowed in their vehicles and closely monitored driver health via their app. Even smaller organizations tried offering some respite to their customers from lockdown anxiety and stress by providing access to webinars on managing mental health. Over time, such actions, whether altruistic or otherwise, provided a significant branding boost to their corresponding companies.

o **Revenue protection:** Everywhere, even large buyers began delaying supplier payments to protect their own liquidity. In industries such as travel and airlines, cancellation requests were rampant. In this scenario, revenue protection became an urgent need for organizations to survive. This was largely done through a combination of contractual enforcements, insurance claims, service obligation extensions, extended credit terms, and delayed or reduced reimbursements. Enterprise software firm SAP introduced flexible financing options for customers in need of extended payments. Employment services firm Globalization Partners, which enables organizations to hire talent in over 180 countries without setting up branch offices or subsidiaries, passed along government grants to customers as cost refunds to help them keep their team members employed.

o **Revenue servicing:** In situations where organizations were still obliged to deliver the product or service despite the disruptions, they responded through service deferrals, advanced notice of product delivery delays, alternate offers, service obligation extensions, or outright cancellations when nothing else was possible. In Norway, international travel concierge beCuriou guaranteed refunds to all their customers and thus retained their confidence.

o **Customer engagement:** As both business procurement and individual consumption nosedived during April–July 2020, brands feared being forgotten by their customers. To stay relevant and present and possibly even increase customer loyalty, organizations deployed a variety of measures. B2B service providers increased their outreach to clients through webinars. Sales staff were urged to double up client calls and emails. Consumer-oriented companies conducted online games and talks. Online newsletters, which had fallen into oblivion, were relaunched. Constrained by social distancing and travel restrictions, the German luxury watch brand A. Lange & Söhne engaged with customers through online events and video conferences. The New Zealand–based dairy cooperative Fonterra took to TV shopping channels in South Korea and online cooking demonstrations in China to engage with customers.

o *Reinvention of offerings:* For many organizations, business as usual was just not possible anymore. Despite all efforts, the external environment was such that it was impossible to claw back to their trend-line revenues. To seek alternate revenue streams, airlines converted their planes into restaurants, while auto manufacturers started making ventilators. Services and products that had previously been planned for the future were now launched into action. The key considerations for the design and delivery of such alternate products and services were a) speed of delivery, b) revenue potential, c) limited upfront investment, d) synergies with core business by targeting existing clientele or by repurposing infrastructure and manpower, and e) unmet needs in the market. While Uganda-based Abacus Pharma recalibrated its product mix to cater to the landscape of changing demands, the Iranian ride-hailing firm Tapsi introduced shopping assistance and delivery services using their resources. Among other initiatives, Bangalore International Airport introduced a food and beverage preordering service that flyers could access via smartphones.

• **Workforce Engagement:** During the lockdown, organizations struggled to operate in ways that had previously been taken for granted. Lockdowns affected delivery staff, employees couldn't come to the office, and business travel became impossible. Soon it was clear that layoffs or pay cuts would need to be made. As conditions stabilized in some countries, employers began to provision for operations with reduced staffing in adherence to prevalent guidelines. Anecdotal evidence points toward a change in pattern wherein CEOs spent much longer on matters related to human resources (HR) during the pandemic. The HR function also became a lot more important during this period. Many organizations coped with such disruption by adopting a combination of measures:

- ○ ***Employee protection:*** The first and foremost concern in this respect was to ensure the safety of employees and protect them from workplace-related transmissions. The first reaction, whether forced by governments or voluntary, was to shut down facilities. Most service-sector organizations managed reasonably well by shifting to a digital mode of working. As things improved in the second half of 2020, better-prepared organizations erred on the side of caution and continued remote working. Best-in-class organizations in the manufacturing, logistics, and other sectors where the physical presence of employees in some capacity was essential provisioned for sufficient safety measures by ensuring safe distancing or an ample supply of gloves and masks. Splitting employees into teams that were required not to access workplaces at the same time, ubiquitous hand sanitizers, temperature taking, and leveraging contact tracing became commonplace. Hong Kong–based logistics platform GOGOX even extended free life insurance coverage to all their logistics partners and their families.

- ○ ***Employee morale:*** Managing employee morale was not easy in the context of remote working, pay cuts, and furloughs. Seeing colleagues lose their jobs was also very demotivating. Virtual team building or counseling sessions didn't prove as effective as envisioned. Successful organizations managed this through greater transparency about financial challenges, substantially higher frequency of communication with employees, providing greater flexibility at work, compensating employees in alternate ways, and management setting an example by taking the most severe pay cuts. Key roles were identified and engaged at the highest level of management to ensure their retention during the crisis. Bangalore International Airport set up a 24/7 helpline to extend support to employees. Some companies, such as beCurio, even saw an opportunity to hire new talent, which was widely available in the early days of mass layoffs. Indian power infrastructure investment trust IndiGrid launched medical packages and well-being programs to provide financial assistance to employees.

- **Financial Periscope:** Organizations big and small faced severe financial stress during the pandemic. Customers delayed or defaulted on payments, new business was hard to chase, and cost of operations went up given the need for extra precautions, reduced supplier options, and required investments in going digital to enable work from home while doubling down on cybersecurity measures. Non-profits witnessed massive declines in donations and grants as their patrons faced financial stress. Best-in-class organizations were fast in projecting worst-case scenarios, forecasting by weeks and months, and reacting early to avoid those. Organizations coped with the ensuing financial disruption by adopting a combination of measures:

o *Cost avoidance and postponement:* Most organizations delayed big investment plans, whether they were in the form of office leasing or renewals, hiring plans, big software or facilities upgrades, or new product launches. Certain investments (e.g., digitalization initiatives) were prioritized over others because this was seen as a way to enable working during the new normal. In the US, purpose-built head-worn devices maker RealWear put new product development on hold and eliminated paid marketing to reduce costs.

o *Cost reduction:* Facing the uncertainty brought about by COVID-19, organizations rapidly cut expenditures to preserve liquidity and reduce costs. This was achieved through furloughs, layoffs, early termination of facilities contracts, and so on. For instance, social network company Hornet decided to go fully virtual and cut office and travel expenses. RealWear negotiated with suppliers to reduce supply and inventory. In Iran, Tapsi had to send almost half their staff on furlough and cut salaries of executives to conserve cash.

o *Leveraging grants/relief:* In many advanced economies, governments opened their purse strings to help companies – small and medium organizations in particular. Many organizations set their financial and legal teams on high alert to lobby, scan, and apply for any available government relief. This went on to become the lifeline for most companies in highly stressed sectors such as food and beverages, aviation, and the like. For instance, the US Paycheck Protection Program (PPP) provided direct incentives for small businesses to keep their workers on payroll and was credited with saving millions of jobs during the pandemic. Globalization Partners secured government grants in every country where they were eligible and passed along benefits to their customers. In Norway, international travel concierge beCuriou was able to secure grants from the government to fund operations.

o *Payables management:* Organizations large and small tried to delay payables as much as they could and push for receivables as fast as possible. This often resulted in unethical behavior as well as violation of contracts, and larger organizations enjoyed a much greater bargaining power in this matter. Some companies, though, went ahead and even made advance payments to their suppliers to help their cash positions. This was done either out of solidarity or to preserve critical or valued suppliers from disappearing. In Uganda, Abacus Pharma was able to negotiate extended payment terms from suppliers on the back of their long-standing relationships and strength of payment records.

o *Raising capital and building a war chest:* Organizations that saw the longer-term impact of suppressed revenues and increased costs due to safety considerations raised funds to weather the storm and also explore potential acquisition opportunities during the pandemic. In India, IndiGrid preemptively raised INR 12.83 billion through a rights issue. In the US, Globalization Partners raised USD 150 million in January 2020 and secured a PPP loan from the government. SOS Children's Villages issued a global humanitarian appeal and raised funds for special needs during the pandemic. Hornet raised a working capital note, allowing them to end 2020 with a 65% stronger cash position compared to 2019.

o *Insurance claims:* For organizations that had insurance for pandemics, business cancellations, and similar disaster coverage, insurance claims provided some relief.

o *Utilizing lines of credit:* This was another key component of survival strategy for large organizations, especially in the context of government support provided to financial institutions as part of pandemic-related relief measures to extend lines of credit to their clients.

• **Operational Resilience:** As the lockdowns affected operations of factories, warehouses, offices, ports, retail outlets, and service stations all around the world, organizations had to first scramble and then put together a systematic plan for dealing with the disruptions. An added dimension to this was the flurry of export controls imposed by governments of major producing economies. These factors called for a complete redesign of operations and supply chains by addressing the following:

- **Work process continuity:** For service organizations, this involved shifting to a full digital mode. This transition involved managing the fast provision of hardware and software for a large number of employees with adequate cybersecurity and privacy measures. For manufacturing and logistics organizations, it was about restarting workplaces by redesigning them and adjusting shifts to allow for social distancing as well as provisioning for other safety measures in line with the latest government and scientific guidelines. Swiss private banking corporation Julius Baer, for example, successfully implemented "Temporary Pandemic Workplace," an initiative to allow employees to access work data remotely in a stable and secure manner. Globalization Partners helped employees set up home offices, and some of their offices prepared mobile hotspots for employees to take home to help address connectivity issues.

- **Supply chain continuity:** Organizations had to overcome the shortage of raw materials and the closure of warehouses, ports, logistics providers, distribution outlets, and service centers. In some cases, prices and fees for such services skyrocketed. While large organizations engaged alternate suppliers by activating existing risk management plans, some even had to invest in key suppliers and customers to guide them as they underwent similar transitions in their own operations. While Abacus Pharma's practice of maintaining a higher level of supply helped ensure operational continuity, Japanese healthcare manufacturer Terumo quickly found alternate suppliers when their syringes and needles plant in the Philippines was impacted by the lockdown.

- **Supply chain diversification:** One of the fallouts of the pandemic was the interplay of the resulting economic stress with geopolitical tensions and ongoing trade wars. Several organizations undertook relocating production and service centers outside of China, with Mexico, Vietnam, the US, Japan, and Taiwan emerging as preferred alternate centers.

In addition to the considerations mentioned in the flywheel, the foundational base of many best-in-class organizations served them well in overcoming the economic fallout of the pandemic. This manifested through the organizations' culture, digital maturity, and risk management systems.

In general, the organizations with a culture of transparency, openness, innovation, and empowerment did much better. They communicated the financial stress and forecast to all the employees frequently and early; explained possible scenarios for pay cuts, furloughs, and layoffs; and obtained buy-in for such measures. Since the pandemic called for fast decisions on measures to overcome localized challenges, those organizations with distributed empowerment and a culture of innovation also fared well.

The pandemic taught all organizations globally the importance of rapidly achieving a level of digital maturity that allowed employees to work remotely and effectively while interacting with the entire diversity of stakeholders. This involved the provision of digital communication and collaboration tools, requisite hardware and software, supply chain management software, and other related tools. While larger organizations had capable in-house systems and sufficient capacity, the ability to leverage cloud-based tools set successful smaller organizations apart from the rest.

Finally, it was the practice of risk management in organizations that enabled them to react quickly and effectively to all the pandemic-induced challenges. The pandemic is a once-in-a-lifetime event, and preparing risk management systems and plans for such events is unusual and even costly. However, organizations that maintained a certain level of risk awareness and preparedness for typical risks related to market, finance, regulations, supply chain, and the like were better equipped to cope more effectively during the pandemic.

Certain other initiatives from the contributing authors' organizations stood out for their speed, novelty, and impact. In New Zealand, Fonterra redirected capacity to produce hand sanitizers. US-based RealWear innovated rapidly by partnering with Tencent of China to develop a joint solution to help healthcare organizations with contactless temperature screening and remote video support, enabling frontline workers to communicate with remote senior staff members. In Uganda, Abacus Pharma housed workers in a local school to comply with a health ministry requirement to house workers near factories in order to meet increasing demand.

Enterprise software firm SAP improved corporate health insurance policies for all employees and their families.

In Hong Kong, to facilitate government health check arrangements, GOGOX launched a saliva pickup service for people placed in quarantine. To measure performance while navigating the pandemic, Japanese healthcare equipment manufacturer Terumo switched from a twice-a-year performance management system to a monthly dashboard-based crisis management system focused on 20 key performance indicators. Power infrastructure investment trust IndiGrid organized weekly townhalls and catch-up sessions to enable transparent two-way communications. Swiss private banking corporation Julius Baer switched to video conferencing and scanned signatures to open new accounts while observing safe distancing.

Witnessing a rapid fall in demand for ride-hailing and a sharp increase in demand for deliveries, Tapsi in Iran quickly designed new offerings to cater to the changing market landscape. To protect their staff, employment services firm Globalization Partners decided that their entire global team would work from home, even in places that hadn't yet seen the virus, and accelerated the deployment of necessary infrastructure. Preparing for growth beyond the pandemic, German luxury watch brand A. Lange & Söhne invested in the expansion of their stores and added locations in Kuala Lumpur, Riyadh, Seoul, Dubai, and Houston.

In this chapter, we have provided a general overview of the survival and rebound strategies of organizations. The subsequent chapters showcase the individual stories of a wide variety of organizations and detail specific examples of their approach. These chapters provide lessons for organizations on coping not only with the ongoing pandemic, but also with other possible unexpected and disruptive events in the future. And while these strategies seem prima facie to be potent in overcoming disruptions brought about by events such as the COVID-19 pandemic, in essence they are also strategies for sound management of organizations under any circumstance.

CHAPTER 2

A. Lange & Söhne

By Wilhelm Schmid (CEO)

About A. Lange & Söhne

In 1845, Dresden watchmaker Ferdinand Adolph Lange laid the cornerstone of Saxony's precision watchmaking industry by establishing the first Lange manufactory in Glashütte. The family was expropriated after World War II. In 1990, the founder's great-grandson Walter Lange revived the brand. Today, A. Lange & Söhne has once again secured a top-tier position in the world of fine watchmaking.

Dark Clouds on the Horizon

In January 2020, shortly after the public holidays, I sat down with our product developers to talk about the prototypes for the next collection. After a "normal" 2019 financial year, the prospects for the watchmaking industry were generally good, despite some uncertainties that, however, were within the normal range. A. Lange & Söhne had just emerged from a sensational premiere. In October 2019, we had presented the first model for a new, sporty, and elegant watch family. The Odysseus, our first watch made of stainless steel, had attracted attention worldwide. For a factory that had until then exclusively used gold and platinum for its cases, this was considered a revolution. With a second Odysseus in white gold with a rubber strap – another novelty for us – we wanted to build on this success in 2020.

We planned to present six new timepieces in April at Watches and Wonders in Geneva, which has become the most important trade show of international precision watchmaking since the demise of Baselworld. As many debuts again were supposed to follow during the rest of the year,

FIGURE 2.1   "Homage to F. A. Lange" anniversary editions, left to right: 1815 Thin Honeygold, 1815 Rattrapante Honeygold, and Tourbograph Perpetual Honeygold.

including three limited collector's editions for a special occasion: the celebrations to mark the 175th anniversary of Saxon fine watchmaking. (See Figure 2.1.) Its founder, Ferdinand Adolph Lange, was also the namesake of our company. The first and second generations of the family had brought A. Lange & Söhne world fame. The brand's high-precision pocket watches were the epitome of "Made in Germany" luxury in the 19th century. They are still highly sought after among collectors all over the world.

After World War II, the family-owned business domiciled in eastern Germany, south of Dresden, was expropriated, and the name A. Lange & Söhne temporarily almost fell into oblivion. In 1990 – immediately after German reunification – Walter Lange, the founder's great-grandson and himself a watchmaker, ventured to start over again. Today, only a few thousand wristwatches are made at Lange each year. They are endowed exclusively with proprietary movements that are lavishly decorated and twice assembled by hand. With 67 sometimes extremely intricate caliber developments, A. Lange & Söhne occupies a leading position in international fine watchmaking.

The special characteristics of the company profile include the duality of being both global and regional, which has also been noticeable in the pandemic, as we will see. A. Lange & Söhne is a global luxury brand that is distributed worldwide and thereby focuses on its own boutiques as well as premium retail. However, behind the fine timepieces is a company shaped by craftsmanship and with regional roots and high added value. Most of the around 750 employees work in the watch production at the headquarters in Glashütte.

Our business model is based very strongly on the interpersonal exchange with our retailers and customers. The first thing I learned when I took over the management of A. Lange & Söhne ten years ago was that I had to meet our concessionaires regularly and that the personal encounters with leading representatives of the company mean a great deal to our end customers.

The 175-year jubilee of Saxon fine watchmaking was to run like a common thread through the entire communication in the anniversary year. It would have also been the entry to a lecture on the relationship between tradition and innovation, which I was to give in mid-February at CEIBS (China Europe International Business School) in Shanghai. I therefore followed the first news of an unknown virus in Wuhan closely. When the conference was canceled at the end of January 2020, and the World Health Organization declared a "public health emergency of international concern" shortly afterward, I had a premonition that many things would go differently this year from how we had planned.

The First Wave

COVID-19 affected the European watchmaking industry – and therefore also A. Lange & Söhne – severely and suddenly. In mid-January 2020, the first COVID-19 infection was detected outside of China, and by the end of the month, the virus had already reached Germany. The Robert Koch Institute – Germany's central authority for disease prevention – assessed the risk to the population as "low to moderate" at the end of February,[1] but the Bundestag declared an "epidemic situation of national importance" just one month later. To contain the pandemic, there were extensive restrictions to public life in Germany – as in many other countries – from

---

[1] Handelsblatt, 28 February 2020, Das Risiko für Deutschland ist gering bis mäßig einzuschätzen.

mid-March 2020. Travel restrictions, business closures, and curfews were ordered worldwide.

The measures led to a strong decline in demand and therefore to dramatic sales slumps, first in Asia and later in almost all other markets too. As early as February, many stores were closed or only open for a few hours a day, not only in China but also in other Asian markets. People stayed at home, avoided travel, and only consumed the necessities. The Chinese tourists who had until recently bought watches in many of our stores worldwide had disappeared.

At times, almost 75% of our boutiques and points of sale worldwide were closed. Many orders were subsequently canceled. The Wempe jewelry chain, one of the most important retailers for A. Lange & Söhne in Europe, found it necessary to temporarily introduce short-time work.[2] The export figures for the Swiss watchmaking industry, still foremost in Europe, had recovered considerably over the summer. For example, the exports in August were only 12% below the previous year's level, after the deficit in April, at the peak of the lockdown, had been at 81%. For the year overall, a decline of 25 to 30% was nevertheless expected.[3]

At the same time, the contact and travel restrictions had enormous effects on the production and working conditions in Germany. We were only affected by the disruptions to the supply chains to a small extent, like the majority of Swiss watch manufacturers.[4] The reason for this was that the parts for our movements are almost completely produced, decorated, and assembled in our factory in Glashütte. Typical supplied parts like dials, leather straps, and watch boxes originate from German or other European suppliers, who, in turn, predominantly produce these themselves. Although there were border closures within Europe, they were not severe or prolonged enough to have a sustained negative impact on the value chain. There were, on the other hand, logistical difficulties in the delivery of finished watches to China and other Asian countries, as many airlines had suspended traffic temporarily.

---

[2]Handelsblatt, 24 September 2020, Kim-Eva Wempe in the interview Geld ist wirklich nicht alles.
[3]Ibid.
[4]Neue Zürcher Zeitung, 4 March 2020, Das Coronavirus trifft die Uhrenindustrie hart.

Riding the Wave

In early autumn of 2020, after the first wave had subsided in Europe and large areas of Asia, it was time to draw up a first interim balance. There were contradictory signals from the watchmaking industry concerning the recovery after the global lockdown. On the one hand, watchmaker shops reported queues in front of their doors for particularly sought-after models. On the other hand, even well-established watch manufacturers had to announce redundancies.[5] As a result of store closures as well as the collapse of international tourism, the exports of the Swiss watchmaking industry decreased by almost 22% in terms of value in 2020. Compared to the quartz crisis of the 1970s, when a technology change brought the watchmaking industry to the brink of disaster, this was comparatively small. The slump was, however, similarly burdensome as the one during the global financial crisis of 2009 and considerably stronger than in other export industries of the country.[6]

Important industry barometers for A. Lange & Söhne were the Watches and Wonders Geneva watch fair, held only digitally for the first time in April, and Watches and Wonders Shanghai, held as an attendance fair again in September. On both dates, it was apparent from the publications and order figures that the interest in our watches and the underlying watchmaking artistry had not diminished. Given the unclear situation, however, we only presented three debuts for the time being, with due caution, instead of the six we had planned: the Odysseus in white gold in two different versions and the Zeitwerk Minute Repeater in white gold with a blue dial in a limited edition of 30 exemplars. We presented the three references of a newly designed Lange 1 Time Zone, which had also originally been planned for the Geneva show, two months later in June, only virtually again. As a watch designed for people who work and communicate in a globally networked world, it fit the mood of the time exactly.

As a result of the continuing travel and contact restrictions, two essential elements of our marketing mix had been taken from us: encounters with

---

[5]Neue Zürcher Zeitung, 17 September 2021, Nicht nur Königin Rolex wird diese Krise gut meistern.
[6]Neue Zürcher Zeitung, 7 February 2021, Corona hat der Schweizer Uhrenindustrie nicht nur geschadet.

people and the direct product experience during factory tours, trade shows, and brand events as well as in our boutiques and at specialist retailers. Compensating for the effects of the pandemic on customer communication and relationships was, therefore, our highest priority. Our marketing department managed to develop visually stunning forms of presentation with impressive speed. After we had launched our debuts digitally, I had a number of Zoom conversations with customers from all over the world – something that neither I nor many of our customers would have thought possible just a few months earlier. Conversations like these take place in an atmosphere that is as pleasant and relaxed as we can offer in our boutiques. We are able to show close-ups of the movements and to simulate what the watch looks like on the wrist.

The measures adopted in Germany to contain the pandemic had the most serious effects on our business processes. To protect employees from infections, the distances between the watchmakers' workspaces had to be increased. In addition, we converted operations in the factory to two shifts. We are unable to perform any factory tours at all until the end of the pandemic. Employees in the administration, marketing, and sales departments have been working from home as far as possible since spring 2020. In this situation, it was of benefit to us that we had already been practicing location-independent work in such central areas as sales and marketing for a long time, and the associated issues of technology and data security had been solved. Meetings now take place only as video conferences. Business trips have been reduced to those that are absolutely necessary.

Since we are thinking beyond the pandemic and assume positive business development in the long term, we have further invested in the expansion of our own stores. In 2020, the locations in Kuala Lumpur, Riyadh, Seoul, and a second boutique in Dubai were added. (See Figures 2.2 and 2.3.) At the beginning of 2021, we opened our sixth boutique in the US, in Houston. We had not planned any large investments beyond these. Our new construction of the factory, put into service five years ago, is designed for growth, in a forward-looking manner, and is state of the art.

It has been particularly reassuring in this situation to know that we have a strong group behind us. In light of an expected recession, Richemont's management already informed the employees of all the subsidiaries in March that, on the basis of a prudent investment strategy and foresighted liquidity protection, the group had the necessary resources to

FIGURE 2.2   A. Lange & Söhne, Dubai.

FIGURE 2.3   A. Lange & Söhne, Seoul.

confront a challenge like the current one. Beyond the financial aspect, issues such as cybercrime, IT infrastructure, supply chains, and international sales logistics are so important to us, and the support of a globally operating group is of inestimable value.

Navigation through Stormy Times

The pandemic is one of the great challenges of this century. Lockdowns, travel restrictions, and canceled trade shows have led us to find creative solutions to maintain our business models under the altered framework conditions. In this regard, the focus has been placed on the human factor. We are taking more care than ever to ensure that our employees, our customers, and the whole company are doing well.

With respect to A. Lange & Söhne, I am pleased that the interest in our watches did not decline in the anniversary year that was so important to us. We were able to carry out all the planned product launches, even if they were predominantly digital and spread throughout the year, including the previously mentioned Lange 1 Time Zone (see Figure 2.4), which was designed for people who work and communicate in a

FIGURE 2.4   Lange 1 Time Zone, launched in June 2020.

globally networked world. We regularly have digital meetings to keep in touch with our markets, retailers, and customers. Even before COVID-19, we already considered digitization an important topic and that has now benefited us. It meant that we were able to use the time during the lockdown profitably to prepare our next steps – from sales by telephone to the question of how we develop our online sales. Among our customers, the pandemic has brought about a noticeable – and, in my view, sustainable – change to purchasing behavior, whereby both these issues became unexpectedly topical. The employees in the factory became accustomed to shift work, and working from home has become a well-functioning routine. Nevertheless, we perceive COVID-19 as a turning point. The "new normal" is a disruptive phase that forces us to shape the change actively and to use the resulting advantages strategically.

The pandemic has made us aware of how quickly and flexibly we can adapt to even the most radical changes. In this way, we have gained new, valuable experience from which we will benefit in the future. But however good the virtual alternatives may be, they are no substitute for the direct product experience, the "goosebumps" feeling that our customers experience when they pick up an A. Lange & Söhne. This is precisely why online sales of watches had only ever played a subordinate role in our business model in the past. There were e-commerce plans in case our customers' buying habits changed at some point; in this sense, we did not meet the development unprepared. But the time had come to press ahead at full speed with our projects in this category.

Digitization will also occupy the industry this year. We will not, however, neglect everything else that is important to us. Cultivating watchmaking artistry, developing exciting timepieces, and expanding our global retail network will remain our priorities. In regard to the future, we are determined and confident. We have highly qualified and motivated employees in whom the typical Lange pioneering spirit is very much alive. And we have used 2020 to ensure that we are ready for when the economy picks up again.

After the Storm

At the time of this writing – February 2021 – the pandemic has not yet been overcome. But effective vaccines are available, and there is hope that most of the population in the major national economies can be protected against COVID-19 by the summer. In individual markets, such as China, the recovery began a long time ago.[7] With contained occurrences of infection, the American and European markets should be able to follow suit by the second half of 2021. By the end of the year, the situation for the watchmaking industry should have normalized to a large extent, although many positive effects may only become visible during the course of 2022.[8]

Similar to after the first lockdown in summer 2020, a mixed picture is still present: in the high-price segment, demand is proving to be astonishingly robust. According to the study "The State of Fashion 2021" by the management consulting firm McKinsey, this can be traced back to the fact that it is hardly possible in the present circumstances to treat oneself to intangible luxuries such as travel or events. And so instead, people are buying themselves jewelry and watches in the upper price range, as these are considered an investment, at the same time.[9] This is consistent with our own observations that strong (i.e., authentic and internationally positioned) watch brands held their own in 2020, as they fulfill the wish for truthfulness, credibility, and lasting value. Brands with this profile have the potential to develop better than the market after the pandemic. This means they have the best chances to emerge from the crisis even stronger.

A. Lange & Söhne has not changed in its essence during the crisis. The craftsmanship that shapes our way of working cannot be completed by working from home. But where we can, we work on demand, remotely, with minimum contact, with consideration for each other and at a distance. Some of this will remain after the pandemic ends. Within the possibilities that their work offers them, people will be able to decide more freely how and where they wish to work.

The year 2020 was a milestone in digital transformation. And the advantages of digitization will last beyond the pandemic. A higher level of flexibility and efficiency, lower expenses for travel, and a reduction in CO_2 emissions – the benefits of remote collaboration have become clear in many situations and will ensure a further impetus for digitization. The infrastructure established, the adapted working methods, and the strongly increased level of acceptance provide a solid basis for this.

Since the watchmaking industry lost its most important attendance fairs, online channels have become even more vital than they already

[7]Neue Zürcher Zeitung, 3 December 2020, Hainan statt Hongkong: Wo die Chinesen seit Corona Schweizer Luxusuhren kaufen.
[8]See also McKinsey & Company, The State of Fashion 2021, page 14. https://www.mckinsey.com/industries/retail/our-insights/state-of-fashion.
[9]Ibid., page 34.

were before. This does not mean, however, that the direct brand and product experience has become obsolete. In fact, in the future, it will come down to the intelligent combination of offline and online to offer the customer emotional added value. The organizers of Watches and Wonders recognized the signs of the times and used the experiences of 2020 to broaden the second digital edition of the Geneva watch fair in April 2021 with interactive elements like live chats and streaming options. For the platform, expanded considerably compared to the previous year, we developed a series of innovative formats that involve the participants as actors in the events. We see a continuing trend here. At Watches and Wonders 2021, for example, A. Lange & Söhne presented exciting new timepieces on a digital platform created explicitly for this purpose. One of them was the Triple Split, which measures lap and split times up to 12 hours. (See Figure 2.5.)

FIGURE 2.5   Watches and Wonders 2021 expanded the digital offerings.

Consumer behavior now demonstrates more sustainability, and this development will continue as well. Timelessness, value preservation, service, and reliability will determine purchasing decisions – far beyond the watchmaking industry – even more strongly than to date. These are aspects on which we have always focused, and the market has recognized these efforts. The auction results achieved during the pandemic are good indicators that A. Lange & Söhne enjoys a strong brand equity. At Phillips' Geneva Watch Auction in November, a rare A. Lange & Söhne Datograph from 2009 in yellow gold sold for the equivalent of USD 208,000, roughly four times its original retail price. Only one month later, an almost new Odysseus in stainless steel changed hands at Phillips New York for USD 81,900, more than almost three times the original sales price. All this shows that a love of mechanical watches is deeply ingrained in people. Neither the quartz crisis almost 50 years ago nor the rise of the smartwatch has been able to change anything about this. After the financial crisis, the watchmaking industry quickly found its center again. I am firmly convinced that it will manage to do so again after the pandemic.

A. Lange & Söhne used 2020 to work intensively on the development of new timepieces, to strengthen the relationships with retailers and customers, to expand digital offers, and to prepare for the reviving global economy. With exciting debuts, an attractive offer for the online purchase of watches, and the first events in the second half of the year, 2021 promises to be a good year for A. Lange & Söhne. Moreover, we are confident and are preparing ourselves with calm, patience, and determination – the classic fundamental virtues of watchmaking – for the challenges of tomorrow.

Never Stand Still

The founder of our company, Walter Lange, who passed away in 2017, once said, "There is something one should expect not only of a watch but also of oneself: to never stand still." To celebrate the 175th anniversary of the Saxon precision watchmaker, the town of Glashütte erected a memorial to him, in which his attitude is expressed by a suggested step forward. We have internalized this and made it the guiding principle for our actions.

The "never stand still" philosophy urges us not to persist in the status quo but rather to work with our gaze directed at new target groups on the further development of an essentially traditional industry, to which we continually give new impetus with scientific findings, technical innovations, and skilled craftsmanship. It is in this spirit that we think beyond overcoming the pandemic and its consequences to the next steps and act with our customers as closely as possible in order to remain successful in the long term. So what exactly are the challenges of tomorrow?

There are three main topics we have to address on a daily basis. First, our employees work in Glashütte, but our customers are located all over the world. We have to bring Glashütte to the world and the world to Glashütte. This is a continuous task that demands our creativity every day anew. The second challenge is the classic dilemma of all luxury brands, of not being able to be exclusive and mainstream at the same time. On the one hand, we must become increasingly well known and continue to grow. On the other hand, our watches are designed for connoisseurs. A. Lange & Söhne should remain an insider brand whose identity is not revealed to just anyone straight away. The third point concerns the relevance of the brand for the next generation. Even if it seems unlikely that young people begin their entry into the world of mechanical watches with an A. Lange & Söhne, they should feel the fascination of the brand and experience the feeling that it can bring them joy in the future.

The Great Lockdown has made us aware of our strengths. We know that with creativity, expertise, flexibility, discipline, and endurance, we can master not only crises but also the challenges of the future. That is why, regardless of all adversities, we have never ceased to invest in growth, to work on the development of our products, and to strengthen our sales channels. All the turning points in our history have taught us that the key to success lies in finding ways out of a difficult situation and growing by doing so.

About the Contributor

 **Wilhelm Schmid** was appointed Chief Executive Officer of Lange Uhren GmbH as of January 2011. He holds a diploma in business administration and was previously employed in senior positions in sales and marketing at BMW in Germany and South Africa as well as at the Burmah Oil Company, Germany, where he started his career.

CHAPTER 3

Abacus Pharma

By Rajaram Sankaran (Group CEO of Abacus Pharma)

About Abacus Pharma

Abacus Pharma, a portfolio company of the Carlyle Group, is one of the largest pharmaceutical distributors and manufacturers in East Africa. Established in 1995 in a small warehouse in Kampala, Uganda, Abacus has since grown to become a USD 100 million+ revenue company, distributing over 600 pharmaceutical products and also becoming the largest parenteral manufacturer in the region. With a wide network of 43 branches, Abacus serves a large percentage of East Africa's population and provides direct employment to over 1200 people. It aspires to be Africa's number one health and wellness company across a wide spectrum of health products and solutions in the next few years.

Backdrop

Access to quality healthcare remains a challenge in Africa, with fewer than 50% of Africans estimated to have access to modern healthcare facilities. The World Health Organization (WHO) estimates that Africa carries 25% of the world's disease burden but has less than a 1% share of global health expenditures. This problem is exacerbated by the fact that Africa still has a mere 3% share of global pharmaceutical production.

This necessitates the need for strong, homegrown pharmaceutical companies with the ability to distribute life-saving medicines to the farthest reaches of the region while also investing in local manufacturing to reduce the region's reliance on imported medicines.

The East African Community (EAC) estimates that East Africa's pharmaceutical market is worth approximately USD 2 billion, with Uganda contributing more than 20% (roughly USD 450 million) to that number. East Africa comprises six countries in the African Great Lakes region: Burundi, Kenya, Rwanda, South Sudan, Tanzania, and Uganda. Kenya is the largest pharmaceutical market in this region, with an estimated market size of over USD 750 million, followed by Uganda and then Tanzania.

With a population of roughly 177 million people and a combined GDP of USD 193 billion (2019), together with an average GDP growth of 6.5% (2018), East Africa is the fastest-growing region in Africa. This region has significant unmet medical needs, and with local manufacturers meeting only 30% of the total demand, the pharmaceutical industry in this region is one of the most attractive investment sectors in the entire continent.

Founded in 1995, Abacus Pharmaceuticals aims to provide access to life-saving pharmaceuticals across East Africa by establishing local pharmaceutical production capability and partnering with international suppliers to provide locally branded generic products or affordable medicines from abroad. We are headquartered in Uganda with direct operations across Kenya, Tanzania, Rwanda, and Burundi, and a presence across the continent.

Starting from a small warehouse 25 years ago, we have grown to become one of the East African region's largest pharmaceutical companies, with annual revenues exceeding USD 100 million in 2019, an increase of roughly 20% from 2018. We have two main lines of businesses: distribution, which contributes around 80% to our top line, and manufacturing, which contributes the remaining.

We opened our own manufacturing plant, Abacus Parenteral Drugs Limited (APDL), in 2009 with an initial investment of roughly USD 30 million and have now grown to become the largest parenteral manufacturer in East Africa, supplying over 35% of the market demand.

In 2019 Abacus reached new heights, with our core Uganda distribution business growing faster than the market, together with new frontiers coming up in the form of our local manufacturing and Kenya business, both of which grew faster than the company.

The increasing importance of local manufacturing to our business was evident in the fact that our manufacturing plant had its highest ever contribution to gross margins in 2019. We also manufactured a record of approximately 70 million units of parenteral in 2019 with capacity utilization of more than 90% in a market where average plant utilization hovers in the 60–70% range.

First Signs

With the WHO declaring COVID-19 a global pandemic on March 11, 2020, it was increasingly evident that COVID-19 would have a major effect on the global economy and completely upend the way the world conducted business. Uganda recorded its first case on March 22, 2020, 11 days after the WHO declaration.

This was also a time when the company was going through a leadership transition. Our newly appointed group CEO, Rajaram Sankaran, had just taken the reins after a successful stint at the global pharmaceutical company Abbott's India arm. The transition happened completely virtually due to the global pandemic. A number of key leadership team members had just joined the organization or were in the process of being hired. To top all of this, the leadership team and board members were in multiple time zones at that time; the countries included Kenya, South Africa, India, Canada, and the US.

The leadership team, accustomed to working in high contact, office-based settings, would now have to pivot to a completely virtual model in a matter of days. The Abacus team was more than ready to take up the challenge.

We had started preparations well before the first case in Uganda was recorded. Cases had already been confirmed in some countries where Abacus operated, such as Kenya, and a number of our suppliers in countries such as India and China had already sounded the alarm.

Abacus has always been an employee-first company, and with employee safety in mind, a newsletter called "Precautions for COVID-19 at Abacus" was circulated to all employees three days before the first case was recorded in Uganda. A slew of measures was announced, with an additional set of measures being taken at our manufacturing plant to ensure employee safety.

Hand sanitizers were installed at key locations within the Abacus premises as well as at all our branches and our manufacturing plant, with all employees requested to use them regularly. The security personnel at all entry points were equipped with no-contact infrared thermometers, and any employees showing symptoms of fever were asked to work from home. Regular fumigation and deep cleaning of the Abacus premises were also carried out. Our customer-facing team (medical representatives and branch employees) were also provided nose masks to ensure safety. (See Figure 3.1.)

FIGURE 3.1 An Abacus Pharma branch with masks and social distancing.

A few days later, the Ugandan government also announced a number of stringent measures to curb the spread of COVID-19 in the country. Four days before the first case, public gatherings were suspended for 32 days with immediate effect. A mandatory 14-day quarantine was declared in government-designated hotels for foreigners arriving in the country, together with a ban on incoming and outgoing travel from highly affected countries.

Restrictions were gradually increased, with public transport also being banned and a 14-day national lockdown declared from April 1, with a nationwide curfew in place from 7 p.m. to 6:30 a.m.

Navigating the Great Lockdown

The lockdown had an immediate impact on the way Abacus conducted business, with management taking measures to ensure smooth functioning of the company during the lockdown. With the government allowing essential businesses to operate with limited staff, all the department heads were asked to identify key staff within their departments/teams who would work during this time.

We arranged for transport for all these employees to ensure that they could commute to and from the office safely. Additionally, our hours of service were reduced by one hour in order to ensure that all employees could reach their homes before the curfew. Face masks were made mandatory at the office.

The Abacus board increased the frequency of its meetings from once every month/quarter to daily, taking into account the rapidly changing business environment. The leadership team effectively leveraged the power of remote working, with regular virtual meetings at all levels, including the group CEO, to ensure proper reporting and collaboration. All team members located in other time zones changed their working hours to ensure that they were available for most of East Africa's office hours.

Meanwhile, with the new CEO taking the reins, a number of key leadership team additions were also made, with the focus on being a diverse and high-performing team.

With one of our executive directors who handled HR transitioning to an advisory role, a new position of group chief human resource officer (CHRO) was created. A new chief financial controller was hired to augment the efforts of the chief financial officer (CFO) in managing the company's finances. A new head of business development and chiefs of staff were hired, who would help facilitate global collaborations and handle strategic projects for the organization.

Looking back, the new leadership team and other strategic hires were key in helping create our effective pandemic response strategy, bringing a fresh perspective from their experience in top companies globally.

The pandemic also had an immediate impact on the heart of our business – our supply chain. Over 80% of our revenues still came from our distribution business, and this was immediately impacted due to scaling down of production in the factories of our key suppliers, the majority of which were based in countries such as India and China.

The raw material supply of our plant was also adversely impacted because the majority of it came from foreign suppliers based in countries such as Saudi Arabia, India, and China. This disruption manifested itself in terms of shipping delays and an increase in shipping costs. Due to Uganda being a landlocked country, the majority of our goods arrive by sea at Mombasa, Kenya, after which they are transported by trucks to Uganda.

Containers that used to take roughly 45 days to arrive by sea now had a transit time of more than three months. The delay happened not only at sea but also at the Mombasa port due to limited employee strength and COVID-19 testing protocols. The increased processing time at Mombasa led to a delay of 15–30 days, contributing to the massive increase in transit time.

Considering the adverse situation, the Abacus team looked at a number of alternatives, such as procuring certain key consignments by air. This, coupled with higher shipping rates, led to an increase in our logistics costs.

New orders were also impacted, with most suppliers refusing to take new orders or taking only small orders until they were back to full capacity. By virtue of operating in a landlocked country and due to its leadership position in the market, Abacus maintains a very healthy stock level compared to its competitors to ensure there is enough supply in the market in the event of a supply chain disruption.

For most of our top products, there was both a strong pipeline of orders and a good inventory level at our warehouses. This ensured that there was a minimal shortage of essential medicines in Uganda and also served as a competitive advantage for us, with Abacus acting as the sole supplier for a number of key medicines in the first few months of the pandemic. We were also able to ensure that our branches, some of which operate in the most remote corners of East Africa and are the only reliable source of medicines to the people in those areas, were well stocked and able to service the people most impacted by the pandemic. (See Figure 3.2.)

Meanwhile, our manufacturing facility had to remain closed for 15 days, from March 30 to April 15, due to a health ministry requirement to house staff at the factory. This led to losses, and a solution had to be found that would meet regulations while also ensuring that the factory kept running. Time wasn't on our side because a plant closure for a longer period could lead to a parenteral shortage in the East African region.

Large-volume parenterals (LVPs) such as Saline and Ringer's Lactate solution were being used extensively for COVID-19 treatment, and any supply disruption could have had a major impact on the pandemic response of East African countries. We found an innovative solution that ensured the safety of workers while also ensuring that the factory kept operating.

We enlisted the help of a local school nearby, which agreed to house the workers. Schools had been closed as per government directives, and this arrangement would provide a single place for accommodating

FIGURE 3.2 Abacus Parenteral Drugs Limited provides essential supplies to the Ministry of Health, Uganda; left to right: Commissioner in-Charge of Public Emergencies Dr. Allan Muruta; Director General of Health Services Dr. Henry Mwebesa; Abacus Board Director Gertrude Wamala Karugaba; Abacus Co-Founder and Board Director Ramesh Babu.

workers while also providing them a source of income during this period. We made sure that all the requirements of the workers were taken care of, including accommodation, food, and transport to and from the factory. Shift schedules were changed to ensure that curfew was followed while not affecting production.

Proper standard operating procedures (SOPs) were put in place to ensure worker safety. Personal protective equipment (PPE) was made compulsory, and social distancing measures were introduced to minimize worker interaction. Machine installations were made remote where possible, and maintenance workers were provided accommodation at nearby hotels to minimize disruption. (See Figure 3.3.)

The pandemic led to a change in the demand landscape across countries, with many once-popular therapeutic areas seeing minimal demand while a number of other therapeutic areas saw increased demand. The populations of the countries in East Africa are some of the youngest in

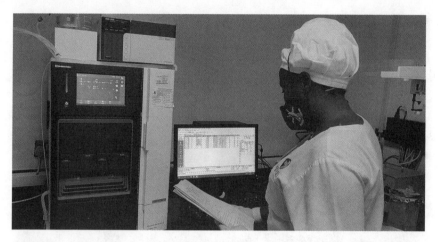

FIGURE 3.3 An APDL quality control team employee at the manufacturing plant.

the world. For example, approximately 47% of Uganda's population is estimated to be below the age of 15. The impact of school closures was seen immediately in decreased demand for a number of key medicines prescribed by pediatricians, especially for cough and cold, with some of these medicines seeing an almost 70% decline in sales.

Our range of locally manufactured eye drops saw a major fall in demand due to ophthalmologists keeping their operations closed for an extended period of time. On the flip side, a few life-saving antibiotics such as azithromycin saw increased demand due to panic buying by pharmacies as well as stockpiling by individual customers. Products such as multivitamin tablets and oral rehydration solution (ORS) sachets also saw an increase in sales, driven by an increase in preventive medication.

A portfolio strategy was designed by the management to ensure that areas of increased demand were appropriately tracked and catered to, which would also supplement the decline in demand for other products. We also created a special Abacus COVID-19 task force, whose job was to ensure regular supply of PPE to customers across East Africa. This PPE included protective clothing designed to protect the wearer's body from various hazards, including communicable diseases. There was a major surge in PPE demand, driven by the increase in preventive measures being taken across countries.

Abacus was receiving regular queries for these products because there was a major shortage of gloves and masks in the market, with local manufacturers still working on repurposing their production lines and being unable to meet local demand. On the strength of our supplier relationships, we were able to procure these products and supply them to our customers at competitive prices.

With the pandemic taking a toll on the economy, the liquidity of many of our customers was affected. Collections were impacted, with many customers requesting an increase in their credit period. A number of our institutional partners also delayed payments due to cash flow issues and a general funds shortage in the region. A subset of these customers even had to file for bankruptcy, with Abacus recovering only a small amount from each of them during the liquidation process. However, we still had an obligation to pay our suppliers.

This is where our relationships, nurtured over 20-plus years, came into play. We were able to negotiate extended payment terms with a number of our key suppliers on the strength of our payment record. We were also offered credit lines by most major banks in the region, in case we needed them. With enough cash in the bank and a strong cash conversion cycle, we faced no major liquidity issues during the pandemic.

However, cost reduction initiatives were still put in place throughout the organization, considering the need to conserve cash in case this situation went on for a longer time. The plant team was able to decrease unit manufacturing cost by roughly 20% in just one year by driving operational efficiencies in the plant.

The Abacus team also embraced the virtual way of work, where possible, which drove additional cost efficiencies. We are proud to say that while we implemented these cost efficiencies, we were still able to ensure that there was no reduction of salaries and no permanent employee of Abacus lost his or her job in 2020. A proper communication line was established with the HR team to ensure that every employee was aware of the steps being taken by management at all times.

Future Outlook

Abacus had planned to expand its reach in its key markets even further in 2020–2021 by opening new branches in Uganda, Tanzania, Rwanda, and Burundi. This would be further supplemented with additional investment in the plant to have a wider portfolio of products. Plans were also in place to expand Abacus's reach to new markets such as French West Africa and Kenya.

A few of these plans had to be put on hold during the first few months of the pandemic. However, with our continued strong performance and the liquidity issues faced by competitors, we were able to capitalize on opportunities presented to us while also restarting most of our expansion projects.

Abacus was able to acquire seven branches in Uganda as a part of company's liquidation process, immediately growing our distribution network in Uganda from 24 to 31 branches (an increase of roughly 30%), at a fraction of the cost of building these from scratch. We were also able to secure USD 12.5 million in funding in record time from the IFC for our plant expansion project, in what was almost an entirely virtual process.

With the pandemic affecting the way we work, there was a significant slowdown in the regulatory process as well for all countries. For example, in Uganda, no registrations were approved between January and June 2020, compared to 40+ products the previous year in the same period. New products contribute 2–3% to Abacus's top-line, and this was lost due to a slowdown in the approval process.

A similar situation was seen for regulators in Tanzania, Kenya, Rwanda, and Burundi as well. However, the situation is slowly changing, with the Ugandan National Drug Authority (NDA) significantly increasing the pace of registration approvals.

The outlook for the pharma industry overall appears positive, with supply chains having now stabilized and most planned projects still proceeding according to plan, albeit with minor delays.

However, there has been a significant decrease in greenfield foreign direct investment (FDI) for both Uganda and Kenya for the period of January to September 2020 compared to the same time the previous year, and it is yet to be seen how long it would take for the rest of the industry to recover. (Uganda saw no greenfield FDI for January to September 2020 compared to USD 416.5 million in January to September 2020; Kenya saw an 85% decrease, with greenfield FDI of roughly USD 200 million in January to September 2020 compared to USD 3.5 billion in January to September 2019.)

In May 2020, the Ugandan government received USD 491.5 million from the IMF, of which 70% was used to boost foreign exchange reserves, which helped keep the currency stable. Exports have also not been impacted in both Uganda and Kenya, and the economies in the region are expected to keep growing, albeit at a slower pace. Imports dipped temporarily due to supply chain disruptions in April and May but have largely recovered.

We have a positive outlook for 2021 and plan to launch a number of initiatives to further grow our business. Abacus plans to launch its Kenya distribution business in the next few months, while APDL plans to expand to Zambia and Malawi while also looking for opportunities in other geographies. The plant expansion project is expected to get started in 2021, with completion expected by 2022.

Supply chains have largely recovered, with FDI inflows also expected to recover in the next few months. The pharmaceutical sector in East Africa has shown remarkable resilience in the face of the pandemic. On the bright side, the COVID-19 pandemic has demonstrated the issues with Africa's reliance on external suppliers for its pharmaceutical needs. Many global suppliers looked inward during the pandemic period, with even the "Pharmacy of the World," India, restricting exports of key pharmaceutical supplies for a short period during the pandemic.

We feel that the pandemic will accelerate the move toward local manufacturing, with many countries in the region enacting more procurement incentives to encourage local manufacturing. This is already happening in Uganda, with the National Drug Authority (NDA) proposing a 25% import duty for eight molecules whose products are manufactured outside the EAC. Our conversations with regulators also indicate the same, with all of them mentioning a major impetus from local governments to support local jobs, considering the economic devastation caused by the pandemic. (See Figure 3.4.)

The EAC, in its 2nd Regional Pharmaceutical Plan of Action 2017–27, has already set a target of reducing the region's pharmaceutical imports

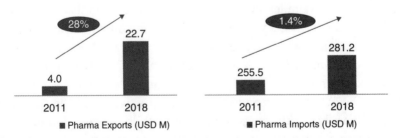

FIGURE 3.4   Uganda's pharmaceutical exports are growing much faster than its imports. Exports are expected to grow at an even faster rate after the pandemic. Source: UN COMTRADE.

from 70% to 50% and has set a target for governments to procure at least 50% of their requirement from local manufacturers. The African Continental Free Trade Area (AfCFTA), the largest in the world in terms of participating countries, commenced trade from February 1, 2021.

These initiatives taken by the African Union, together with many more at the East Africa level – for example, the East African Community Medicines Regulatory Harmonization (EAC MRH) initiative – will accelerate the move toward local manufacturing of pharmaceuticals in East Africa and make the region more self-sufficient in the long term. There is a huge opportunity for players who wish to serve this soon-to-be "East African single market."

The pandemic has also made suppliers more risk-averse compared to the situation previously. Earlier, many suppliers used to be open to long-term bookings for their most popular products. Abacus had approached one such supplier with a proposal for booking a year's worth of supply, but it declined, citing that they were taking only short-term bookings to manage risk better. The working capital issues facing smaller players have worsened, impacting their expansion plans. This should hopefully change in the long term.

The pandemic has also brought to the fore new ways of healthcare delivery and has accelerated their growth in a market where most people outside of cities lack access to good healthcare facilities. In a recent consumer survey conducted by the Boston Consulting Group (BCG) in October 2020, 61% of consumers in Uganda and 69% in Kenya reported reduced frequency of health facility visits. In the face of this new reality, many healthcare providers in Africa are accelerating their adoption of tools such as telemedicine and remote patient case management. Kenya has seen a number of such telehealth platforms experience a surge in demand, with examples including companies such as 360 Health and Wellness, Access Afya, SASA Doctor, The Daktari, and Byon 8 App.

Online pharmacies have also grown, such as MyDawa in Kenya. In Uganda, the United Nations Population Fund (UNFPA) partnered with SafeBoda, a popular ride-hailing app, to launch a "personal health shop," where users could order and receive reproductive health commodities at their doorsteps. With the substantial growth in the adoption of digital tools during the pandemic, East African governments are expected to encourage investment in digital health and similar emerging areas.

The COVID-19 pandemic has had a positive impact on the East African pharmaceutical industry, with the disruption of global supply chains further highlighting the fragility of the African health system and the need to have strong, local players. With prior experience in handling the Ebola and AIDS epidemics, Uganda's national pandemic response strategy has succeeded in controlling the number of cases. (See Figure 3.5.)

Abacus had a solid pandemic response, driven by strong and diverse leadership at all levels, deep supplier and customer relationships nurtured over many years, a best-in-class supply chain, and most importantly, its employees, all of whom were willing to embrace change and go the extra mile for their company. As articulated beautifully by Richard Branson, "A company's employees are its greatest assets, and your people are your product." We are sure that all of these learnings from our pandemic response will ensure that we are even better prepared for similar events in the future.

FIGURE 3.5   Abacus team with the president of Uganda, discussing ways Abacus can continue to support Uganda's COVID-19 response; left to right: Abacus co-founder and board director Ramesh Babu; Abacus group CEO Rajaram Sankaran; President H.E Gen. Yoweri Kaguta Museveni; Uganda's state minister for investment and privatization Evelyn Anite; Abacus co-founder and board director Rasik Haria.

About the Contributor

Rajaram Sankaran is the Group CEO of Abacus Pharma, East Africa's leading pharmaceutical distributor and manufacturer. With over 20 years of cross-functional experience in the pharmaceutical space spanning several global markets, he is driving the next phase of growth for Abacus in Africa. He has worked at multiple global pharma and consulting companies in the past, including AstraZeneca, Ranbaxy, Torrent Pharma, Frost & Sullivan, and most recently, Abbott, where he served as the strategy and business development director for the India region.

References

Abacus Pharma website. www.abacuspharma.com

APDL (Abacus Parenteral Drugs) website. www.abacusparenteral.com

BCG Report. "Building Resilience: COVID-19 Impact & Response in Urban Areas: The Case of Kenya & Uganda." https://www.bcg.com/en-za/building-resilience-covid-19-impact-response-in-urban-areas

Deloitte insights. "The Economic Impact of COVID-19 on East African economies." https://www2.deloitte.com/content/dam/Deloitte/tz/Documents/finance/Economic_Impact_Covid-19_Pandemic_on_EastAfrican_Economies.pdf

IFC Project Information: Abacus Pharma. https://disclosures.ifc.org/project-detail/ESRS/43844/abacus-ii

Ministry of Health, Uganda. www.health.go.ug

Mohamed, Nazeem. "The East African Pharmaceutical Sector: Opportunities and Challenges." https://www.unido.org/sites/default/files/files/2018-03/Nazeem%20Mohamed_FEAPM_East%20Africa_Inside%20the%20Pharma%20Maret_0103 2018%20Bonn.pdf

Mutembe, Danny. "East Africa: The next pharmaceutical manufacturing platform." https://insights.omnia-health.com/hospital-management/east-africa-next-pharmaceutical-manufacturing-platform

National Drug Authority (NDA), Uganda website. www.nda.or.ug

Overview of EAC (East African Community). www.eac.int

Sarki, Ahmed M., Alex Ezeh, and Saverio Stranges. "Uganda as a role model for Pandemic Containment in Africa." https://www.ncbi.nlm.nih.gov/pmc/articles/PMC7661999/

"Stronger communities: Abacus Pharmaceuticals, a case study by the Carlyle Group." https://www.carlyle.com/impact/abacus-pharmaceuticals

Ugandan Bureau of Statistics. www.ubos.org

"Uganda's Emergency Response to the Pandemic, A Case Study." https://thinkwell.global/wp-content/uploads/2020/09/Uganda-COVID-19-Case-Study-_18-Sept-20201.pdf

WHO (World Health Organization) reports. www.who.int

World Bank Open Data. http://data.worldbank.org

CHAPTER 4

Bangalore International Airport

By Hari Marar (Managing Director and CEO)

About Bangalore International Airport

Bangalore International Airport Limited (BIAL) was established as a private public partnership (PPP) enterprise to build, own, and operate the Kempegowda International Airport, Bengaluru (KIAB). KIAB, which is the third largest airport in India, handled around 33.5 million passengers in 2018–19, during which period it was also one of the fastest-growing airports in the world. The shareholders of BIAL include Fairfax Financial Holdings, Siemens, the government of Karnataka, and the government of India. BIAL has embarked upon a massive USD 2 billion capacity enhancement program, scheduled to be completed and operationalized in 2022. The company is also developing a sustainable, smart, and vibrant airport city in its campus.

Backdrop

"Now there is one outstandingly important fact regarding Spaceship Earth, and that is that no instruction book came with it."

Operating Manual for Spaceship Earth
by R. Buckminster Fuller

I often talk to my daughter about negotiating the multiple journeys that lie ahead of her; one of the things I find myself telling her is that life doesn't come with an instruction manual. As a parent, I can prepare her for several things, but there will be curveballs along the way. Those are the times that will call upon all her strength and wisdom.

In the past 16 months, these little conversations have come back to me very often, reminding me that this is my "no instruction manual" moment, one that I would have to negotiate with my team at BLR Airport (BIAL), with some parts fortitude, a dash of wisdom, and dollops of courage – all at the speed of light.

Just as COVID-19 was beginning to impact our lives, I was on a visit to Heathrow Airport in London and involved in a series of interesting meetings that allowed us to think about the choices we needed to make and the investments that were necessary to influence the future of aviation in our respective countries. During one such meeting, I received a message from the executive assistant requesting an urgent appointment. He and my CFO wanted to have a critical discussion as soon as possible. They briefed me about how the COVID-19 crisis was escalating and suggested that we set up a task force to deal with the situation. The team had been tracking developments ever since the situation in China had begun to worsen. Everyone felt that it was time to respond and start taking proactive actions.

There was a feeling of unease in the pit of my stomach. In hindsight, however, I can tell you there was no way I was prepared for what came next. In fact, I can safely say that nobody in the world was prepared for or really understood the magnitude and impact of what was coming our way. I, for one, felt the whiplash and G Forces that a Formula 1 driver must feel when negotiating dangerous turns and avoiding potential crashes at very high speeds – all while ensuring that the car does not careen out of control and end up in a flaming heap on the racetrack.

Before I share how we at BLR Airport managed this crisis, let me give you a quick background on where we were as an airport and the kind of growth trajectory we were seeing.

Taking Off

Around 1998 when Bangalore began being touted as the "Silicon Valley of the East," it was obvious that the gateway to this world needed a befitting mantle as well. When the brand-new Bengaluru Airport was inaugurated in 2008, we got off to a flying start, going from 8 million passengers to 32.3 million passengers in FY 2019–20. (See Figure 4.1.)

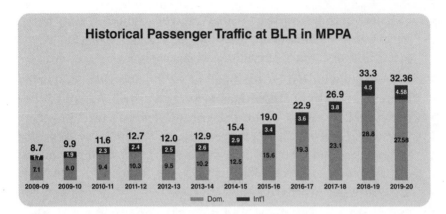

FIGURE 4.1 Passenger traffic at BLR (in millions of passengers per year).
Source: Bangalore International Airport, Ltd.

We were running out of space for our passengers and, encouraged by this growth, we embarked on a massive expansion plan valued at approximately USD 1.8 billion. We worked toward a second terminal, one that would be a point of reference for the world of aviation in multiple ways. We were just about halfway through the development of this infrastructure in January 2020, with most large value orders already placed, when the global pandemic hit us.

Getting Organized

On my return from London, the first thing I did was call for a meeting with my leadership team. During discussions, the complexity and breadth of potential issues were evident to everyone. As a result, the first thing we did was to set up multiple task forces.

As I discussed it with the team, we realized the need for nimble decision-making and accessible leadership, and we empowered on-the-ground teams to execute and take action, employed diligent passenger monitoring, and took a collaborative approach across the entire ecosystem. With that in mind, we drew on people from across the entire organization (see Figure 4.2) to set up the following task forces at BIAL:

1. **Steering committee chaired by** me in my role as **managing director and CEO, supported by my leadership team, enterprise**

risk, and corporate affairs team. This team connected every morning to take stock of developments and make key decisions that would cascade down to the organization and stakeholders.

2. **War group, chaired by the head of enterprise risk, supported by representatives from various verticals in BIAL and other personnel engaged in on-the-ground operations**. The group monitored developments on the ground, continuously apprising stakeholders and others of key operational actions. This team was empowered to make decisions and was the heart of our pandemic response group, which continues to date.

3. **Stakeholder group chaired by the COO, supported by multiple stakeholders** within the BLR Airport ecosystem. The focus of this group was to discuss mitigation solutions as relevant to each partner and escalate concerns or issues. This way the ecosystem would work as one.

4. **Surveillance group chaired by the head of BIAL security, supported by representatives from various internal and external verticals.** This group was focused on the contact tracing of passengers arriving at BLR Airport.

The teams hit the ground running, and this approach is what helped us negotiate this crisis in a way that kept our heads above water. This system

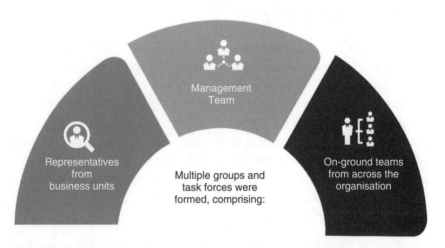

FIGURE 4.2   Task forces utilized at BIAL.
Source: Bangalore International Airport, Ltd.

of functioning ensured that decisions were made without any delay and we moved into action mode very quickly.

From February onward and well into June, the steering committee met twice a day; sharing morning breakfast and evening tea with each other over our Microsoft Teams calls. While these meetings helped us stay on top of things effectively, they also brought us together as a team and were often the only time some of the leaders got the chance to laugh a bit with each other before stepping back to manage their teams and the unfolding crisis. I must take a moment here to reflect on how critical this was as we were steering the BIAL family through a crisis, and it was imperative that we helped each other along as well.

Understanding Needs

We realized we had to start with the basics, and at each stage several questions emerged:

- What was the best chemical for sanitization?
- What cleaning protocols and schedules should we follow?
- How could we ensure procurement speed and efficiency without breaking the bank?
- What would make the passenger feel safe to fly again?
- How could we ensure that we mitigated people's fear of physically touching a surface or screen?
- How would we manage deliveries that were stuck in the supply pipeline, both domestic and international?
- What was the best way to keep passengers and other stakeholders updated about changing regulations?
- How would we keep cash flow intact while ensuring our employee salaries and jobs were protected?
- What was the best way to manage our financial stakeholders and ecosystem?
- How should we take care of our concessionaires and aviation stakeholders and work together with them to stay financially viable and yet emerge stronger?

Each question required a mini-task force that explored what was out there and came back with ideas and options. Once we decided on the way forward, implementation was done in record time.

Our Approach

While these issues were evolving, my leadership team and I had several discussions on how to deal with the entire situation in a holistic manner. Yes, we knew we had to stay afloat; however, we also needed an approach or an internal map to navigate this situation. Several global consulting firms reached out, and we heard them out and decided how we could adapt what we heard into a framework that worked for us at BIAL.

This is how we came up with the **3As: Accept, Adapt, and Advance**. We applied this thinking across the board, and I reiterated it every chance I got:

- **Accept** the current situation.
- **Adapt** to it by innovating and revisiting paradigms. Nothing was fixed and everything could be questioned.
- **Advance** by focusing on what would best serve the current situation and also deliver benefits in the future.

The other thing that was very clear to me and my colleagues was that nothing was cast in stone, least of all our budgets. The parameters that we always thought were constant suddenly appeared both uncertain and variable.

We asked ourselves, how does one build a budget, create forecasts, or plan with any kind of certainty in such a scenario? It was then that we decided to apply the principle of progressive calibration. I told the board that we would be revising our budgets every quarter based on the evolving scenario, while ensuring three things:

1. Protect jobs and pay employee salaries on time.
2. Maintain safe and efficient operations.
3. Honor our commitments and relationships.

As I look back, what helped us most in navigating the potential financial fallout was our commitment to financial discipline. We had built a strong business model with no inherent comorbidities; organizations with high levels of debt, low levels of cash, or negative cash flows were the ones likely to be hit hard. We were financially healthy and hence could navigate the crisis as long as we were ensuring we followed the spirit of progressive calibration.

Focusing on Cash

The lockdown meant our revenues were impacted overnight. But 80% of our expenses comprised personnel costs, payments to the government, financing costs, and maintenance costs for upkeep of airport systems and facilities. These expenses continued to add up, threatening to choke our cash flows.

While we had no problem with our project cash as our equity portion was already spent (giving banks a lot of assurance), we needed to find ways to reduce our expenses to take care of the operational cash problem.

Our immediate response was to set up a program that we called BIAL 2.0. A crack team led by some of our brightest minds dove in to identify organization-wide opportunities for cutting costs and increasing efficiency. This was achieved in the specific areas of cash conservation, cost optimization, and process innovation.

However, this was not enough because the lockdowns were extended several times. Even when domestic commercial operations resumed, there were several capacity restrictions and route restrictions.

My CFO and I were clear that we needed to engage with our financial stakeholders and work out the best way forward. We reached out to our lenders for a loan moratorium, a move that had the industry-wide support of the Reserve Bank of India (RBI). We reached out to the government to relax our concession fee, property tax, lease rental, and related payments for a fixed duration. The government considered most of these positively. Once again, I think we got this kind of response because of positive relationships that we had built historically and the spirit of mutual trust, respect, and support that has been the hallmark of our interactions. The entire team at BIAL can be credited for building such an amazing rapport with the government, and it really worked for us when we needed it the most.

Another huge achievement in this difficult time was the way our teams focused on collection of receivables from all our partners. We had one of the most stellar receivables performances across the industry (and across other industries, for that matter). This was only possible because of the collaborative spirit of everyone involved and also the relationship of trust and respect we had built with our stakeholder partners – airlines, ground handlers, fuel farm, cargo operators, and so on.

A bright spot during this time was the cargo volumes, which were a major positive for the entire industry. Not only have cargo volumes recovered faster than passenger volumes, but they are expected to grow above pre-COVID-19 volumes by 2022, reinforcing Bengaluru as a key hub for cargo in South India.

Minimizing Touch

One of our key issues concerned how we were going to enable passengers to go through the terminal without touching surfaces. This simple question led us to develop a contactless check-in process from parking-to-boarding, with emphasis on minimum touch and minimum exposure between passengers and airport personnel. Passengers can use their mobile phones to scan the bar code on the kiosk, giving them a complete control over the check-in experience. We were the first airport in the world to roll out this contactless passenger journey, crucial in these times but equally relevant for all times.

Biometric-based passenger identity verification was already a widely accepted solution that had been under trial at BLR Airport. These systems, which use facial recognition to identify passengers, have always held the promise of speeding up passenger processing time from curb to gate. During this time, we partnered with airlines to drive adoption and facilitate passengers with ease.

Our partners across multiple government agencies were extremely collaborative during this time and were equally open to making necessary changes. As a result, we moved to the adoption of automated passenger screening systems, eliminating the need to pat down passengers and lowering security processing time to keep everyone protected.

With the resumption of domestic flight operations on May 25, 2020, we ensured maximum safety across touchpoints. Passengers experienced contactless dining and retail, with almost total elimination of human contact at outlets. Flyers could preorder features and benefits through smartphones using the "FSTR by BLR" tab on the official website of BLR Airport or through self-ordering on FSTR kiosks or by scanning QR codes displayed across the Terminal.

All these measures were aimed at reassuring passengers that it was safe to fly and that air travel was the safest option in these times.

We Are Here for You

While we reassured passengers, it was equally important for us to reassure our employees. It was only natural that job security and safety of themselves and their family would have been at the top of our employees' minds. We wanted to turn this on its head and see what we could do that would leave our employees feeling they had better odds in December 2020 than in January 2020. The first thing we did was to assure each employee that their jobs and salaries were safe. We also took several measures to ensure their safety and security was of utmost importance:

- Health and safety were prioritized, and only essential operations staff were permitted to be present at the airport during the lockdown announced by the government of India in March 2020.
- Executive communication provided employees of BIAL and the airport community with updates in real time. World Health Organization (WHO) advisories on protective measures were continuously updated and circulated among employees.
- All employees had to undergo temperature screening before entering offices. Offices and common areas were sanitized frequently.
- Sanitizers were made available at offices and at over 700 locations in the terminal.
- Mandatory e-training modules on the nature of the virus and its prevention were rolled out for employees. For everyone working at BLR Airport, an in-depth training program was organized to drive awareness and prepare them with adequate knowledge on dealing with COVID-19.

- Dining at cafeterias was restricted, and employees could place an order digitally and collect food.

- A 24/7 helpline service was launched to extend support to employees on personal and work-related matters.

- Counseling support was also available to employees and families.

- As cases were escalating, hospital beds were scarce, and employees were nervous. As a result, we also converted a sports complex into a full-fledged COVID-19 care center, managed by a medical partner. All this was turned around in a week's time.

- In April 2020, as a responsible corporate entity, BIAL launched a joint initiative, "Namma Chethana," to provide 3,500 daily meals to the stranded workers, daily wage earners, villagers, police officers, and those working in the unorganized sector across Chikkabalapura district. Furthermore, over 428,500 meals and 7,750 grocery kits were distributed to the needy during the lockdown.

We did two additional things that I believe were really bold measures given that our top line was quite close to zero.

- In May 2020 BIAL paid eligible employees their bonus for the recently closed financial year. The teams had worked hard the previous year and we had celebrated some outstanding achievements as an organization. As a result, the entire team, supported by the board, was clear this was the right thing to do.

- In the spirit of advancing forward, the current need was to identify alternate revenue streams so that we would be more diversified. In the process, we would give employees a chance to be entrepreneurs while they worked at BIAL. We conducted a Shark Tank for our employees wherein more than 100 ideas were submitted by teams and 6 were finally chosen to go ahead into the implementation stage. We put together a jury comprising some of the BIAL leaders, external investors, and fund managers. This process really energized the entire organization.

Care is one of the key values at BIAL, one that has come to the fore during this pandemic. Not just care for our passengers, but care for each and every one of our employees, especially during a time when they stood up and went the extra mile.

A Way to Construct

The area where the pandemic hit us very hard was project expansion and construction. During a site walkthrough, my CPO told me that we were staring at a potential risk of about 600 crore (more than USD 80 million), due to material not reaching us in time.

Many of our supplies were being imported, which slowed down significantly in January 2020, with China shutting down and several European factories closing down. We attempted to mitigate this by identifying alternate vendors from other geographies who could supply some of these items. At the same time, we started working with government agencies to expedite clearance of several items that were stuck in ports. While we couldn't solve this entirely, I was quite happy with the extent of recovery that we did manage.

However, problems were only mounting. On March 23, the government suspended all construction activities across the board. During the initial phase of the lockdown, no construction work was permitted, and we were well aware of the risks involved.

An idle workforce with no entertainment or work in huge labor camps is a recipe for disaster. We had to act fast, and we did. On one side we worked with the government to see if work could be restarted, and on the other we isolated the camps, conducted regular checkups for them, implemented activities to engage them, and assured them of their payments.

As with personnel, finances, and operations, our project verticals also saw the best minds rolling up their sleeves to arrive at solutions almost overnight.

- Plans were drawn up to ensure minimal disruption to more than 120 projects, involving more than 50 project managers across the campus.
- Virtual platforms were created to bring together approximately 30 internal and external stakeholders to collaborate on a monthly average of 60 work concepts on terminals, landside, and airside.

What I am particularly proud of is that the projects team worked in collaboration with the contractors and their workforce, and at no point were hygiene and on-site safety standards compromised.

- Posters, signage, and awareness sessions (or as we termed them, "myth-buster sessions") were organized for the airport community, in coordination with National Disaster Response Force (NDRF).
- Doctors and nurses were deployed on shifts to tend to the sick and take care of emergencies.
- Project offices and labor camps, including living quarters, were sanitized regularly.

However, the inevitable could not be stopped. Anxiety about their loved ones back home and their own fears meant that a large number of the workforce migrated back to their hometowns. A 10,000-strong labor force trickled down to about 2,500 at its lowest during this phase. Our efforts continued to keep as many as we could, while continually supplementing them with those who were willing to come back.

These measures and focused action on part of the team reassured the government, which gave us permission to begin construction again. In June 2020, we resumed work on our critical projects, knowing that we were in a race against time and had a lot of catching up to do.

Family

While we are one company with about 1,300 employees, we are also the custodian of an ecosystem with 27,850 employees. We had to look out for them too, and most of them had to pay us fixed rents or royalties. I kept asking my team these questions:

- How do we treat them?
- Do we ask for money from them at a time when we need it the most?
- Do we enforce contracts?

Fixed partner fees were waived, and instead a framework was established, where we moved to a variable fee format linked to returning passengers. This approach became a benchmark for others in the industry to follow and was so widely encouraged across the industry that global CEOs of some of these companies have reached out to me appreciating the gesture.

When I look back, I realize that there were no straightforward answers. Even so, my teams thought of these questions and found solutions without anyone asking them to. As the custodian of the organization's culture, I am exceptionally proud of this.

Building for Tomorrow

Considering the past 16 months from the moment of that phone call when I was London until now, a few things stand out for me:

- Power of a collaborative approach and partnership between multiple stakeholders in the ecosystem
- Empathy and compassion toward our employees, partners, stakeholders, and vendors
- Multiple stakeholders coming together as one to arrive at solutions and deliver a superior customer experience
- Going contactless and raising the bar on technology-enabled solutions for passengers to provide safety and reassurance
- Communication, communication, communication, to ensure consistent, transparent, and regular communication with all stakeholders

If there is one thing that helped us make it all come together, it is the belief that we are all building for tomorrow. And if we are to thrive, we must partner and work together to achieve the vision that we have set for ourselves.

What Lies Ahead

Two decades ago, 9/11 changed the face of global aviation. The security protocols institutionalized in the years that followed became the norm. The current pandemic has changed the game again, bringing with it the "new normal" – one that will establish aviation as the safest mode of travel. Even as we speak, it remains unclear how long the pandemic will last, as countries and governments work toward vaccinating citizens.

Industry Outlook

The pandemic has caused the worst disruption in the history of the aviation industry. With multiple lockdowns and restrictions across the world, passenger numbers plummeted to levels seen a decade ago. The fall in passenger traffic has had a severe impact on the financial viability of stakeholders across the aviation value chain.

There has been a gradual recovery in domestic aviation in India with the easing of lockdowns. However, recovery of international traffic has been very slow, given that countries are wary of opening borders because of fears of a second or third wave of COVID-19, as was witnessed in the US and UK in December 2020 and which continued to be visible in India in 2021.

Despite the nonuniform recovery, we are hopeful that based on a rapid pace of vaccination, improved testing protocols, and a globally accepted health passport, the aviation sector may achieve pre-COVID-19 numbers by 2024.

Company Outlook

At BIAL, we expected the recovery in domestic passenger traffic to be faster than international traffic, which did happen as COVID-19 cases dropped and economic activity gained pace. However, the recent resurgence of COVID-19 cases in India and new travel restrictions present a clear risk to this recovery.

We believe that the demand will come roaring back! Underlying fundamentals for demand in air travel haven't changed. As soon as health protocols are in place and vaccination is completed, demand will return to normal. Our job is to be prepared with capacity, thus we are focusing on three main areas:

1. Developing and investing in digital capacity
2. Investing in and completing the physical capacity program – our existing projects
3. Investing in and developing the airport city

As a result, we are pushing hard to work with international and domestic carriers to focus on developing Bengaluru as the new Gateway to India.

Long-Lasting Impact on the Industry

The pandemic is likely to have a lasting impact on the aviation industry, accelerating the adoption of digital technology features that might otherwise have taken years to implement. A significant change is the shift to touchless travel and biometric identity systems, both of which we have successfully rolled out at BLR Airport.

Health checks at entry, relentless levels of sanitization, safe-distance measures, hygiene kits at boarding, in-flight sanitation, aircraft filtration systems, and much more are likely to continue for the foreseeable future. Travel patterns will evolve with time as passengers slowly decide to travel like they used to. Airports and airlines must provide constant reassurance on safe travel measures and share information on the ever-evolving scenarios.

During this phase, the most significant disruption we saw was in the financial viability applicable to airports, airlines, regulators, and partners alike. The way I see it, airlines will have to reorganize and learn to thrive in a low-demand environment until new protocols and confidence measures enable the industry to recover.

Regardless, the real test of the success of the new business models rests on a higher degree of collaboration between various aviation stakeholders. This collaborative effort, much like what we experienced at the peak of the pandemic, will help us enable a safe and seamless travel experience for passengers.

I expect that air cargo will continue to play a critical role in transporting essentials across the globe, reinforcing its significance in the aviation business.

In 2019, there were 200 million air passengers in India, but COVID-19 put a damper on the incredible growth story. However, the slew of measures put in place could enable the aviation industry to reset, plan, innovate, adapt, and continue as the safest mode of travel.

Growth Opportunities

There are several key areas where we can grow:

1. This is going to be the era of the platform business. We must leverage the fact that we are already a natural platform and develop a digital platform that can offer an ever-growing range of services to passengers.

2. We can use biometric technology and manage the challenge of identity management, travel document authentication, health pass clearance, and more to improve process efficiency and passenger experience at airports.

3. We need to identify and understand changing customer needs and expectations and cater to them in a proactive manner.

4. There will be a resurgence in and increased focus on acquiring experiences rather than assets. Airports can be places that orchestrate magical experiences for their customers so that the airport experience becomes the most memorable part of the travel experience. (See Figure 4.3.)

5. New and emerging technologies will help airports transform to become smart, sustainable campuses that bring together AI, ML-based analytics, IOT-based asset management capabilities, and new predictive insights.

6. Airports can tap into the emerging "gig" economy and a far larger and more exciting talent market to be able to deliver this ambitious vision.

FIGURE 4.3 The airport terminal beckons passengers.
Source: Bangalore International Airport, Ltd.

Conclusion

"Twenty years from now you will be more disappointed by the things you didn't do than by the ones you did do. So, throw off the bowlines, sail away from the safe harbor. Catch the trade winds in your sails. Explore. Dream. Discover."

Mark Twain

Humans are social animals and flourish through shared interactions. We thrive on discovery, on the intrinsic need to go out and experience, touch, and feel. Business is not made by cold transactions that are carried out on a virtual medium. You need a firm handshake. You need to look people in the eye. You need to build confidence. You need the dinners to make the deals. In the long run, these human instincts will result in people traveling again. Of course, this will require appropriate modifications, and we will all need to realign ourselves accordingly. But by all indications it will certainly happen.

About the Contributor

Hari Marar is the managing director and CEO of Bangalore International Airport Limited (BIAL), the operator of the Kempegowda International Airport Bengaluru, the third largest airport in India. Hari is also the chairman of Bangalore Airport Hotels Ltd. and Bangalore Airport City Ltd. (BACL), which are the subsidiaries of BIAL. BACL is developing the airport campus into an aerotropolis, or airport city, which will be home to multiple businesses such as IT parks, business parks, healthcare, biotechnology, a knowledge park, retail, entertainment, dining, concert arenas, and hospitality. His vision is to transform the airport into a global leader and role model in the areas of sustainable practices, innovation-led progress, and technology leadership. In 2019, Hari was appointed to the four-member Heathrow Expansion Advisory Board. Hari is also the chairman of the Karnataka water sustainability task force of the Confederation of Indian Industries.

CHAPTER 5

beCuriou

By Edward Wendel (CEO and Owner), Celina Sofie Gylthe (COO/CFO), and Kenneth Cai (Cofounder and Travel Design)

About beCuriou

beCuriou is a niche travel company targeting high- and ultra-high-net-worth (UHNW) discerning clientele across the world, in addition to organizing group trips for quality-oriented firms in the legal, finance, property, technology, and energy sectors. The value proposition is to provide the best combination of personal service, sophisticated insight, and competitive prices.

The company started in 2013 in Oslo, Norway, and now has offices in London, Singapore, and Cape Town, along with a Paris office opening in 2021. Moreover, beCuriou has been among the fastest-growing companies in Norway for several years (according to *Dagens Næringsliv*) as well as one of the fastest-growing companies in Europe in 2019 (per *Financial Times*).

beCuriou focuses on recruiting a diverse set of talent and industry-leading skill sets with backgrounds from luxury travel brands such as Singapore Airlines, Swiss hospitality, finance companies, private banking/wealth management, and clients with science and economics university degrees.

beCuriou has also taken a leading role within Impact Travel by building a bridge between high-end travel, ESG (environmental, social, and governance), and finance. Through our ESG partnerships across our destinations, we create opportunities for our clients to visit organizations that we support, meet the social entrepreneurs, and experience local community projects, giving a unique educational and memorable insight into the challenges and opportunities at our local destinations.

Industry

The travel and tourism sector accounted for 10% of global GDP and amounted to USD 9 trillion in 2019, according to the World Travel and Tourism Council, making travel and tourism three times the size of agriculture. This was predicted to increase by 3–4% for 2020, according to a report published by UNWTO in January 2020.

The estimate from UNWTO for 2020 is that international tourist arrivals plunged 60–80% in 2020.

The value chain in the tourism industry is fragmented, with limited coordination among the small and medium enterprises (SMEs) that make up a large portion of the sector. Online travel operators have taken a large part in the industry, especially in the mass market.

beCuriou set out to have the most robust balance sheet in the industry, and the AAA-rating from Bisnode/Dun & Bradstreet has always been a strong value proposition for our clients. This stood us in good stead in 2020 and has become an even stronger selling point during the pandemic.

From its outset in 2013 until 2019, the company grew by 32% on average per year in revenue. The budgeted growth for 2020 was 25% but ended with a reduction of 70% in revenue. However, with strict cost controls, professional and strict follow-up of providers in the value chain honoring their debts (e.g., making the owners accountable), governmental support, securing grants for the company's innovation projects, plus the performance of the investment portfolio of the company, we ended up with a solid plus, and only 14% lower profit before taxes compared to 2019. (See Figure 5.1.)

The First Signs: When COVID-19 Hit

The scale of the pandemic was not something beCuriou or anyone in the travel industry was prepared for. Our financial management and operations, however, enabled us to maintain a level head and to mobilize our diverse team to approach the situation in a calm, constructive, and well-organized manner.

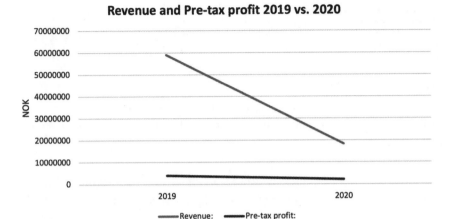

FIGURE 5.1   Revenue and pretax profit, 2019 versus 2020.
Source: beCuriou AS, rounded to nearest NOK 10,000

The First Few Months

The year 2020 was off to a good start with an increase in demand and revenue, but as soon as COVID-19 spread across the globe, we saw a rapid decline in revenue, which hit us in March. (See Table 5.1.)

Typically, our demand consists of big-ticket, tailor-made trips (often USD 50,000–200,000 or more) reserved several months in advance; however, the demand we now saw was almost solely for urgent one-way flight tickets from clients and their friends and families who were stuck abroad and not getting through to their traditional travel agent or airline call centers. Our in-house flight handling, International Air Transport Association (IATA) license, and the greatest flight expertise in the industry allowed

TABLE 5.1

Months:	Jan and Feb 2020 vs. 2019	Mar and Apr 2020 vs. 2019
Revenue change:	+14%	−78%

Norwegian Air Travel, January-April - 2020
TERMINAL PASSENGERS - transfer and infants included

	January			February			March			April		
	2020	2019	Change	2020	2019	Change	2020	2019	Change	2020	2019	Change
Domestic	2 320 618	2 306 053	0.6%	2 328 824	2 357 162	-1.2%	1 240 526	2 783 639	-55.4%	326 775	2 416 730	-86.5%
International	1 432 569	1 416 326	1.1%	1 505 831	1 482 973	1.5%	705 924	1 694 680	-58.3%	22 289	1 796 758	-98.8%

FIGURE 5.2 Norwegian air travel decline in the first part of 2020. *Source:* https://avinor.no/konsern/om-oss/trafikkstatistikk/arkiv *(Avinor owns most airports in Norway.)*

our clients to get home safely and in a timely manner. Figure 5.2 illustrates the rapid decline in international flights in Norway, which by April was down 98.8% from 2019 levels.

We also had to contact all the clients who were due to travel in the next months. We took it upon ourselves to make sure our clients felt confident that they were getting the best service at any given time – and not only limited to travel management. Doing so meant understanding the totality of each client's individual interests and assisting with legal advice, cancellations, postponements, insurance claims, credit valuations, and more.

The Operational Challenges

The arrival of COVID-19 also resulted in a wide range of operational challenges that we needed to address.

Liquidity For most businesses in our industry, liquidity, or lack thereof, was the primary concern in the short term, as many of the travel agencies condition their financial balance by fluctuating trends in demand. For us, however, we had a very high liquidity ratio and equity level, and as a result we guaranteed refunds for all our clients. Knowing that their funds were safe instilled confidence in our clients, contrary to the situation with many other travel companies.

Credit Risk We have also always run credit risk analysis to make sure our own and our client's funds are safe, even if we were met with resistance and questions, as this is not standard procedure among the SMEs in the travel industry.

This credit risk analysis became an important tool to identify the risk element and a way to prioritize the time and level of action needed to be taken, especially when it came to the airline industry (of which several went into restructuring and bankruptcy in the following months). In some instances, we were confident that the providers were still solid and able to make refunds, while in others, we took quick and drastic action (including threat of legal action) to ensure we were prioritized when refunds were made possible.

Reducing Overhead   Internally, we also negotiated with suppliers to reduce our fixed costs, especially focusing on those that were not themselves as much affected by the pandemic (such as our rent, phone, and technology providers). We have always focused on having tight cost controls; however, the pandemic made it even more important.

Team   Moreover, most of the team were put on part-time furlough, including the owner himself, Edward Wendel. Leading by example instilled a feeling of solidarity and that "we were in it together." The partial furlough was key because labor is one of our major costs.

The furlough system was explained in detail, and the owner also made sure to understand and help out regarding each person's individual concerns and make adjustments where there was a personal need.

Keeping the whole team alert, informed, and engaged during this extreme period was imperative, we decided. Team meetings were continued every week. And we kept almost everyone on partial payroll – above the needed work capacity – to maintain the team feeling among our highly valued colleagues. We also did our best to help everyone be as optimistic as possible and prepared for future opportunities for beCuriou – where the main differentiator will always be having the best people in the industry serving our customers.

Navigating Through the Great Lockdown

Though we were now in a situation with 5–10% of revenue in comparison to previous years, we were prepared to focus on what *was* possible instead of waiting for better days. With the world in lockdown and restrictions making it very difficult and complicated to travel, we decided to take a multi-angled approach to use this to our benefit. Our thoughts were many, and putting all our eggs in one basket could become a costly affair in this uncertain time.

Business

We soon realized that we had to look at alternative ways to stimulate demand. Luckily, many of our clients from Scandinavian, where there is an internal travel market. Capitalizing on this demand could provide a revenue stream while international travel was restricted. In order to do so, we decided to apply for a grant (not a loan) from Innovation Norway (the Norwegian government's most important instrument for innovation and development of Norwegian enterprises and industry). It was important that we applied for a grant, as opposed to a loan, to maintain our AAA-rating that had given us a competitive advantage among other travel providers. Innovation Norway deemed our grant application and proposal interesting, and we secured a grant of more than NOK 1 million (approximately USD 120,000). This enabled us to reduce the furlough amount and work on becoming the leading high-end DMC (destination management company) in Norway.

We also stimulated demand by focusing on the future and came up with the slogan "Det er lov å glede seg til fremtiden," which translates as "You're allowed to look forward to the future," and ran ads in the financial newspapers. (See Figure 5.3.)

This attracted positive attention. First, it focused on a positive message and sharing information about the competitive rates we could secure if booked ahead (with flexible policies, of course). Secondly, beCuriou was visible when the rest of the travel industry was lying low. Taking a contrarian approach in both our action and content proved rewarding, and we managed to increase our revenue to 50% of 2019 levels in June and July. (See Table 5.2.)

Moreover, we proactively reached out to all our clients to hear how they were doing and share our updates and that we still had a AAA-rating. We thought this was more important than ever to do now.

FIGURE 5.3   One of the company's print ads, featuring the new slogan.

TABLE 5.2

Months:	May 2020 vs. 2019	June 2020 vs. 2019	July 2020 vs. 2019
Revenue Change:	–96%	–58%	–56%

Liquidity

Liquidity had always been a focus and of great importance to us as well as the privilege of having capital. This all became even more evident during COVID-19. Even with a good liquidity level, we took further measures to secure our cash flow, such as placing employees on furlough, which reduced our highest fixed cost to between one-third and one-quarter of 2019 levels.

In addition to our successful grant application, we were also active in pushing for further financial support together with the Federation of Norwegian Enterprise (Virke). We did so by taking part in industry discussions and being active on social media platforms such as LinkedIn. We also made a clear decision not to take any loans and only apply for funding in the form of grants in order to keep our solid footing (AAA-rating).

Instead of focusing on international travel for our Norwegian customers during a time of travel restrictions and quarantines, we focused on travel within Norway. Though we didn't receive the full grant amount, our application was at least successful, and the total grant amount was more than NOK 1 million (approximately USD 120,000). We have already seen some of the positive effects as a result of it.

In addition to reducing labor costs, we also made an effort to cut back other fixed costs, including office rental (e.g., negotiating rent-free months for the Oslo office), and to cut back on licenses for those on furlough. On average, we managed to reduce other fixed costs by about 35–40% (2020 vs. 2019 levels).

People

We've always been a diverse team, with backgrounds ranging from finance and economics to hospitality and real estate, making sure we have a variety of perspectives where we constantly challenge each other. Our individual differences become our strength as a team, and the pandemic made this evident in so many ways.

We have a high level of financial and legal understanding, missing in similar SME travel companies, where the management and owners quite often have a mindset of short-term cost-consciousness, employing individuals mainly with basic tourism backgrounds and limited academic education.

We fought several airlines when they stopped processing refunds through the BSP (Billing and Settlement Plan), which is an IATA electronic billing system for running and simplifying the interchange of data and funds between travel agencies and airlines. For most of our cases, we managed on behalf of clients and ourselves more quickly than most to eliminate all outstanding refunds with the airlines.

We might be different in many ways, but like most other companies within our industry, we had to drastically cut costs and furlough most of our employees – at least mostly on a partial basis. It was important for us to be open and honest about the situation but at the same time offer support and a listening ear. We also kept our weekly team meetings, where we came together on Zoom and were able to "see" each other (at least virtually) and share any news, updates, input on how we could try to use the pandemic to our benefit, and the occasional joke to lighten the mood. These meetings have certainly played a role in making sure we never lost our strong corporate culture.

We also kept our office in Oslo open every day in adherence to all government guidelines. Being visible, not just online and on social platforms but physically in our office, was important for us. It showed our clients that we were still open for business and that we have the resources never to give up and can use the pandemic as an opportunity to grow further into the future.

Moreover, the pandemic provided an excellent opportunity to get hold of the best talents that would otherwise show little interest in working for an SME travel company. We had applicants from some of the world's top banks, NGOs, family offices, and more. As a result, we decided to invest in doubling the size of our team with employees and new offices in Singapore and Cape Town. (See Figure 5.4.) This decision created optimism and a belief in the future among our employees on furlough.

Investment Plan

Though we cut costs during the pandemic, we also focused on investing in the future. We invested in both new talent and new offices, as previously mentioned, as well as new technology. When it comes to the latter, after careful consideration and guidance from our advisory board, we finally took on the job of upgrading our database/CRM system. With

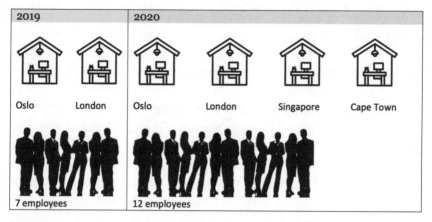

FIGURE 5.4 The company added offices in Singapore and Cape Town.

substantial investment in new technology (in what is considered the best CRM system worldwide), we intend to strengthen our client relationships, improve our clients' experience, and improve operational efficiency and the easy sharing of information. We also hope to gain more information about what drives our client's decisions and preferences and how we can successfully grow our client base.

We also invested more time in keeping in touch with our existing UHNW clients and reaching out to new potential UHNW clients worldwide, especially by utilizing our Impact Travel focus. We define Impact Travel as traveling in a way that empowers local communities and protects our earth. With global coverage on travel, we cooperate with local high-end travel partners, distributors, and ground handlers; we create a bridge between quality travel experiences, finance, and social and environmental change.

Moreover, we also reached out to our existing corporate clients and those with the potential of becoming clients, as they typically plan a year in advance and also because the other event companies were more or less closed. We also used timing as an argument, because we knew that we were in a stronger position to negotiate with our providers if we were early rather than waiting for the vaccines to be completely rolled out and for the demand to pick up, potentially outgrowing supply at certain destinations. This was a strong argument for corporate travel that typically has a set budget.

In terms of prospecting potential clients, we identified several hundred across the globe and looked at how we might connect with them through mutual connections. For those with a philanthropic interest, we also used the angle of potentially partnering with their foundation or a foundation they support. Through our new highly skilled international employees, our network widened exponentially.

Future Outlook

Although 2020 was off to a good start, with the pandemic and the global travel restrictions and uncertainty, it took a sharp downward turn. However, with our strong financial foundations, diverse team, and structured and dynamic approaches, we turned the challenge into an opportunity to grow.

We are optimistic for the industry overall but believe new habits in digitalized interaction will lead to a significantly reduced level of corporate travel, because many physical meetings will be replaced with video conferencing.

For the leisure market, we predict a big pent-up demand that will be seen as soon as travel is allowed without health risks and quarantines. When these are eliminated and the vaccines work as hoped for, we believe that the third and fourth quarters of 2021 will represent a strong rebound potential for us, as the inclination for travel is very high—something we already see clearly in new booking requests from our clients.

beCuriou focuses on top-end products and advanced content and experiences. We have a strong belief that our niche and bespoke service with a deeper sophistication level among our staff has great potential for future growth in our industry. We have therefore decided to use the opportunity to increase our capacity with new staff and offices in Asia, Africa, and in France/Switzerland and have recruited senior staff from private banking and other luxury travel agents. This is something we feel we are quite alone in doing at the moment.

We have also observed that the top-end segment, and especially the younger generation, often has a strong interest in philanthropy. Our special partnerships with carefully selected local philanthropic organizations will add an important differentiator for our chosen segment. This also goes for the top-tier law firms and other companies seeking the best talent from universities. Today's generation of talent expects their employers to have a serious ESG stance. Because it is important to our customers to create a corporate culture and bonding within the organization, assembling all employees for company trips will become a lot more significant than traditional events and parties. We see that introducing engaging local ESG activities organized by our professional ESG analysts/advisors has become an important part of why our corporate clients chose us. Consequently, Impact Travel will be an important continued growth opportunity for beCuriou going forward.

Learnings from the Great Lockdown

Many lessons have been learned from the pandemic – both in the travel industry as a whole and for beCuriou specifically. We have all learned to work a lot more efficiently by digitizing many of our meetings and thereby saving time and reducing carbon emissions. We believe the whole corporate sector will reduce their travel demand and be a lot more selective in choosing which meetings require physical attendance. Furthermore, we have had time to invest in making our value chain and processes more efficient by implementing new IT platforms and increasing team members' competence in our industry-specific systems.

We also believe the owners and leaders in our industry have learned to build more financial resilience toward the inherent risks connected to travel. Our fragmented industry has a large number of SMEs, frequently started by founders who "love to travel, so I will start a travel company" – often with a small amount of equity and risk capital allocated in the companies. The industry has limited governmental oversight, leaving it to owners and managers to set the levels of risk buffers. The pandemic has to some extent forced out some of the weakest players and mandated that companies provide more robust service while owners and leaders focus better on the financial aspects of running a business. This will hopefully create more safe and sound service providers for travelers, and we see clients being a lot more aware of travel company risks now than before COVID-19.

We expect that COVID-19 will linger for some time but also that demand (especially for holidays) will return as soon as vaccines are rolled out more widely. Business travel might be reduced as a result of increased online communication and a focus on sustainability.

We have also experienced that clients are far more appreciative of the personal service and advice we offer, after learning how many of the online operators and airlines were totally unprepared to handle the extreme number of cancellations and refund claims. Many new clients have come to us who value having someone to fight for their rights with travel providers such as airlines, hotels, and tour operators. In this sense, the pandemic actually strengthened our position in the market space. And clients appreciate us continuing to challenge many of the traditional industry norms.

About the Contributors

Edward is a business economist with 20 years' experience from various wealth management positions at Norway's largest bank, DNB. Through his extensive personal and corporate travel experience, Edward believed there was room for improvement around the high-end segment in relation to personal service, sophistication, and competitive pricing. As a result, he founded beCuriou together with Kenneth Cai, who added valuable luxury service background from Singapore Airlines and Swiss hospitality.

Celina Gylthe joined beCuriou at the early stages in Oslo and has been instrumental in developing the company's client handling and setting new benchmarks for the company's operational standards and efficiency. She has a BA in economics from Durham University and opened the London office in 2015.

Kenneth cofounded beCuriou together with Edward to challenge the traditional thinking management of the hospitality industry. Kenneth has a BBA in hospitality management from Switzerland and adds a valuable luxury service background from Singapore Airlines.

CHAPTER 6

Fonterra

By Karen Smyth (Fonterra GM Risk Assurance)

About Fonterra

We are a cooperative owned by nearly 10,000 farming families. Our farmer owners have long realized the strength of coming together as a co-op and how it can enable them to take their milk to the world. From humble but pioneering beginnings, we're now the largest exporter of dairy products in the world. Through our global grass-to-glass supply chain, we collect, process, store, ship, and distribute more than 4 billion MT of nutritious dairy products to 140 markets. Our 22,600 employees across the globe believe dairy is well placed to play an important role in helping feed the world's growing population, which by 2030 will have another 1 billion mouths to feed.

Dairy is an integral part of our food – as an end product like milk or yogurt, or as input for products like cheese in pizza. It is essential in both food service and packaged food categories. Given its intrinsic presence, dairy is a microcosm of the food industry, with dairy consumers' preferences influenced mainly by the same trends affecting the food sector.

We work with our farmer owners on a cooperative approach. Each day we pick up and process their milk, and we have an extensive network of support people who can assist farmers with everything from farm productivity, profitability, and environmental improvements to milk quality, safety, health, and animal welfare.

In recent years, the dairy industry has been at the center of the carbon emissions debate. In New Zealand, we pioneered low-carbon dairying, with the on-farm carbon footprint being one-third of the global average, due to our extensive and highly efficient pasture-based farming system.

But we know we need to do more and that's why almost half of our cooperative's farmers now have tailored Farm Environment Plans and we are targeting 100% by 2025. It's also why we've made farm-specific emissions profiles available to all farmer owners, which will give them a baseline to work from and help them identify opportunities for further improvement.

Cows are part of our family. Our cows spend more time on pastures than anywhere in the world, and we place a high emphasis on their health and welfare. This means that they live longer, more productive lives and produce some of the highest-quality milk on the planet. None of our cows are given hormones for producing extra milk, and this activity is banned across New Zealand.

The global dairy market reached a value of USD 718.9 billion in 2019. The rising demand for milk and milk-based ingredients was evident around the world. This can be attributed to population growth, rising incomes, health consciousness, and the thriving food and beverage industry. Another growing trend has been a rise in the demand for natural products free from additives, artificial preservatives, or chemicals.

First Signs

New Zealand announced its first case of COVID-19 on February 28, 2020. By mid-March, it was becoming clear that COVID-19 would significantly affect our business and the economy at large. In the third week of March, we announced our interim financial results. While the results were well received, there was a lot of uncertainty around what impact COVID-19 would have on our business. While it was not practical to answer all the questions farmers and employees had, we did commit to keeping everyone updated, and we communicated regularly.

On March 19, 2020, borders were closed to nonresidents. In the next two days, New Zealand introduced an alert system to inform citizens about the severity of the situation in the country. On March 25, the alert level was moved to its highest tier, and the country entered lockdown.

The effects of COVID-19 were felt in every part of our business – from rural New Zealand to global markets. Our global COVID-19 response was managed through our Comprehensive Incident Management Framework. Globally, across all business units, our teams focused their incident response teams to ensure we had a coordinated approach from the CEO down through all business levels.

Throughout the pandemic, the safety of our employees was our number one priority. As an essential business, we were in a privileged position to continue to operate within strict guidelines designed to keep our employees safe. We quickly transitioned approximately 8,000 office-based staff globally to working from home by introducing new technology for connection, upskilling, and adopting more flexible and adaptable working practices. Our teams started maintenance programs to get our New Zealand manufacturing sites ready for the next season with reduced staff (vulnerable workers were not allowed on-site) and applied additional safety protocols.

Also, in the early days, it became clear that our business's most significant impact would center around the food service industry. With hotels, restaurants, bakeries, and catering sectors being forced to shut down, we could face a sharp dip in demand. This could also potentially be one of the last industries to recover.

Getting products to our customers on time is an essential part of our supply chain operations. The vast majority of our products (about 1.4 million metric tons) leave through the Port of Tauranga toward the north of New Zealand. Our partnership with New Zealand's logistics leader Kotahi and Maersk, the global shipping company, proved hugely valuable in managing this disruption, and we continued to move products to our customers. During these times, the value of our strong strategic partnerships came to the fore as they provided us with the service options and container and vessel capacity to ensure our dairy products were moved around the world.

During the Great Lockdown

We had recently unveiled our new purpose and strategy, and just before the pandemic, we had launched "Good Together," the umbrella that brings together our purpose, strategy, and values. "Good Together" gave us the clarity to know what we needed to do to keep our people safe and support their well-being and keep our operations running as we focused on areas where we could make a difference for the environment and the

New Zealand economy while continuing to provide quality nutrition to the world. We also developed a psychosocial recovery model and created "Good Chat" dial-in sessions to support mental well-being for our people, and we have had over 5,000 people globally connect around the world and get support via these sessions.

Several changes were made to our global operations. In China, our food service teams moved from customer visits to virtual training sessions and livestreams to demonstrate how to use our butter and cheese. In New Zealand, our farmers continued to keep their farms operating, and our teams ramped up production to provide dairy to supermarkets for the influx of panic buying and home bakers. To help small businesses in New Zealand, we committed to paying our vendors within 10 days from receipt of their invoices.

With hand sanitizer in short supply in New Zealand, we redirected two million liters of our high-grade ethanol for use in sanitizer production. When one of our medical nutrition customers put in an urgent request for more hydrolysate (a fast-absorbing whey protein used to provide nutrition) to feed hospital patients, including those suffering from COVID-19, our teams quickly responded and extended production by one month, and partnered with Air New Zealand to get the life-saving cargo to the customer.

Case Study 1

Fonterra farmers, factory workers, teams from the US, and even some of Air New Zealand's crew did their bit to help patients suffering from COVID-19. Hydrolysates – a fast-absorbing whey protein used to make high-protein beverages, and easy for patients to drink or to provide nutrition to those intubated – was in high demand after COVID-19 was detected in the US.

One of Fonterra's customers, a medical nutrition company, played a prominent role in the COVID-19 response and had an urgent request for more hydrolysates to help provide nutrition to patients. The order was for about 15% of what we would typically produce in a whole season, and they

FIGURE 6.1 Fonterra ramped up production of hydrolysates, a fast-absorbing whey protein, to provide nutrition for intubated COVID-19 patients.

wanted it "yesterday," but the team rose to the challenge and got to work. Given the criticality of getting the product to the customer, we worked with Air New Zealand to charter a direct flight to get the product to the customer as quickly as possible. (See Figure 6.1.) We're always proud of the difference our products make in people's lives worldwide, but it's another level when it could potentially save lives.

Case Study 2

Lockdown really showed the character of our people and the resilience of our business. Our employees who were able to work from home did so. Those in front-line roles, such as our tanker drivers and operational staff, continued to work, and we did everything we could to take the very best care of them, with extra precautions to ensure their health and safety. (See Figure 6.2.)

FIGURE 6.2 Even when COVID-19 levels were lowered, Fonterra maintained higher restrictions at its operation sites.

Case Study 3

When research technologist Richard Lloyd, at Fonterra's Research and Development Centre, packed up his laptop to work from home for the lockdown, he also got the okay to take the 3D printer with him to put it to good use for the community.

With protective gear in short supply, Richard used the printer to produce orange frames for protective visors for the area's essential health workers. (See Figure 6.3.) Along with the free visors he made, Richard linked up with Shields Up, who coordinated the production of the shields around the country through crowdfunding.

FIGURE 6.3 Fonterra Research Technologist
Richard Lloyd used an office 3D printer
to produce frames for protective visors for
essential health workers.

Case Study 4

When two of our team from Fonterra's Clandeboye manufacturing site
heard that there was a shortage of hand sanitizer in their local community,
they knew they had to do something about it. Saskia and Andrew Lewis
put their labor of love, a boutique gin distillery called the Humdinger, to
good use and started producing batches of hand sanitizer in their spare
time. (See Figure 6.4.)

FIGURE 6.4   Saskia and Andrew Lewis from Fonterra's Clandeboye site, put their boutique gin distillery to good use and produced hand sanitiser.

When schools closed, we let school principals know that they could send home milk from our "milk for schools" program to families that needed it. We also redirected nearly one million servings of milk to community groups, including the Salvation Army, Kiwi Harvest, Eat My Lunch, and Whānau Ora. We lent a homogenizer to COVID-19 Vaccine Corporation (CVC) to help speed up their effort in producing a vaccine in New Zealand. In many of our markets, including China, Thailand, Sri Lanka, the US, and Vietnam, we donated products to healthcare professionals and community groups.

Navigating the Great Lockdown

The impact of COVID-19 was felt in every region we operate in. However, our farmers and employees came together as one team and kept our business running. This was helped in large part by New Zealand having very few (in some places zero) community cases of COVID-19. Our food service business in China was hardest hit – when restaurants, cafes, and the like closed down. Having an on-the-ground team helped us immensely to understand the situation firsthand and direct our strategy.

Projects were prioritized, and those that couldn't be put on hold were given exemptions to continue under strict internal COVID-19 protocols. With international experts not able to travel to New Zealand to be part of project work, we employed technology known as HoloLens from Microsoft – enabling them to take a virtual tour of the project in real time from anywhere in the world and keep updated with developments.

Our sales team had to adapt to a whole new way of selling. In China, our teams conducted home cooking demonstrations, attracting more than a million online viewers. Our team took to television shopping channels in South Korea to sell more than USD 1 million of functional nutrition in just one hour. The changes we made enabled us to continue to operate.

At a time when many businesses have not been so fortunate, we've been able to stay open, keep employing people, and give back to communities. As an "essential business," we have been in a privileged position to continue to operate during all COVID-19 alert levels. This is not something we've taken lightly. When New Zealand moved down to Alert Level 3, we continued to work with the precautions we had in place for the highest alert, Level 4. To this day, many of these precautions remain in place.

Clearly, it's not a singular action that Fonterra took that delivered success; instead, several actions came together to help New Zealand communities and our global family of customers and employees. Our farmer owners, tanker operators, and manufacturing teams kept the milk processing going and also produced additional ethanol and hydrolysates. Our supply chain teams kept the products moving. We dynamically adapted our product mix as global markets have shut and reopened – redirecting products around the globe to meet changing demands. We increased our emphasis on "well-being" and "connection," which will continue as a core part of our business practices. Our ability to keep operating and the support we have provided our communities have improved how our staff, farmer owners, and New Zealanders feel about Fonterra and the dairy sector as a whole.

During COVID-19, we achieved our highest ever reputational scores. We also saw an increase in our Net Promoter Score with our farmers as pride in their role in New Zealand was reignited, and we experienced an overall positive media sentiment. We couldn't have done this without the support of our entire global value chain, and we have worked extremely closely with customers, suppliers, and communities.

Future Outlook

While there have been challenges for us at Fonterra, it has certainly not been all doom and gloom. Despite the food service industry being so severely impacted, we see some positive trends resulting from COVID-19.

Some key trends that have accelerated due to COVID-19 are about how food is prepared in-store, how customers engage with their suppliers, and how consumers are now purchasing their food.

1. We are now seeing significant simplification of the menu items that our food service customers are operating, mainly to keep staff farther apart and reduce the amount of labor in kitchens to preserve the health and safety of their employees as they prepare food. We've seen food service operators cut their menu items by 50% to focus on the core items – which means we need to ensure we stay relevant in these core menu items.

2. Another trend is reducing labor in restaurants – to ensure employees are protected from COVID-19 risks and ensure the restaurant's costs are being managed. Labor costs typically amount to approximately 30% of their total expenses. We expect restaurants to outsource more and more of their food preparation to large-scale industrial kitchens off-site to continue managing their costs in these challenging times.

3. Digital technology will change the way customers order from us, how we sell to our customers, and how everyone will order our food from restaurants forever. During the pandemic, delivery and takeout often have been the only way food service operators can sell to consumers. This is a big reminder that we need to make sure the great products we create from our New Zealand milk are fit for delivery and takeout. A great example is what we are doing with our mozzarella innovation to ensure products like pizza are still piping hot and the cheese is still stretchy when it arrives at homes.

In the wake of COVID-19, we are already seeing heightened awareness from people about their health and immunity. As a result, food-as-medicine is taking off again. The importance of science in consumer choice will likely increase, with significant implications for both products and production methods.

Although a lot of these trends were on their way before the pandemic, COVID-19 has accelerated them as businesses have had to pivot and, in many cases, change their business model. Some of these changes were initially brought in to help businesses manage through the short-term, but we expect to see many establishments continue them as a permanent part of the way they do business.

In times like these, the key to success will be mindset – embracing change and thinking differently while putting ourselves in our customers' shoes. In addition to this – we must have a firm focus on our return on capital. We must ensure that capital investments deliver against their business cases – which is where our innovation agenda will play an important role.

We have the opportunity to leverage our sustainability value proposition and to really differentiate our precious New Zealand milk while also entering into new categories with new products where our sustainability, innovation, and efficiency give us a competitive advantage. A big part of this will be all about focusing on the things we can control. For example, we can't control when governments relax their various lockdown rules or put them back again, as we see in many countries. And we can't control when our food service customers can start operating again. However, despite these challenges, we can still look at ways to get closer to our customers and support them so that we are their preferred supplier when they are open for business.

Learning from the Great Lockdown

COVID-19 has made us rethink several aspects of how we do business and how we respond to rapidly evolving circumstances. Some of our key learnings include:

1. **Importance of agility:** The best-equipped companies will look to rapidly adjust their strategies to fit with the "new normal" dairy world post-COVID-19. Several already underlying trends are likely to be accelerated by COVID-19.

2. **Sustainability:** Sustainability already has been gaining traction for years. Assuming consumer spending power is not too badly hit, it is plausible to imagine a post-COVID-19 world where sustainability

will have an even more significant impact on consumer purchasing. Increased supply chain scrutiny is likely to take place.

3. **Plan for scenarios:** Along with pharmacy and some high-tech industries, dairy has undoubtedly been more sheltered from the global downturn than most sectors. And unlike the long 2008 economic crash, a faster rebound in demand is expected, with China in particular helping. In fact, in New Zealand dairy sales have gained strength during the pandemic, and the industry has proven itself to be a durable part of the New Zealand economy.

4. **Proactively adapt:** It will be critical for dairy companies to capitalize on sales channel shifts, with customer-led operating models that allow companies to take advantage of these opportunities.

5. **New categories:** In the wake of COVID-19, we are already seeing health and food-as-medicine taking off again. The importance of science in consumer choice will likely increase, with significant implications for both products and production methods. This could also act to accelerate the advance of dairy alternatives.

6. **New customer behaviors:** We believe the secret to our success going forward is all about applying our solutions in a different way to provide the most support to our customers. We have already seen how well our China food service business has bounced back. They have shared their learnings with us, and we have already applied some of these to our new strategy. In particular, we are looking at all the new online behaviors we have been following and how we can best capitalize on these.

While economists are expecting the world economy to continue to recover from the lows of 2020, growth will not be evenly spread. We will need to continue to monitor the impact and flow of the effects of COVID-19 in our markets and keep adapting as necessary.

About the Contributor

Karen has been with Fonterra for 11 years and in that time she has had a number of senior management positions. While in the role of GM Preparedness and Response, which she moved from earlier this year, she led our crisis and incident management teams in response to a number of issues across the co-op.

Karen led Fonterra's COVID-19 crisis response, and while she says at times the task at hand was daunting, ultimately she was inspired by the way everyone at Fonterra joined together to successfully face the many challenges COVID-19 brought, which in turn saw the co-op come through the pandemic in good shape.

CHAPTER 7

Globalization Partners

By Nicole Sahin (CEO and Founder) and Debbie Millin (COO)

About Globalization Partners

Globalization Partners simplifies global remote team building by making it fast and easy for companies to hire anyone, anywhere within minutes via our Service as a Solution (SaaS) global Employer of Record (EOR) platform powered by our in-house worldwide HR experts. Companies find the talent, and we enable them to hire that employee without the complexity of setting up costly international branch offices or subsidiaries. The way our platform works is that we put our customers' talent on our already existing, in-country payroll, which spans 180+ countries. We're legally the employer of record, but the customer gets all the normal benefits of having global team members without setting up international entities, managing global benefits, or figuring out complex global tax matters.

Before launching Globalization Partners in 2012, one thing was clear to the founder, Nicole Sahin: There was an opportunity to innovate in the international expansion space. Global growth was a priority for many companies, but the red tape doing business in foreign countries made it challenging and time-consuming for companies to go global.

Almost ten years later, Globalization Partners has fundamentally shifted the way companies hire talent worldwide. We make it possible to hire team members via our fully compliant global Employer of Record platform, within hours of finding the right talent – easily.

We're proud to be the clear market leader in an industry we led from the outset, and while 2020 ended up being a positive year for us as a company overall, the year as a whole certainly didn't go off without a hitch.

Any startup founder or high-growth company executive knows that building a business from the ground up is full of curveballs. Even after nine years of high-growth madness, 2020 stood out as one for the record books. The initial period of March through June was the most stressful because we were steering a fairly large ship through a storm without a compass or any data to help us chart a new course.

When the lockdown started, we knew we had to react quickly as a company to preserve the foundation we had built and that we also had to reassess our strategic plans. We also knew we needed to take very rapid steps to survive and become stronger and more resilient. The challenge of pivoting quickly, without any data or insight into what might happen, was extraordinary and unprecedented.

What We Expected in 2020

Globalization Partners closed a minority investment round in January 2020, and we planned to grow at full speed before COVID-19 hit. We had recently expanded our revenue team and started hiring in England and Ireland to sell into Europe. We also had plans to hire a GM in Singapore to lead our Asia Pacific sales team expansion.

Before the beginning of the pandemic, we hit at least 20% quarter-over-quarter growth but only sold global expansion services to companies headquartered in North America. Our 2020 plan was to take the business that had found radical success in North America and replicate that in Europe and Asia. We also planned to invest heavily in our technology team, with the theme of "automate everything." Our business of employing team members worldwide on behalf of other companies is, by nature, a human-centric business. Still, much of what our high-value team members do around the globe can be automated. We intend to build a highly scalable and customer service-centric business by using technology to make repeatable tasks go away, so that team members can focus on supporting our customers and their team members with personable, high-touch service.

To accomplish this, we had planned to double revenue and staff for the year, bringing in 180 internal employees over the course of 2020 to our existing team of 186 people. In the end, we hired almost the same number of internal employees as originally intended, and our revenue grew about 40% for the year to roughly a half-billion annual recurring revenue (USD). We consider ourselves extraordinarily lucky to have grown our revenue line while also executing our plans to build the business's operations and technology side for future growth.

When the pandemic began to make itself known, like all executives, we tried to navigate in a completely unpredictable environment. We charted a course that would enable us to succeed or at least survive based on multiple variables. We were also acutely aware of the lives that depended on us – not only our team members but also our customers and their employees around the globe.

When It Began

When we first started hearing about COVID-19 in early Q1 via our internal employees in China, we weren't yet sure that this would be a global pandemic. The information we were receiving in the US initially wasn't very clear. The evolving situation resulted in us deciding to close our global offices and go completely remote in early March 2020, somewhat ahead of when other US companies started considering the same.

As a company with offices in every corner of the globe, including countries that don't have a normalized work-from-home culture, we were concerned about the impact of closing all our international offices. Did our vital finance team members have Wi-Fi and proper workspaces to work from home? How could we collaborate and keep our team spirits high? Despite the risk to the business, it seemed the right thing to do to get ahead of the pandemic in terms of protecting our team members' lives. We made the calculated choice to let everyone work from home, even in places that hadn't yet seen the virus.

Fast and Bold Actions to Protect Employees

Once we chose to go fully remote, we realized that some of our teams would struggle more than others to continue working. In the US, working remotely is common, at least a day or two per week. Our teams in India and Mexico, among others, were facing a more drastic transition and lifestyle shift. In many countries, working remotely is not a part of the mainstream business culture, and Internet infrastructure in private homes was often less reliable than workplaces.

While it was anxiety-inducing and required backup plans to make sure the business could still run if many members of our team were unable to effectively work from home, we made the decision that we were better off enabling our team to protect themselves by working from home versus going into the office and risking their health.

Having set the home office shift in motion, we needed to make sure that our teams worldwide had the right infrastructure set up to work from home and had contingency plans in case of widespread illness or Internet failures. To make sure that people were equipped to connect and work without interruption, our executives worked directly with our in-country HR and managerial leads worldwide to smoothen the transition, creating individual plans for each home office, such as buying home office wireless boosters.

Employees appreciated that we put their safety first and doubled down on their commitment to work. There was a sentiment that we were all in it together, and our team members valued that we prioritized their health. We were impressed by the team spirit and everyone's commitment to getting through the pandemic together.

Some offices prepared mobile hotspots for employees to take home, should they have connectivity issues. Many communities – rural and urban alike – were experiencing slow or intermittent wireless Internet connections. This can significantly impede business, so it was worth doubling down on resources early on. Logistically, we were lucky to be set up well before the pandemic, with everything in the cloud and most meetings already being held over video. Globalization Partners was in a unique position to switch gears quickly and effectively.

Realistic Recalculations and Our Biggest Business Challenges

In mid-March, which is usually an extremely high-demand month for Globalization Partners, new business dried up completely. Over 70 new customer agreements expected to close within two weeks suddenly stopped negotiations. Companies everywhere froze operations, especially hiring plans, because nobody knew how their business would be impacted. This sudden halt left executive teams worldwide scrambling to function and create clarity in an environment where there is none. Our well-laid plans suddenly were thrown into "pause" as we ourselves paused hiring while our CEO and CFO scrambled to forecast worst-case, mid-range, and best-case scenarios.

Existing customers also reacted, not knowing what this would mean for their business and working through their own contingency plans. We reached out to every one of our customers to see how we could help them. Some customers did reduce their staff. We helped others navigate salary reductions or other adjustments to keep their team intact and reduce their costs while we rode out the storm together. We also offered additional services at no cost to help customers who were continuing to hire – many of whom were making shifts and hiring in different countries than they might have originally planned.

It was intimidating to see the calculations for our worst-case scenario, but our business needed a plan for every possible outcome. We expected to lose about a third of our recurring revenue customer base, assuming our customers would be terminating people they hired via our Employer of Record solution as they tried to cut costs. Ironically, this loss of revenue would come with a lot of work because if our customers were terminating team members around the globe, we would have to handle those terminations with as much grace as possible for all parties during a nebulous legal and emotional time.

Meanwhile, governments around the world were putting slap-dash regulations in place to stop companies from terminating employees. Keeping up with fast-changing regulations in over 180 countries to protect employees during a pandemic was our core job function. We were obligated to our customers – and their team members who trusted us – to do it well.

Another challenge in March 2020 was that our finance executives estimated that in the worst-case scenario, up to 30% of their team would not be able to work from home at all due to inadequate infrastructure and lack of dependable Internet connections. A significant portion of our billing team is in India and Mexico. At that time, we knew that if our teams in Mexico and India were unable to function, we'd be facing huge roadblocks as a company. Getting money in, out, and around the world is critical to our business, so we were more than prepared to pivot if all hands were needed to stay operational. Our finance and technology teams scrambled to ensure operations would continue no matter what.

Once we had a plan in place and had carefully thought through all contingencies, we pivoted and executed. It took about two and a half weeks to get there, during which the executive team found ourselves suddenly at home and cut off from one another except through video calls, planning through one of the most stressful and unpredictable periods of our careers.

By early April, we had our plan in place. CEO Nicole Sahin led an all-hands call and spoke with our entire team globally about what we expected for the business and the numbers behind the worst-case scenario. We had calculated that we might lose up to a third of our recurring revenue and that the economy (and our revenue) might not recover for up to a year. Beyond that, our survival plan was to hunker down and build the technology underlying the business so that we could come out of the pandemic as an even more dominant market leader in our space. It was important to our leaders to be transparent, and we knew people were worried about the survival of the business and their jobs. We were clear about what we asked of our team: understanding, hard work, and collaboration, with the promise that the worst was behind us. It was going to be a rocky road, but we'd get through it together.

Preparing for the Road Ahead

In the global Employer of Record industry, it took our customer base until about June to figure out how COVID-19 was going to impact their business, what their new financial situation was going to be, and how that would impact their hiring plans – but at the beginning of the pandemic we didn't know how quickly that turnaround would happen. Meanwhile, we came up with our strategic plan, and it was communicated to every employee in early April. Our strategic plan was to hunker down and build.

In January 2020, we received USD 150 million in private equity funding. We knew that if carefully managed, we could use the pandemic period and the economic downturn to continue building the underlying infrastructure of the business, laying a strong foundation for the undoubted success ahead. We wanted to come out of the pandemic stronger and knew we had a once-in-a-lifetime opportunity to take strategic advantage of future opportunities.

Thankfully, our worst fears were not realized. Our global teams set up home offices wherever they could – some even converted closets into cubicles – and were ultimately successful. We didn't have even one employee who was unable to make remote-work work. We suffered relatively few customer terminations and surprisingly few problems with collections. Our costs were lower due to the lack of travel and in-person events, and we paused on our plans for office space expansion while our team continued to work remotely. We got a Paycheck Protection Program (PPP) loan from the government, which helped because we didn't know how hard our customers would retract on payments. Beyond that, we felt fairly comfortable with liquidity because we had planned carefully for this type of event since the company was founded.

Thanks to years of contingency planning and structuring our business for maximum financial stability at the outset, we maintained our firm footing. Also, the timing of our minority investment added to our resiliency.

Supporting Our Customers

Once we'd overcome the initial shock and our teams were once again operating at full speed, we looked to our customers. Everybody was going through a crisis, so we asked ourselves how we could use our resources and pivot to be as helpful as possible in getting through this situation. We have always believed in providing exceptional customer service, and if our customers were going to go through hard times, we wanted to help. Our business philosophy has always been to do right by our customers and our employees, and the business, in turn, will take care of itself. That philosophy proved itself again during the pandemic.

We'd assumed many companies would be laying people off, and we wanted to help save jobs, so the right decision was clear to us: reallocate resources from new product line launches to help our customers by being maximally flexible wherever we could. We also went out and got government grants in every country where we were eligible and, in the spirit of those programs, passed those savings on to our customers as a direct refund of the costs of keeping their team members employed. Specifically, in Australia, we received a boost payment of AUD 100,000 and credited this grant to our customers with Australian employees. We also received government support in Singapore, which we passed on to our customers with Singapore-based team members.

Many of the companies we serve were not directly eligible for government programs, so this grant sharing helped them keep their employees on board. If we got a refund, that went back to our customers. That meant we had a direct impact on their business and helped save jobs all over the world.

Once we were confident that we did right by our customers, we moved to restart marketing efforts. We knew that when the economy stabilized, the market would be booming with demand for the global remote workforce. This is exactly what we could help companies achieve. We were increasingly sure that leaders would come out of the pandemic having learned that they could build a global remote workforce by hiring anyone they wanted anywhere in the world.

With the gift of retrospect, we can say that we read the market right, which led us to maintain and accelerate our market leadership position. Google analysts told us in December 2020 that Globalization Partners' market presence was significantly greater than that of our competitors in terms of share of voice, and our lead widened significantly during the pandemic. This is likely because most companies in our industry pulled back spending during 2020, whereas we moved, carefully and strategically, full steam ahead on our newly charted course.

Another decision made in Q2 was to accelerate our technology investments. Automating expansion was already on our technology roadmap, and the remote reality we found ourselves in made these technology advancements more pressing. Our engineers accelerated this evolution to help companies hire internationally, facilitate remote onboarding, and continue their expansion plans, pandemic or not.

Accelerating into the Region Best Positioned to Bounce Back

As a result of our team moving to remote working, regional divides melted away as we all switched to digitally communicating with our colleagues. Besides, that shift made hiring in a new country no longer as daunting as it was pre-2020 for many companies.

Asia Pacific and Europe were already major components of our expansion plans. While other companies scaled down, we accelerated hiring in Asia Pacific by onboarding our General Manager for Asia ahead of schedule. This was a somewhat risky bet but calculated, because we saw governments there handling the pandemic so much better than the rest of the world. We expected a faster economic recovery in Asia Pacific, and we chose Singapore as our hub to enter the wider APAC region from a revenue perspective.

We saw the stock market bounce back around the world in Q3 and knowledge-based companies like ours recovered a semblance of "business as usual," albeit from our living rooms and kitchens. Globalization Partners' team in Asia Pacific overachieved on targets in 2020, as did our team in Europe. We targeted the latter region from our innovation center in Ireland – another product of the lockdown that we have been able to grow, training every new hire remotely.

We are very fortunate that the pandemic's impact on our liquidity wasn't as drastic as expected. We had sufficient cash to fuel the company's expansion in Asia and Europe. However, we still decided to reallocate resources through 2020 toward longer-term revenue, operations, and technology efficiency, because we didn't know how long the economic slowdown would last.

Our Employees Came Through for Us

From a human perspective, there were many challenges that we could not foresee, but that brought us closer as a company. Our executive team worked hard to be incredibly supportive and proactive with our employees and acknowledged that we were all having challenges, both personally and professionally.

We encouraged our teams to use Zoom for talking to family and staying in touch with friends and ensured all our teams had Wi-Fi and home workspaces, even if whole families were working from home.

At the start of 2020, we had hired a Global Community and Culture Lead with a focus on growing and maintaining our employees' well-being – something that we doubled down on when the world went into lockdown – and we had the infrastructure in place to continue this support. Like many companies, we set up online social events focusing on storytelling and employee recognition – both to keep our group unified across the globe and to acknowledge the wins amidst a tough year. We partnered with a global organization called Water for People, where we helped fund clean water solutions in Malawi. We hosted our first annual Rockstar Awards – an internal global celebration where we gave out awards to employees nominated by their peers. We also continued to have consistent companywide staff meetings, enhanced our internal communications, and started hosting weekly mindfulness sessions and workshops on resilience and vulnerable leadership. The team has been great about letting us know what they need, and then we partner together to find solutions.

One of our team's suggestions to respond to the lockdown was to set up a COVID-19 task force and make sure our website had up-to-date information about each country we have a presence in. Thanks to this initiative, we instantly pivoted our marketing to be less about "hire this person and expand your business" and more about giving people the most up-to-date resources and cutting through the noise.

Our executives called on their networks for useful data. We are looped in on policies worldwide, so as governments changed legislation regarding terminating employees, COVID-19 relief packages were rolled out. Expert HR recommendations were also disclosed, and our team leaped into motion, sharing information with all our customers.

We reached out to every single customer to ask how we could help them, and we temporarily offered additional HR services for free. Some teams came up with policies to help our customers handle their international employees with IT support. Meanwhile, others coached our customer companies to reduce salaries to avoid layoffs, and our marketing team created content to guide companies on managing their workforces remotely.

Fortunately, our people were able to work from home well. We did our best to support employees, but what's commendable is that our employees came through for us. A large part of our employee population is based in the US, so besides the pandemic, we were also living through civil unrest, which had a major impact on many team members, making an already difficult year even more challenging.

All around the world, our people were dealing with stress, and yet our team was willing to work hard through the storm. They delivered in a way that will always inspire us.

Uptick Thanks to New Business Models

We had expected Q2 to be the first quarter in which company revenue would contract due to the pandemic, but we actually stayed flat – a very unexpected and welcome blessing. By June 2020, companies had cemented their shift to remote work, and this new model led to an uptick in our global hiring business in Q3. Our flatlined revenue numbers started to modestly increase in Q3.

By September, companies knew what the impact of the pandemic would be on their business. They had started to realize that working from home was positive for business, and some began thinking about hiring in new jurisdictions. To provide perspective: by the end of 2020, we had 300 internal employees with annual recurring revenue of USD 500 million. As we look ahead to 2021, we plan to more than double our internal employees to 650 and have an expected USD 750 million in annual recurring revenue. Our revenue mix in 2020 consisted of 90% coming from North America, with 5% from Europe and another 5% from Asia. In 2021 that is changing to 75% from North America, 15% from Europe, and 10% from Asia. Whether this increase in companies' hiring practices was to test out market demand or access the best talent worldwide, they were coming to us to help them do so.

Technology and software companies that power virtual communication and online learning saw significant growth, and many organizations began expanding development teams, customer support, and sales teams. With many visa restrictions in the US, we also saw companies seek to retain talent in their home countries due to their inability to relocate to the US during the pandemic. Our business makes the potential of a global remote workforce easy, and we were extraordinarily well positioned to help companies take advantage of the new trend toward global remote work.

Internally, we continue to hire around the world and interview remotely. We've hired hundreds of people who have worked with us for months but have not met any of their team members in person. For a global company, that happens periodically every time you hire the first person in a new market, but the levels to which we hired to great success in 2020 were astounding. We attribute a lot of our success in this area to having an effective onboarding program and wonderful company culture. We've also doubled down on our training and internal technology. Though many of us have never met in person, our teams always say they feel like they know everyone so well. This is because we had already built the baseline systems and processes well before remote work became the norm.

Some key elements of our onboarding program include:

- First-week plan: key conversations with new co-workers to help the new hire get to know their team.

- Internal pulse checks: each team member fills out weekly check-ins using software called 15Five, which gives their manager and leadership a view into their focus areas and growth objectives.

- 30-, 60-, 90-day checkpoints: documented expectations and a 90-day check-in with the manager to ensure their first three months were effective.

There's a lot of fear around hiring people you've never met. But once you take the leap, it can be as easy as or even easier than in-person recruiting. What *is* interesting is the change in how people looked at Globalization Partners and why they were coming to us. Traditionally, we had been all about sales expansion, but now we help clients hire people around the world who may not be able to expatriate for a visa or for COVID-19-related reason. Our solution has facilitated employers to grow teams quickly and allow their employees to work from wherever they live, in full compliance with laws and regulations.

Transparency, Even About Uncertainty

The total absence of data and predictability as we watched the pandemic unfold was extremely stressful and frustrating for leaders. Yet we needed to provide direction for our teams. As a leader or CEO, it's your responsibility to project confidence and develop a plan.

In the interests of providing stability to our employees even while leadership was still trying to find its footing, in March 2020 we communicated to employees that we would not require people to come back to the office until the end of the year. We continued to monitor the situation and readjusted our predictions in Q2. At that time, we made sure our teams knew that they would be working from home until April 2021 at the earliest.

Of course, we loved being in the office, united and inspiring each other. But to get to the office in many cities, you have to take public transportation. Our ongoing outreach signaled that our people felt uncomfortable about getting on commuter buses and trains, and our priority was protecting our employees' physical and mental health. Being transparent about this allowed everyone to plan for the coming months.

We also overcommunicated at every opportunity. We spoke directly to the entire company every couple of weeks about what was going on during the pandemic's early stages. Our executive team listened carefully to the teams, which was as important as our upfront communication. Plenty of companies talk about promoting that type of empathy and transparency, but periods of uncertainty are when it's time to put those traits into action.

What's Ahead?

Not everyone wants to work in the office every day, and the pandemic forced us to reevaluate this social norm. Employers are now on an accelerated path to adapt to global remote work.

Globalization Partners was ahead of the curve because of our company's nature – we knew that being global and partially remote was a competitive advantage. We, like our customers, questioned hires near our offices in Boston, thinking carefully about each job: Does this role need to be here anymore?" Many positions no longer need to be filled within driving distance of our headquarters. Without the pandemic, would we have gotten to the point where, as a culture, it was normal to not meet employees or go to meetings in person?

Mass remote work has accelerated global hiring and work trends by 10 to 15 years – companies no longer hire simply based on proximity. This new business model is dominating knowledge-based industries because it's more strategic to build around talent hubs, not just where your product is sold. Now, leaders are thinking strategically and targeting great tech talent hubs. For example, they're targeting South America to stay in line with North American time zones, and hiring in Eastern Europe to be close to Berlin and London time zones but in lower-cost jurisdictions. These areas have great talent pools that companies now realize they can access.

As well as the trend toward hiring internationally, leaders are now looking to an asset-light approach: hiring employees worldwide to explore market demand before setting up infrastructure. Companies want to have people in local markets but don't want to invest time and resources into setting up a local entity to do so. A whole host of companies are looking for a solution to unburden their HR teams when hiring where they lack presence because they can now have both remote employees and lighter administration overhead.

Having navigated a global pandemic and seeing our team's resilience, we have every confidence that we will remain the market leader into 2021 and beyond. Also, we positioned the whole industry for growth through consistent communications, which increased demand for services that only an Employer of Record can offer. Today, companies that might never have considered hiring abroad are accessing the best talent for their open positions simply by looking further afield.

The Future of the Industry and Global Business

We believe the next pandemic is highly likely to happen again during our lifetimes. It will become part of basic contingency planning for companies to think about building their businesses to avoid being caught off guard when the next global lockdown hits.

We learned many lessons in 2020 that are important for businesses when preparing for the future:

1. **Build for the worst-case scenario from day one.**

   From a financial perspective, we had always built the company with a potential recession in mind, having worked through 2008 and seen how quickly that decimated much of Silicon Valley. Cash is king and always has been. Our business by nature is high risk from a cash perspective because we take on the liabilities of global employment for our customers. Specifically, we have to pay the team members our customers employ through us, whether or not the customers pay us.

   From day one, we always secured deposits against the risk of having to pay long notice periods if our customers went bankrupt and collecting accrued liabilities related to employment terms as we go. Some of our competitors reduced their requirements to be more competitive, but we stuck to our plan. This paid off in dividends for us as well as our customers – they already had incurred the full cost of their global employees and didn't have to come up with unexpected cash, and we were secured against the possibility of customer bankruptcies.

From a team-building perspective, avoid giving yourself an easy way to cut costs when you need to by building responsibly the first time around. Globalization Partners was spared the need to conduct massive layoffs in 2020 because we were operating in a fiscally responsible way and hiring people in emerging market jurisdictions while still building a highly talented team. We also always future-proofed our business by hiring in cost-appropriate jurisdictions for the talent we needed. This allowed us to emerge from the recession faster and did not give any investor the opportunity to suggest that we "restructure" our team later.

For example, our highly talented business development team for North America is based in a jurisdiction where compensation dollars go much further than hiring in San Francisco or Boston. There's a time to hire high-value talent in high-cost jurisdictions, but finding easy ways to hire remote workers at the outset saves you the pain of laying off team members when they most need their jobs.

2. Secure cash reserves or a line of emergency credit – before you need it.

One of the reasons our company weathered the storm was that we had cash. We were fortunate enough to have run the company with significant cash deposits and not to have played games with our cash reserves, even during an unbelievable bull market with no end in sight. Having an emergency line of credit is critical. As soon as the pandemic hit, new loans dried up at banks. It is impossible to secure a line of credit when you most need it, even with cash in the bank. Don't wait until that moment.

3. Don't underestimate the value of a strong company culture.

Team spirit set us apart in 2020. We have always taken the perspective that investing in a work hard/play hard company spirit with a positive company culture would pay off in dividends, and it did. It took unbelievable grit and perseverance for our team members worldwide to work hard every day despite heartache and school kids suddenly being home, but they did it. We wouldn't have made it without the dedication and brains of our team members.

Among other things, we value communication, leadership, and fun. We make it a point to celebrate employees' wins inside and outside the workplace. Globalization Partners has created several programs that aim to unite its employees and recognize their contributions to the company. These include the Rock Star Awards, for which employees nominate a coworker who goes above and beyond and deserves special recognition. There were winners in every department and every region; winners were given a monetary bonus, and the entire company was given an extra day off to use any time during the summer. Globalization Partners also maintains an internal newsfeed for employees to share their personal wins, life achievements, and happy moments to keep international and remote teammates connected across the world.

As a company with such a widespread and remote workforce, it is vital to get creative and think outside the box. We host many programs and initiatives that encourage employee innovation, creativity, and togetherness. We use technology to enhance the human experience – whether it's sharing photos of a global charity drive, tapping into an internal team and their background and resources to learn from each other, or employees sharing book recommendations and photos of their pets and children. We also have a video-first policy when using Zoom.

To encourage connectivity and collaboration, Globalization Partners implemented Slack as the organization's primary employee collaboration tool, which is helping to connect teams around the world. As part of this, we have also implemented a tool called Donut, an initiative to improve engagement and introduce people virtually who don't know each other.

4. Great technology is worth the investment.

Being online and in the cloud as much as possible is critical to weathering a storm like COVID-19, and it's harder to go digital in the middle of a crisis. For example, if people are equipped to work from home long-term, that will help in the event of a future pandemic. We are also happy with the number of people we helped take new positions at our customer companies, many of whom had been stuck in their country throughout 2020 and were unable to accept jobs that required relocation. Since companies used our solution across the globe to employ great professionals, we helped many people secure job opportunities that might not have been available to them before remote work became commonplace.

COVID-19 gave global remote team building a booster shot, and, in response, we gave our customers access to fantastic employees around the world. We are certain that international remote teams will become part of every company's platform in the future. Coming out of the global recession of 2020, we have learned many lessons and have much to be grateful for, not least of which is the strong foundation we established during our "hunker down and build" strategy we undertook during the pandemic. We are confident we are now well ahead of our competitors and will remain the market leader, due in no small part to our ability to weather the storm as a team.

About the Contributors

Nicole Sahin's mission is to eliminate barriers to doing business internationally and building global teams. As founder and Chief Executive Officer (CEO) of Globalization Partners, she is recognized for having created an innovative solution that enables companies to hire great talent anywhere in the world, without the complexity of setting up international branch offices or subsidiaries. Businesses are able to bypass the legal, HR, and tax complexities of hiring in another country, while getting all the benefits of a global team.

Nicole holds an MBA in international management from the Middlebury Institute of International Studies. She splits her time between Boston and San Diego, loves to travel, and is inspired by the belief that making it easy for people to expand internationally and work seamlessly across borders ultimately makes the world a more exciting and open-minded place.

Debbie Millin is Chief Operating Officer (COO) of Globalization Partners and a founding member of the executive team. With over 20 years of operational, project management, and client relationship experience, Debbie specializes in supporting companies that are experiencing rapid growth to scale their systems and processes.

By 2020, Debbie's leadership led Globalization Partners to be recognized by the Financial Times as one of the fastest-growing companies in America. Debbie serves on the Advisory Board for both Special Olympics of Massachusetts and the Commonwealth Institute and has been a member of multiple nonprofit and private boards throughout her career. She is a frequent speaker on topics including women's leadership, entrepreneurship, rapid-growth companies, and global expansion.

CHAPTER 8

GOGOX

By Steven Lam (Cofounder and CEO) and Eugene Lee (COO)

About GOGOX

Established in 2013, GOGOX is the first app-based logistics platform in Asia committed to providing extensive logistics services through innovative technology. Formerly known as GOGOVAN, the company has a competitive and diverse business portfolio, from van-hailing and instant delivery to customized logistics solutions. GOGOX instantly connects individuals and businesses with millions of logistics partners to fulfill all sorts of delivery needs, redefining the delivery experience by providing speedy, agile, and convenient logistics services that are unmatched. Over the years, GOGOX has expanded its businesses from Hong Kong to Singapore, Taiwan, Mainland China, South Korea, India, and Vietnam.

Backdrop

When COVID-19 first emerged, it appeared mainly in Asia. But within a couple of months, it had spread across the globe, becoming a pandemic that brought the world to a halt. People were told not to leave their homes; cities went into lockdown and country borders were closed. However, as a technology-based logistics company, stopping is exactly the opposite of what we do at GOGOX.

Founded in 2013, GOGOX is the first app-based logistics platform in the Asia-Pacific region. The company started from our first business, Boxful, a lunchbox advertisement company. As that business was operating, we quickly learned that logistics services in Hong Kong were unconsolidated and inefficient. They lacked any type of operational infrastructure, and pricing was obscure. Despite all the challenges, we saw great potential in the logistics industry, which led to the establishment of GOGOVAN, our brand for the next seven years. In 2020, we rebranded to GOGOX to better represent our increased suite of logistics services and solutions.

In the beginning, we offered a van-hailing platform that instantly connected users with our logistics partners in Hong Kong via our mobile application. But we soon realized that our hometown was not our only market. As pioneers aiming to unleash the untapped potential of the logistics industry, we set our sights on conquering the entire Southeast Asia market. Over the years, we have expanded our business to Singapore, Taiwan, South Korea, India, Vietnam, and China. Today, we offer an extensive service portfolio, from van-hailing and instant delivery to customized logistics solutions, covering more than three hundred cities and eight million registered drivers under our network.

In under ten years, our small logistics business has grown to be proudly known as Hong Kong's first unicorn startup. However, would this distinction be enough to serve as our armor and protect us in the battle against COVID-19?

First Signs of COVID-19

We were on a management trip in Yilan, Taiwan, on January 11, 2020. Although COVID-19 was already in the news, it didn't cause us too much concern because everything around us was normal. We thought the situation would be like the previous Middle East respiratory syndrome (MERS) outbreak in Korea in 2015, alarming but controllable. Even when Steven flew to Switzerland to attend the World Economic Forum, COVID-19 wasn't anywhere on the agenda.

However, when we returned to Hong Kong, we experienced a completely different dynamic. Confirmed cases of COVID-19 were increasing and more people in the city started to wear face masks, reminiscent of the troubling severe acute respiratory syndrome (SARS) outbreak in 2003. On February 9, 2020, Hong Kong officially entered its first wave of COVID-19, and throughout the month, parts of China were placed in lockdown, and drivers were unable to return home. We began to sense that COVID-19 was something completely different from what we had initially thought.

There was one particular moment where the severity of the situation really hit us — we had a zero-completion rate for deliveries in China. We were overwhelmed by this unexampled figure. China is our largest market, and if that zero figure lasted for longer than a week, we wouldn't have a business to run. The fear grew as we started to worry if our other markets would also hit zero completion rates.

Navigating the Great Lockdown

It was terrifying to see how quickly COVID-19 spread across the world. Every day, our markets around Asia were seeing increasing numbers of confirmed cases. However, our #growordie company culture empowered us to strive through the challenges.

In early February 2020, we held a town hall meeting with all markets, where we presented the ugly truth — the dissatisfying business numbers and our operational concerns. We believe that transparency is key to crisis management, and as the CEO of the company, Steven wanted to ensure everyone knew that he would stay and overcome any challenges with them side by side.

We are a family of 2,000 staff members across Asia, and we knew that our members have families to support and children to raise. We had to make them feel safe and let them know that they were being taken care of, especially during this difficult time. It was inevitable that we had to execute cost control, and as the captain, Steven stepped up and announced that he would only take one dollar as his salary. Then he asked the leadership team to undergo a pay cut as well. It was not an easy decision, but it was the right one. These initiatives and the quick rebound of our China market bought us some time to buckle down to revise our strategies and sufficiently prepare for this unprecedented journey.

When you are at war, it is advantageous to have a centralized command center and choose the right battleground to start the fight. Hong Kong was our most resourceful and mature market, so it made sense for us to navigate the storm from the location we were most familiar with.

Hong Kong is a very interesting market. Things are always happening in the city, and people change very quickly. We observed two very particular transformations in Hong Kong during the pandemic: the surge of home delivery and the reduced digital divide. These changes exponentially grew our business's potential, particularly GOGODelivery, a door-to-door same-day delivery service, and GOGOBusiness, which specializes in providing logistics solutions to small and medium-sized enterprises (SMEs). Compared to 2019, we recorded a 200% year-on-year growth in new user registrations, while service demand from market segments, specifically public administration and defense as well as accommodation and food service activities, increased 152% and 122%, respectively.

During the first wave of COVID-19, Hong Kong saw a shortage of face masks, and people were very concerned about safety while leaving their homes. In response, we quickly launched a proxy buying service under GOGODelivery, offering a hassle-free shopping and delivery experience for users and encouraging them to stay home. Proxy buying caters to all sorts of daily needs, from grocery shopping and buying household essentials to food delivery. This service's magic is that it goes beyond the Internet, helping to reach local shops with little to no online presence. Our users can place orders for what they need from any shop, and our drivers will go buy it for them and deliver it to their doorsteps. The new feature was enthusiastically welcomed by the public, as we saw sharp increases in new user acquisition, order numbers, and brand awareness.

In March 2020, Hong Kong recorded the second wave of the outbreak. To facilitate the Centre for Health Protection (CHP) health check arrangements and increase the efficiency and speed of sample collection, we introduced a door-to-door saliva specimen pick-up service for inbound travelers and those placed in quarantine. Although we offered the service at cost, this initiative was able to reach more than 30,000 new users, and we had the great potential to turn them into loyal users. We soon expanded the service to all private clinics, laboratories, and private hospitals, penetrating into the new e-health market.

Extending our expertise to helping the local community was something we needed to and were honored to do. Nonprofit organizations, underprivileged families, and disabled individuals throughout Hong Kong were having difficulties getting face masks and sanitizing product supplies. We organized many community events to collect donations of these supplies from the public. Thousands of masks were received and redistributed to families and organizations in need of them, lighting up their dark times with love and care.

The Logistics Flywheel

The milestones we achieved in Hong Kong provided a shot of confidence to our other markets and showed them a path to move forward through this tough time. It also gave us the motivation to take on the bigger challenge: the e-commerce segment.

COVID-19 has accelerated the development of business transformation as companies urgently have felt the need to embrace the digital world. We are not talking about having a simple website; the new era of e-commerce requires a more advanced business infrastructure and agile end-to-end logistics solutions.

In our opinion, the pandemic has expedited the adoption of e-commerce by three years, particularly in the Southeast Asia (SEA) region. The online population grew tremendously in 2020, with 400 million new users joining the Internet; 70% of SEA's population now has access to the Internet.[1] E-commerce is expected to be a core segment to unlock because 90% of online users are likely to keep their online habits post-pandemic, a segment that's worth several billion dollars.

The role of logistics is no longer confined to delivering a package from one place to another. It should now act as a flywheel,[2] facilitating e-commerce evolution and transforming into a business solution that empowers businesses to capture and unleash the value and potential of the digital world. The flywheel effect was introduced by Jim Collins in 2001 and serves as an analogy to describe the process of using the right strategy to lift a heavy wheel and keep it rolling toward greater success. For us, the rapid rise of e-commerce is the flywheel that will drive the logistics industry forward. (See Figure 8.1.)

To assist local SMEs, we offer a more complex range of logistics solutions that meet the needs of businesses of different scales in different markets. GOGOBusiness provides companies with the highest level of logistics efficiency. From dedicated customer team service and routing optimization to driver management, the order cycle is completed on the same day with affordable costs.

---

[1]Internet users in the world 2020 by Statista, https://www.statista.com/statistics/617136/digital-population-worldwide/

[2]Jim C. Collins, *Good to Great: Why Some Companies Make the Leap and Others Don't* (Harper Business, 2001).

FIGURE 8.1   The flywheel effect.

In Taiwan, we launched fulfillment services, supporting marketplaces, and chain-brand companies with a range of services from storage to shipping, going beyond simple delivery. Our team in Korea focused on the retail trade industry and achieved 62% year-on-year growth in terms of order volume.

Meanwhile, social distancing measures in Seoul contributed to a 130% increase in ad-hoc delivery order requests. In Singapore, we have witnessed a significant surge in business delivery and recorded a five-fold increase in new users, in which accommodation and food service activities had the highest service request, with over a 300% year-on-year growth. The swiftly revised strategies in our other markets empowered us to capture market needs according to the rapidly developing COVID-19 situations and ongoing changes in local government policies.

The strategy to tackle the SME market has always been about value, delivering extra product benefits that contribute to better efficiency. COVID-19 has challenged us but also reinforced another part of our company's ethos, #Daretoventure. We have become more than a last-mile delivery company, evolving into a multifaceted, technology-led logistics company that offers agile and efficient logistics solutions.

In addition to business performance, the safety of our users and logistics partners has always been a top priority in our daily operations. We rolled out global safety measures to enhance the service level to be as safe as possible for both users and logistics partners. At our Hong Kong headquarters, we provided an income protection scheme to couriers who participated in the door-to-door saliva specimen delivery initiative, as well as free life insurance coverage to all logistics partners and their families, hoping to offer them a more protected work environment with extra benefits. (See Figure 8.2.)

FIGURE 8.2   In addition to business performance, safety is a top priority.

People Management in the New Normal

Running a business is tough, but managing people is an even more arduous task, especially in the new normal.

One interesting fact about our company is that three of our four founders were fresh graduates when they started the business. When there were fewer than ten employees in the company, things were pretty straightforward. Today we have a great talent team to take care of the thousands of staff we have, and COVID-19 presented us with some bumps in the road. We are a very young company with intelligent and dedicated employees who are mostly millennials and Generation Z. We spared no effort in

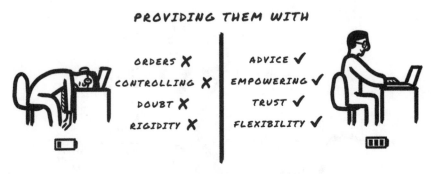

FIGURE 8.3   A safe working environment was essential for all employees.

ensuring a safe working environment for every member of our team in the pandemic. We executed work-from-home procedures and provided face masks and sanitization necessities to all essential employees. But we knew these efforts alone weren't enough. (See Figure 8.3.)

Fairness was the first issue we had to address at a very early stage. Like many companies, we have departments that work in shifts, and the nature of some departments makes it extremely difficult to work remotely. Our customer service team, business team, and finance department went back to the office regularly to keep the wheels rolling, while other teams were able to work from home. Although no one spoke out about it, we felt the need to address this. The founders and department leaders would go back to the office whenever they could to work alongside those departments, indirectly expressing their gratitude for their dedication to the company.

Engaging with those working remotely was a completely different challenge. In Asia, the home office concept is relatively new; although some employees were excited at the work-from-home policy, others were not as fond of it. Within a few weeks, we noticed that work efficiency began to drop and engagement became weaker and sparser. We tried to introduce a timesheet exercise to keep track of work efficiency. However, we quickly realized it wasn't the right tactic because it brought up questions around micromanagement and trust. One of the lessons learned from working with the younger generation is always ensuring that they feel valued and respected, offering them advice instead of presenting orders, and empowering them whenever possible but not controlling them. Therefore, we decided to invite all middle managers to be more involved in strategic meetings, giving them more visibility on the business. Most importantly, they were tasked to improvise according to the market's lockdown situation and company strategies. We provided them with trust and the flexibility to lead and execute as they see fit, and in return, teams became more engaged.

Also, our employees' mental health is something we take very seriously, so we decided to ensure that our office was always available if any employee chose to work there instead of at home. When they worked from home, we made sure they were not working excessively, striking a healthy work-life balance.

From a management perspective, our leadership team was also having a hard time maintaining good communication. Conversations became cold; the team was distant, and members of management within markets and teams were worried. Sometimes doing business is more than just revenue. Creating and embodying the values your team believes in is much more important, particularly in dark times like this. It took many in-depth chats and genuine understanding to rebuild the connection.

What We Learned from COVID-19

Platform and sharing economies have greatly disrupted the way we live and do business. Over the past decade, we have been fascinated with the new economy, but COVID-19 has shaken things up and led us to rethink our strategy.

Our management philosophy has always been "Imagine for ten years, plan for five years, action plan for three years, execute it in one year," but COVID-19 was never in the picture. We know it's cliché to ask "what if," but what if there was no pandemic? Generally, we believe the digital surge and business transformation would have happened at a much slower pace, investing more time in educating people on the value of logistics. If everything went as planned, 2020 was the year for our international growth, building our Korean market to become the second Hong Kong, our second-most profitable market. However, there aren't any what-ifs in real life. Instead, the pandemic has taught us just how important it is to build a business that can resist any uncertainties, big or small.

Like many other startups, we used to chase after aggressive expansion, valuing something that looks good on paper over our business's long-term quality. One of the amendments we made during COVID-19 was to rectify our mentality and search for better business efficiency, growing the company in a healthier and more sustainable way with a strong foundation that can stand up against any kinds of black swans in the future.

Reverse Engineering

Over a period of 18 months, we reversed our approach and shifted our focus to the fundamentals — our product, our people, and our brand. At the product level, we put more time and resources into our products as our investment in the future. We migrated our seven-year-old app server infrastructure from a basketball court to an airfield, providing ourselves with better grounds for greater achievement. Also, we launched our integrated API suite and unlocked agile seamless logistics integration for businesses of all sizes. The product and engineering transformation set a more robust infrastructure for us to scale up and execute our new "flywheels" at a much faster speed. (See Figure 8.4.)

Besides upgrading our products, we also worked with our team to make sure they comprehend the challenges ahead in the new normal and to tackle them with the right characteristics and beliefs. Back in 2013, we created three company values — #nobullshit, #noevil, and #daretoventure. After seven years and much growth, we decided to refresh the culture we embody to better respond to the world today.

PAST

LOOKING FOR
MARKET EXPANSION

NOW

BUILDING STRONGER
FUNDAMENTALS AND
HIGHER EFFICIENCY

FIGURE 8.4 The new flywheels.

Our company's DNA doesn't come from founders and senior management but from our managers and juniors who demonstrate our standards and values throughout their work and the daily interaction with users, driver-partners, and the community. We formed an Employee Engagement Team and invited members across markets and teams to discuss the characteristics we exemplify daily and the culture we want to build for the future. It helped us understand more about the type of company our employees enjoy working at and how we might get there.

Today, we are a company that values #nobullshit and #daretoventure and embraces the culture of #topofyourgame, #growordie, and #deliverhappiness. With stronger products and people, we wanted to let the world know that we are ready for the challenges and opportunities that the future will bring. So, we rebranded.

GOGOVAN was who we were for seven years. But we bid the brand farewell on July 8, 2020, as we entered the eighth year of our journey, with new branding as a celebration of how far we have evolved. GOGOX is a new identity that symbolizes our commitment to providing eXtraordinary eXperience to individuals, business customers, and logistics partners with our eXpertise and to drive eXponential growth for enterprises with efficient logistics services and technologies. We are immensely proud of our achievements, especially when times have been tough, but we are excited to show what the newer and stronger us can deliver.

Future Outlook

Frankly speaking, we are still not out of the woods yet, but at least we are on the right track. Efficiency sits at the core of our business now; we have scaled up our products and rebranded to enable ourselves to capitalize on greater opportunities. Our marketing and growth strategy are more dedicated to enhancing the user's journey; a holistic approach is in place from activation to retention. We are aiming to build more flywheels to equip ourselves with the right DNA against any global crisis in the future. (See Figure 8.5.)

Logistics and delivery are industries that have not been accelerated over the last 20 years. The emergence of e-commerce has forced the industries to evolve to satisfy altered customer behavior. There are expectations

* MANAGEMENT PHILOSOPHY
# DNA OF GOGOX

FIGURE 8.5   The company's new identity helps define a path for the future.

for more advanced service levels and more instant and real-time logistics services. The development of intra-city logistics will further facilitate the adoption of e-commerce and home delivery, a more connected living infrastructure enabled by technology and data analytics.

The world has changed, and we have to change with it. Information will be shared seamlessly with the increasing adoption of digital technology. Consumer behavior will continue to transform and require more complex data analytics to understand. Automated vehicles and smart city development will further reshape our industry. The logistics evolution will be centered around connectivity and efficiency, requiring the traditional service to develop a new set of more agile and instantaneous solutions.

There is an interesting equation awaiting us to crack: what will the future look like when logistics is further exposed to the influence of digitalization with advanced technology such as artificial intelligence and robotics accelerating in the post-pandemic era, along with the growing influence of Generation Z?

About the Contributors

Steven Lam is the cofounder and Chief Executive Officer (CEO) of GOGOX, which was founded in 2013. He is responsible for developing the overall business strategy and driving the growth and profitability of the business across the region. Steven earned a bachelor's degree in business administration with a focus on global management from the Haas School of Business, University of California, Berkeley.

Eugene Lee is the Chief Operating Officer (COO) of GOGOX, overseeing the strategic direction and operations in GOGOX's seven markets. The combined entity is now Asia's largest logistic delivery platform. Eugene continues to chart the company's expansion plan, evolving and improving the company's operational processes, engagement, efficiency, and productivity, as GOGOX takes on its next phase of growth and progress.

CHAPTER 9

Hornet

By Christof Wittig (Founder and CEO)

About Hornet

Hornet is the world's top gay social network, with over 30 million users, providing a community home base that is available anytime, anywhere. Amplifying the radical, affirmative power of the LGBTQ+ community with cutting-edge technology, users feel comfortable sharing their experiences with friends who understand and validate their life. Hornet has become the number one gay app in markets such as France, Russia, Brazil, Turkey, and Taiwan, and is rapidly expanding its sizable user base in the US.

Backdrop: Social Networking for the Gay Community

The social networking industry is sometimes dubbed the oil industry of the 21st century, alluding to its increasingly pivotal role in managing interpersonal relationships, the formation of opinion in societies, and its ability to extract oligopolistic profits from their dominant position in the marketplace due to network effects.

However, the industry is undergoing constant change, and the market leaders are experiencing clear signs of disruption. Innovative social media formats such as mobile, chat, or ephemeral video challenged the status quo and prompted large acquisitions, such as those of Instagram and WhatsApp. Later, entire subcommunities left the one-size-fits-all networks and found their own spaces, starting with young millennials (Snapchat and TikTok), business users (LinkedIn), news (Twitter), or athletes

(Strava). The arrival of TikTok and Clubhouse shows the ability of new entrants to routinely build very large audiences in short periods of time.

At their inception, gay apps were narrowly defined as dating apps, introduced and led to this day by Grindr. Hornet, which I cofounded in 2011, and other gay apps initially followed this lead and carved out niches in certain regions or subcommunities. Grindr continued to battle allegations of being much too dating- and sex-oriented, and toxic for minorities within the gay community, with initiatives like the now largely abandoned Kindr campaign.[1] The need for a more community-oriented app became apparent.

Hornet recognized the opportunity to provide a more inclusive place for the LGBTQ+ community, as well as the market openings in social networking, and pivoted in 2016 to become the world's gay social network. By including content and influencer programs into the app, Hornet created a safe space for gay men to contribute, connect, and communicate over their interests rather than for dating purposes or in heteronormative and often unsafe environments.

In subsequent major releases, Hornet was first among gay apps to introduce a feed (Version 3 in 2016), to add news articles (V4 in 2017), to elevate the feed to be the app's home page rather than a grid of guys nearby (V5 in 2018), to add the Hornet Badge of authenticity (V6 in 2019), and most recently to add ephemeral video stories to the home page in fall 2020 (V7).

Today, with over 30 million diverse users, Hornet provides a community home base that is available anytime, anywhere. Amplifying the radical, affirmative power of the gay community with cutting-edge technology, users feel comfortable sharing their experiences with friends who understand and validate their life.

In 2020, prior to the effects of COVID-19, we expected to grow our paying users from 37,000 by 30% to close to 50,000, and our social networking users from around 450,000 daily active users (DAU) by 30% to over 600,000. We expected to increase engagement metrics, such as chat messages or feed activity, by 10% per user and revenue by 30%, turning

---

[1] #KindrGrindr: Gay dating app launches anti-racism campaign, https://www.bbc.com/news/newsbeat-45573611

a small profit after reinvesting additional revenue in additional hires. Hornet hadn't planned to spend any funds on marketing, just as we had not in 2019, and intended to grow purely organically.

First Signs: March 2020

Hornet's product and design team was meeting up for a "Design Sprint" during March 10–15, 2020, in Istanbul, Turkey, to test new product features with focus group users in my presence. (See Figure 9.1.) After that week, we were slated to travel to Cape Town, South Africa, to meet for the quarterly product and engineering offsite as well as the annual executive offsite.

FIGURE 9.1   The "Design Sprint" in Istanbul, March 2020.

The news reports were already tense in February and early March, with COVID-19 cases skyrocketing in various parts of the world and Italy going into full lockdown on March 9. The situation rapidly deteriorated further during the week of March 10, while we gathered in Istanbul, and we started to see a heavy impact on our business:

- Daily active users (DAU) dropped 2% that week and continued to drop 2–3% every week until it hit a trough on April 24.
- Nearly all premium brand partners of Hornet (e.g., Gilead, Panasonic, LiveNation) put their advertising campaigns on hold by the end of March.
- User subscription revenue softened only slightly and was supported by renewals and a generally strong performance earlier in the year. However, since Hornet makes a significant portion of its user revenue in various emerging markets, the drop of the Russian ruble, Turkish lira, and other currencies by some 20% from March 2020 onwards was also immediately hitting the revenue top line, denominated in US dollars.
- On March 13, a senior key engineer based in Prague, slated to travel to the offsite in Cape Town, fell ill to COVID-19.

All of us who had traveled to Istanbul and were scheduled to travel to Cape Town on March 16 decided to cancel our trips and return to our respective hometowns.

Based on the initial read of numbers and the general news, the executives anticipated a steep drop in revenue. We convened on Zoom (a platform the widely distributed company used since 2015) in an extraordinary board meeting on April 2 to review Hornet's economic assessment (see Figure 9.2) and to hammer out the details of a COVID Preparedness Plan (**Plan CP**). We decided on a raft of measures to weather the crisis, including:

- Acceleration of community digitization to make Hornet a COVID-19 winner
- Cost reductions by going fully virtual across the entire company, without offices or travel, and other cost-saving measures

Economic Update
COVID-19 Pandemic

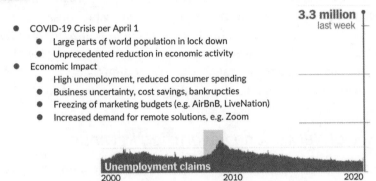

- COVID-19 Crisis per April 1
  - Large parts of world population in lock down
  - Unprecedented reduction in economic activity
- Economic Impact
  - High unemployment, reduced consumer spending
  - Business uncertainty, cost savings, bankrupcties
  - Freezing of marketing budgets (e.g. AirBnB, LiveNation)
  - Increased demand for remote solutions, e.g. Zoom

FIGURE 9.2　Hornet's economic assessment from the beginning of the pandemic.
Source: Hornet

- Converting 20% of the entire team compensation for two quarters to equity and future bonuses, which was unanimously and gratefully accepted by all team members, as they valued the promised job security
- Raising 1.5x monthly revenue in a Working Capital Note to fortify our balance sheet
- Appointing a COVID czar to calibrate the tone of Hornet for the hardships ahead, reprogramming most of our campaigns toward staying at home, wearing masks, and other socially responsible behavior

During the Great Lockdown of 2020–21

There were many implications for both our business and our industry in 2020–21.

Social Networking Usage

Generally, social networking usage was only slightly disrupted by COVID-19. Facebook's DAU barely dipped in 2020 in the US, Canada, and Europe and grew moderately throughout the year in the rest of the world, not very different from the trends observed in 2019. Facebook family's (including Instagram and WhatsApp) DAU grew stronger, also in line with the 2019 trends.[2] Newcomer TikTok grew strong from 500 to 700 million monthly active users (MAU) in the first half of 2020,[3] and strong new players (Clubhouse) emerged as in prior years: Clubhouse started in April 2020 and went from a few thousand users in May 2020 to three million as of January 2021.[4] However, since social networking markets in general were already pretty saturated, COVID-19 didn't steeply accelerate their growth rates as it did for video calling (Zoom) or online food delivery.

Social Networking Advertising Revenue

Initially, when COVID-19 hit, advertising revenue plunged in Q2 and Q3 2020. In Q4 2020, this trend reversed, as businesses started to adapt to the increased digitization of economies and acceleration of direct-to-consumer models, while offline retail locations still remained partially or fully shut. This benefited digital, highly targeted, direct-to-consumer advertising revenue. For instance, at Facebook, the seasonally strong Q4/2020 saw a 43% increase over Q1/2020, while the respective spread in 2019 was only 30%.

Dating Users

Dating apps took a deeper drop in Q2 2020 than social networks but also rebounded strongly in Q4, as users looked to reconnect or find new friends or partners online.

Hornet's User Numbers

Our user numbers initially dropped moderately by 5% in 2020 but then fully recovered in line with the industry. (See Figure 9.3.)

However, Hornet's composition of users – social networking versus dating users – changed dramatically in 2020 as we continued to ship social networking functionality. Social users on Hornet rose from around 450,000 average daily active users at the beginning of 2020 by 30% to over 600,000 by the end of 2020. (See Figure 9.4.)

[2]Facebook Q4 2020 earnings, https://investor.fb.com/investor-events/event-details/2021/Facebook-Q4-2020-Earnings-/default.aspx
[3]https://www.cnbc.com/2020/08/24/tiktok-reveals-us-global-user-growth-numbers-for-first-time.html
[4]https://www.businessofapps.com/data/clubhouse-statistics/

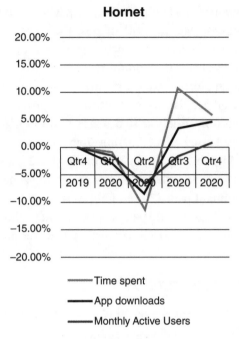

Hornet

──── Time spent

──── App downloads

──── Monthly Active Users

FIGURE 9.3   Hornet's user numbers.
Source: Hornet

User Behavior Cohorts 2018-20
Avg DAU

── Social

FIGURE 9.4   The evolution of Hornet's user composition.
Source: Hornet

Social usage would be a feed-based activity, where people, independent of location, would engage on posts or post their own content, together with many other users in a public space, organized around common interests pertaining to the LGBTQ+ community.

Engagement on Hornet exploded. The average number of chat messages sent per user per day jumped from 24 to over 30 at the peak of COVID-19 and has now solidly settled at 28, some 20% higher than in 2018.

Video stories, launched in Version 7 in October 2020, became an instant hit. (See Figure 9.5.) By the end of April 2021, some 25,000 user-generated videos were posted every week, triggering some 1 million users to watch them a total of over 250 million times.

In short, from a user metric perspective, Hornet achieved all its ambitious goals to grow as a gay social network in 2020, despite COVID-19.

Hornet's Revenue and Costs

Hornet's revenue developed K-shaped in 2020. Advertising took a beating while user revenue continued to grow strong.

Advertising revenue plunged sharply, as it did for peers in the industry, and has not rebounded, partially because of increased barriers for smaller advertisers to earn revenue through marketplace headwinds (such as GDPR and IFDA). The premium direct business barely had a heartbeat in Q2, but in Q4 2020, it came back with one of the strongest quarters of new insertion orders (mostly for 2021 flights) since 2018.

Subscription revenue from users, on the other side, barely budged in Q2/2020 but continued to increase rapidly thereafter, continuing its trend of fast-rising user revenues stemming from Hornet's now well-differentiated position as a social network. (See Figure 9.6.)

From January 2020 to January 2021, the number of paying users at Hornet rose by 45%. On the revenue side, though, in subscription prices denominated in emerging market currencies such as the Russian ruble or the Turkish lira – which plunged some 20% versus the US dollar in Q2/2020 – the dent was bigger and has not yet fully recovered because many of these currencies remain below their dollar value compared to a year prior. (See Figure 9.7.)

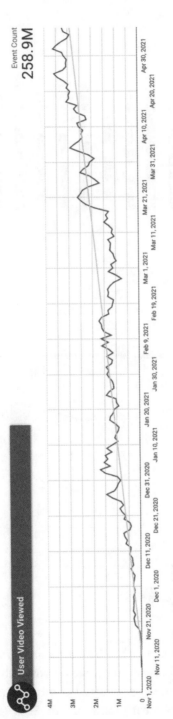

FIGURE 9.5 User video views.

Source: Hornet

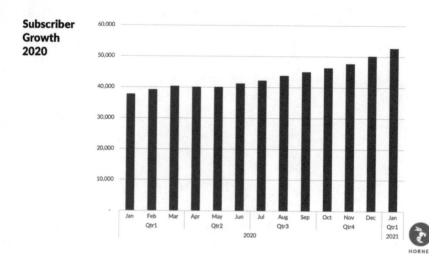

FIGURE 9.6 Subscriber growth in 2020.
Source: Hornet

Hornet Revenues

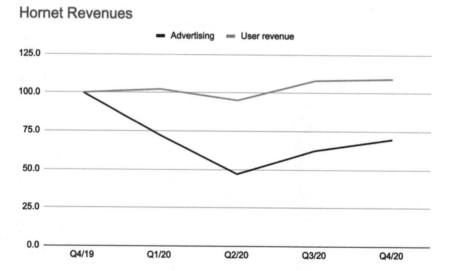

FIGURE 9.7 Company revenues in 2020.
Source: Hornet

Hornet costs adjusted in Q2/2020 through variable cost of goods sold (COGS: app store revenue share, server cost, advertising sales commissions) and the cost savings realized through Plan CP. By working fully remotely, we saved nearly 50% of our SGA (Selling, General &

Hornet Costs

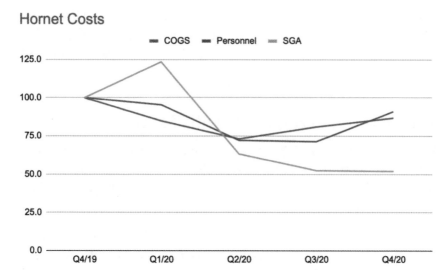

FIGURE 9.8 Company costs in 2020.
Source: Hornet

Administrative expenses – especially office leases and travel). (See Figure 9.8.) Since Hornet has always operated largely remotely, adopting Zoom many years prior for video conferencing, we barely missed a beat when switching to 100% virtual work from home.

In the end, we managed to eke out a profit in 2020 despite massive headwinds to our top line, thanks to our strong sense of mission and community within the team and our already distributed workforce.

Navigating the Great Lockdown

Hornet engaged on several fronts to successfully navigate the Great Lockdown.

What the Organization Did for Liquidity

Through a combination of cost reductions, compensation deferrals, and strong user subscription revenues, despite foreign exchange rate headwinds, we were able to turn a profit in Q3/2020 and contribute a neutral cash flow from operation by Q4 again. In addition, we raised a Working Capital Note, offering attractive interest rates in a generally low-rate environment, so that the cash ending on December 31, 2020, was overall 65% higher than at the end of 2019.

What the Organization Did with People

We at Hornet felt that COVID-19 was a chance to accelerate the adoption of gay social networking while offline resources were unavailable: gay bars were closed, travel disrupted, and pride parades canceled. This resulted in two major outcomes with respect to our users and our team:

1. There was no idling our *team* but rather a need to accelerate product rollout to add missing social networking features such as ephemeral video stories as soon as possible. We decided to move full steam ahead, retain all team members, and even add senior engineers. To manage cost, we asked for a 20% haircut on everyone's compensation (executive team 25%, CEO 50%) in exchange for stock options and future bonuses. Since there was great alignment around the mission and the need to pull together during these times as a company, every member joined the voluntary pay deferral for the proposed six months.

2. There was an opportunity to educate our *users* about the need to connect to their community, anytime and anywhere, especially during the Great Lockdown. Hornet appointed a COVID czar with a background in infectious diseases and mental health issues pertaining to the LGBTQ+ community, who would calibrate all messaging to frame COVID-19 as an example of why the community and the digital access to it mattered more than ever before. Campaigns like the #GreatGayStayIn allowed people to connect socially from their homes while staying physically distanced to protect other members of our communities from infections. (See Figure 9.9.)

FIGURE 9.9 Social media campaigns helped people connect while remaining physically distanced.

What the Organization Did with Investment Plans

Since Hornet felt COVID-19 would be a big catalyst to move the gay community to more digital connections, we decided to accelerate the investment to add missing social networking capabilities, such as ***ephemeral video short stories***. We planned to launch Version 7 with such capabilities at the end of the six-months-long COVID preparedness period, and so it did on October 7.[5] (See Figure 9.10.)

---

[5]Hornet Version 7 Launch announcement, https://hornet.com/about/v7-video-stories/

FIGURE 9.10 The pandemic served as a catalyst for more digital connections.

At the same time, we reduced our exposure to advertising revenue and continued to explore new avenues to user revenue by introducing the virtual in-app currency **Hornet Honey**, also a long-sought project that was accelerated as part of COVID-19.[6]

What Happened Across Regional Markets

The shifts and swings were wider in markets that managed COVID-19 relatively poorly, such as the United States and Brazil, and were much less pronounced in countries that emerged faster or remained less affected due to their specific geographies, such as Russia or Taiwan. We observed that the announcements of lockdowns made users wary for a few days or

[6]Hornet launches Honey as in-app currency, https://hornet.com/about/award-posts-honey/

weeks, before adjusting their habits and embracing social media to stay in touch with others. As of March 2021, the countries with the biggest volatility were those that were deep in a new wave, especially Brazil and France. Taiwan, on the other end of the spectrum, with just above 1,000 cases and only 10 deaths, barely registered any changes to the longer-term trajectories.

Future Outlook

We believe social networking will not only remain a backbone to our societies but, thanks to the experiences and proliferation of new technology as well as new habits formed under COVID-19, will continue to benefit from a COVID-19 accelerated digitization of many aspects of our lives, including working from home, online shopping and food delivery, homeschooling, and digital entertainment, from Netflix to live-streamed concerts.

We also believe that the increased fragmentation of social networks by user interests or communities will continue and that we at Hornet are perfectly positioned to take full advantage of these changes as they pertain to the LGBTQ+ community.

At the opening of 2021, we have fully recovered with our user-generated B2C revenues to pre-COVID-19 levels and have reduced advertising revenue as part of our revenue mix, making us less dependent on the whims of B2B markets.

We believe that Hornet's social networking proposition will take hold in more and more markets and will eventually disrupt the way gay apps are seen anywhere in the world, allowing us to grow our global user base by 10 times, once reaching certain tipping point thresholds, as the company has already successfully done in over a dozen markets.

Learnings from the Great Lockdown

The Great Lockdown felt like a massive catalyst for the digitization of society. Innumerable societal activities were jolted into the digital space, and the need to connect to one's community for personal connections made no exception. It is difficult to list all the benefits, as they will be widespread and very individual, such as the ability to move into a larger home in a less expensive city due to working from home, but also the ability to find support in one's community, like the LGBTQ+ community, no matter where in the world you live or what access to such resources are available locally.

No doubt, lots of brick-and-mortar businesses and many analog LGBTQ+ resources will be permanently disrupted or fail due to that change, such as iconic gay bars in San Francisco or canceled sports, arts, and cultural events, but the upside is increased reach, efficiency, and societal learning and etiquette of how to best leverage digital tools for interpersonal connections.

Hornet as a digital solution to connect parts of our societies has been and will be a big beneficiary of these changes, and the company is even more confident than before that it was on the right track investing into tools for meaningful connections formed through social media, rather than often relying on proximity and in-person meetups.

While I cannot say whether these developments are good or bad per se, they were bound to happen anyway. For those who were privileged enough to do so, COVID-19 has created a more level playing field to transition more of their lives to the digital realm.

At Hornet, a digital disrupter, we see COVID-19 as a massive catalyst to drive positive change for our business for years to come.

About the Contributor

 **Christof Wittig** is a serial software entrepreneur and investor. He is founder and CEO at Hornet and managing partner at Strive Capital. Christof also serves as director of fundraising for the Gay Games 11 in Hong Kong in 2022. Christof has been an investor and/or board member in various companies, including Enish (TYO:3667), Metago, KeepSafe, VirtaHealth, Black Medicine, Moviepilot, Boxfish, Cerebral, and App Annie. Christof holds a master of science in management from Stanford University's Graduate School of Business, where he was a Sloan Fellow in the class of 2004 and author of the case studies on MySQL and Google's Android. He also holds a Dipl.Ing. from Technical University Munich.

CHAPTER 10

IndiGrid

By Harsh Shah (CEO and Board Member)

About IndiGrid

IndiGrid is the first Infrastructure Investment Trust (InvIT) in the Indian power sector. It owns 13 operating projects consisting of 40 transmission lines with more than 7,570 circuit kilometers length and 11 substations with ~13,550 MVA (Million-Volt Amps) transformation capacity. IndiGrid has assets under management (AUM) worth ~INR 20,000 Cr (USD 2.70 billion). The investment manager of IndiGrid is majority owned by KKR.

Backdrop

The outbreak of the COVID-19 pandemic was the largest economic shock the world has witnessed in decades, causing a collapse in global economic activity despite the unprecedented support policies of governments and organizations. The COVID-19 pandemic not only brought to the fore business challenges from a commercial point of view, but it also shook us out of our state of inertia to examine business policies and question the sustainability of historic business models from an environmental, social, and governance point of view.

With favorable oil prices, positive global momentum, and an upswing in domestic manufacturing, the Indian economy was progressing well toward achieving the vision of a USD 5 trillion economy. According to International Monetary Fund (IMF) data, India's GDP grew by 4.2% in financial year 2019–20, higher than the emerging markets and developing economies' collective GDP growth of 3.7% in the same year. However, due to the impact of the pandemic and the ensuing lockdowns, India's GDP shrank 7.5% in Q2 FY 2021, after seeing a record contraction of 23.9% in Q1.

The Indian power sector, too, has not been spared from the effects of the pandemic. COVID-19 stress-tested the Indian power sector at a time when the sector was already in financial disarray and in urgent need of transformative reforms. Despite recent government reforms like creating a single national power grid, boosting access to electricity for its citizens, and promoting the dynamic growth of renewable energy, some of the toughest, most needed reforms are still pending.

At IndiGrid, we have been committed to vanguard the sector transformation, and this put us in good stead when faced with the COVID-19 pandemic. We not only reported resilient growth during the Great Lockdown, but we also announced six acquisitions, doubled our team size, and increased distribution to our investors while maintaining robust electricity availability for the nation to ensure an uninterrupted power supply in these volatile times.

IndiGrid, backed by KKR, is India's first power sector Infrastructure Investment Trust (InvIT), formed in 2016 with the goal of democratizing ownership of the power infrastructure in India and providing reliable electricity to all. Four years ago, we embarked on our growth journey, built upon solid fundamentals of transparency, governance, and providing superior risk-adjusted returns to unitholders. In its short but eventful existence, IndiGrid has come a long way, from 2 power transmission projects with 1,930 circuit kilometers and 6,000 MVA transformation capacity to 13 assets with ~7,570 circuit kilometers length and 13,550 MVA transformation capacity.

Since listing on the stock market, our assets under management (AUM) have increased more than threefold from INR 38 billion in June 2017 to INR 205 billion in March 2021. (See Figure 10.1.) Over the last three years, we have announced 15 consecutive quarterly distributions for our investors, delivering an ~88% absolute return since the IPO (including distributions and unit price movement until March 2021), making Indi-Grid one of the most attractive yield platforms in India on a risk-adjusted basis. (See Figure 10.2.) We accelerated this journey by achieving firsts and successes, such as acquisition of our first regulated transmission asset, foraying into the solar sector, acquiring a first intra-state asset, inducting KKR as a sponsor, and being the first public InvIT to do rights issuance, to name a few. All this puts us firmly on track to achieve our aim of becoming Asia's most admired yield vehicle.

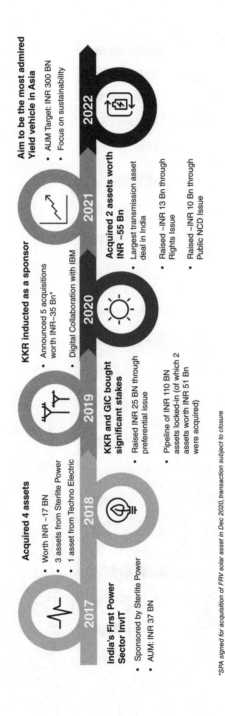

2017

India's First Power Sector InvIT

- Sponsored by Sterlite Power
- AUM: INR 37 BN

2018

Acquired 4 assets

- Worth INR ~17 BN
- 3 assets from Sterlite Power
- 1 asset from Techno Electric

2019

KKR and GIC bought significant stakes

- Raised INR 25 BN through preferential issue
- Pipeline of INR 110 BN assets locked-in (of which 2 assets worth INR 51 Bn were acquired)

2020

KKR inducted as a sponsor

- Announced 5 acquisitions worth INR ~35 Bn*
- Digital Collaboration with IBM

2021

Acquired 2 assets worth INR ~55 Bn

- Largest transmission asset deal in India
- Raised ~INR 13 Bn through Rights Issue
- Raised ~INR 10 Bn through Public NCD Issue

2022

Aim to be the most admired Yield vehicle in Asia

- AUM Target: INR 300 BN
- Focus on sustainability

*SPA signed for acquisition of FRV solar asset in Dec 2020, transaction subject to closure

FIGURE 10.1 IndiGrid's increase in AUM.

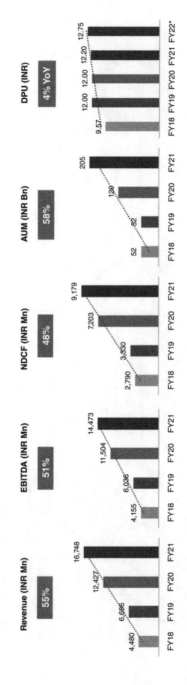

FIGURE 10.2 The company's numbers. *(Source: Bloomberg)*

During the Lockdown

The pandemic and resultant work from home (WFH) corporate pheno-menon has compelled India to strengthen its ability to maintain the security of supply, boost system flexibility, and better integrate its power hardware and software for effective preparedness in the face of such an existential crisis, thereby making electricity more indispensable than ever. The advent and success of digital technology, too, critically depend on the availability of a reliable electricity network. Power transmission was therefore classified as an "essential service" during the lockdown. How-ever, this blessing brought with it a new set of challenges:

- **Change in Demand Patterns:** The demand pattern of electricity changed during lockdown due to lifestyle changes emerging from reduced business activity and the emerging trend of WFH led to an increase in residential load demand and a decrease in commercial and industrial loads. This distressing situation created new chal-lenges in the technical and financial activities of the power sector, which required power utilities to initiate contingency and disaster management plans to tackle the volatile situation.

- **Change in Generation Patterns:** From approximately 72.5% of the energy mix in a one-month period before the lockdown, coal/thermal power plants' share fell to below 66%. In absolute terms, this resulted in a 25% decrease in thermal power production in a month-on-month comparison on both sides of the lockdown announcement. The short-fall was met by an increase in the share of all other sources, including hydro and other renewables, given their "must run" status.

- **Financial Tightening:** The already strained health of electric util-ities, especially distribution companies, took a hit as revenue collec-tions eroded. The industrial consumers (and their cross-subsidies) and state government payments and transfers got sidetracked, while residential consumers increased their demand but not their payments. The revenue collection of states was severely impacted as economic activities came to a halt. Further, the state governments redirected their resources for funding relief measures such as food distribution, direct cash transfers, and providing consumers with a moratorium for payment of electricity bills. In a similar vein, the Union Power

Ministry also issued directions to provide three months' moratorium to distribution companies to make payment to generation and transmission companies and reduction in Late Payment Surcharge (LPS) from 18% per annum to 12% per annum.

- **Risk-Planning:** On the flip side, the COVID-19 crisis also highlighted the benefits of closer cooperation between relevant players at every level, including the distribution companies, the system and grid operators, and the regulators through the Central Electricity Regulatory Commission. On April 3, 2020, India's population responded to Prime Minister Modi's appeal for "Challenging the darkness of COVID-19" and switched off their lights for nine minutes during the evening hours. The national system operator POSOCO successfully managed a demand reduction of 31 GW versus an anticipated 12–14 GW, thanks to the coordinated response between state and national dispatch centers. There are many other such instances where the Indian power sector showcased impressive emergency coordination of system operation, management of reserves, and line maintenance across India, demonstrating that no state can be an island.

With predictability and stability being the bedrock of our philosophy, IndiGrid and especially its asset management team have been up to the task during this period and have been instrumental in ensuring safe navigation through the lockdown and maintaining the national grid without disruption. Fortunately, our core strengths (see Figure 10.3) enabled us to address several key areas during COVID-19:

1. **Safety: The Key Priority**

   In the face of COVID-19, when businesses were succumbing to pay cuts and job cuts to stay afloat, we at IndiGrid prioritized people's safety and well-being above all. The team, which is used to working collaboratively, had to quickly change gears to adapt to working from home. The biggest challenge that first needed addressing was to ensure the safety of each one of our employees, whether on the ground or in remote locations. With digital readiness, workforce flexibility, transparent and two-way communication, supportive policies, and empathy, we ensured that we all stood together in this war against COVID-19. The platform also launched supportive medical packages, vaccination drives, and well-being programs to provide financial assistance in these tough times.

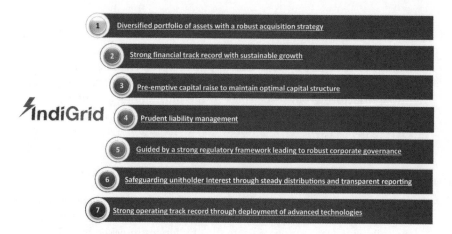

FIGURE 10.3 IndiGrid's core strengths.

2. Impact on Operations

Due to the lockdown, our scale of expansive networks, and ensuing logistics and labor issues; there were challenges in on-the-ground maintenance and surveying. However, these were quickly mitigated because the government listed power transmission as an "essential service." Additionally, the fact that our revenue depends on availability and not actual power supply also insulated our revenue to a large scale. Through our robust operations, we maintained availability of over 99.50% during FY 2020–21. There was also a decline in the number of trips per line on a month-to-month basis. Thus, our operational robustness helped us to maintain strong asset reliability and to limit the impact on operations.

3. Disruption of the Supply Chain

Even though power transmission was declared an "essential service," there were disruptions in the supply chain as a lot of the third-party service providers and vendors faced operational, working capital, and labor issues. Even though IndiGrid does not constantly supply raw material, the supply of spare parts for repair is critical. Similarly, the business is significantly dependent on other service providers like tax, valuation, regulatory, diligence, and so on, and the resilience planning and agility of each vendor also impacted the supply chain.

4. Impact on Collections

Delayed payments coupled with revised priorities resulted in working capital stress in the sector. Though the business carries minimal collection risk due to the point of connection (POC) mechanism, the event did lead to a timing mismatch. The collection efficiency dipped to sub-50% in the June 2020 quarter before rebounding to over 126% by March 2021.

While the impact was transient, it did challenge the management to devise a strategy to overcome the temporary hump as, on the one hand, the cash inflows were constricted due to COVID-19, but on the other hand, IndiGrid as an InvIT had to provide predictable and steady distribution to its investors. We won over the working capital mismatch through factoring the receivables in the outstanding payments on the back of our AAA rated cashflows. To add to that, our prudent liability management framework allowed us to maintain headroom to fuel growth as well as work on reducing our incremental cost of borrowings.

5. Value Accretive Growth: Deal-Making During COVID-19

In line with the strategy of focusing on value-accretive acquisitions to provide superior total returns to its investors, IndiGrid consummated the following transactions despite the challenges imposed by COVID-19 (see Figure 10.4):

- India's biggest transmission asset deal: Acquired NER-II from Sterlite Power for INR 46.25 billion
- First Solar asset: Signed SPA for the acquisition of the first solar asset, i.e., 100 MW FRV asset from FRV Solar Holdings XI B.V (transaction subject to closure)
- First cost-plus regulated asset: Acquisition of first cost-plus asset, i.e., Parbati Koldam Transmission project (PKTCL) from Reliance Infrastructure at an indicative EV of INR 9.0 billion
- Third-party acquisition: Jhajjar KT Transco Private Limited (JKPTL), an asset acquired from a third party for INR 3.1 billion.
- Gurgaon Palwal Transmission Limited (GPTL) for INR10.8 billion
- East North Interconnection Company Limited (ENICL) was acquired from Sterlite Power for ~INR 10.2 billion

The completion and signing of these transactions despite the lockdown is a testament to its commitment to increase unitholder value on an ongoing basis. It has been possible due to seamless and untiring collaboration across the entire IndiGrid team, including finance, asset management, legal, and secretarial. At present, IndiGrid's AUM is INR 205 billion. It is present in 17 states and 1 UT. There are 40 lines across ~7,570 circuit kilometers and nine substations of ~13,550 MVA transmission capacity. To further support its growth momentum and create leverage headroom, IndiGrid preemptively raised INR 12.83 billion through the first ever rights issuance by a publicly listed InvIT in India, which was oversubscribed with a 125% subscription. The platform also became the first listed InvIT/REIT in the country to issue public debt securities, which got subscribed ~25 times.

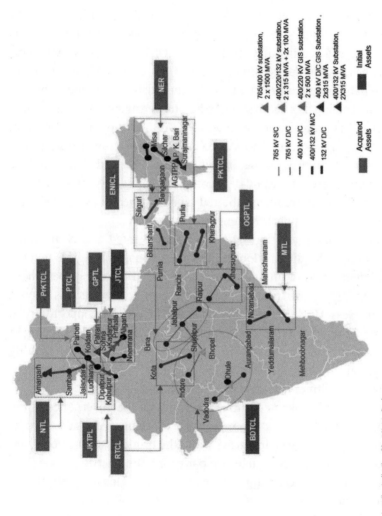

Location Indicative, Chart Not to Scale
SPA signed for acquisition of FRV solar assets (transaction subject to closure)

FIGURE 10.4 Acquired assets.

Future Outlook

The challenges of a global pandemic, nationwide lockdown, unprecedented collapse in global economic activity, and the aftermath have left behind a lot of scars, as well as long-lasting learnings.

The infrastructure sector, which is historically considered a traditional, manpower-heavy sector, has also been jolted to awareness of its inadequacies and redundancy during the COVID-19 period, with new measures now being devised to ensure optimal utilization of resources. While the pandemic exacerbated many of the existing challenges the sector faces, it is acting as a catalyst for India's power market reforms, which have been under way for some time. More importantly, it is clear that public resources are needed to strategically create a sustainable power infrastructure. Similarly, immediate measures are needed to mobilize capital from private sources by deepening the capital avenues for infrastructure projects and reducing the red tape historically associated with infrastructure and the power sector.

Application of innovation needs to be accelerated across the value chain, including the digitization of grid operations, smart grids, energy efficiency interventions, and adoption of advanced metering. Decarbonizing the energy sector through renewable energy projects has been a work in progress. However, this crisis has also given us an opportunity to advance the adoption of renewable energy and energy storage, keeping in mind the lower cost of operations of renewable power plants, the steadily decreasing capacity utilization factor of coal power plants in the country, and India's commitments to global climate change goals.

The government also needs to make sure that the governance of the distribution sector is adequate to meet those challenges and safeguard its electricity security by investing heavily into the transmission sector, given the increasing need for renewable grid parity and the electric vehicle (EV) revolution. There is also an urgent need to reassess global supply chains and trade dynamics.

To facilitate all this, governments can establish a policy environment that is conducive to supporting the creation of project pipelines and new business models that drive asset monetization. InvITs have recently been the preferred asset monetization solution for the capital-starved infrastructure sector, helping address the lack of funding avenues and options for flipping mature assets to free up capital for developers while also attracting private capital through an efficient framework.

Since IndiGrid's inception, key tenets of its growth strategy have included sustainability, digital transformation, and a long-term reliability-focused asset management framework. Predictability and stability are the foundation of our philosophy, but these principles found new meaning and applicability during the Great Lockdown. We learned several things during this time:

1. **Be prepared.**

   Preparation of disaster management plans has always been looked at with some skepticism. Thanks to an up-to-date policy framework around human resources, disaster recovery, IT, health and safety, quality, and asset management, IndiGrid was able to quickly adapt to the unprecedented situations stemming from the pandemic. Having alternate contingency plans in place allowed the business to mitigate critical risks like supply chain collapse, an inaccessible workforce, logistical logjam, and digital breakdown. IndiGrid has also been conscious and nimble with its capital management framework. Thanks to our prudent liability management, our AAA rating also was given a vote of confidence by our investors during the rights and public NCD issue where the transactions were oversubscribed despite volatile market conditions.

2. **Build a transparent and winning culture.**

   Employees are the backbone of any organization. It is therefore imperative that this most important corporate resource is motivated and healthy. A combination of isolation, limited human contact, and fear and anxiety took a toll on the mental and physical well-being of the employees. In addition, the feeling of burnout, change in working lifestyle, and blurring lines of work hours left a lot of us feeling overwhelmed. This underscores the need for a permanent employee support system to care for employee safety, mental health and engagement, and productivity. Transparency up and down all levels of the organization is paramount in such situations to maintain a strong and healthy culture. Without open communication, the struggles employees face may go unrecognized, which can impact their productivity. In a similar vein, recognizing employees is more critical than ever. At IndiGrid, valuing all stakeholders, including employees, regulators, and customers, has been a part of the DNA since its inception. Supportive HR initiatives like the work enablement policy provided for extended insurance and medical claim coverage, vaccination drives, flexible work hours, and other well-being offerings, which helped ease the anxiousness for employees. Weekly townhalls and catch-up sessions were also scheduled to ensure two-way, transparent communication.

3. **Invest in technology.**

With rare exception, operating digitally has been the *only* way to stay in business throughout enforced shutdowns and restricted activity. In a contactless world, where the majority of interactions were virtual, a functional digital platform became the prerequisite for the implementation of work-from-home policy. Every business, however big or small, needed smart digital solutions to ensure continuity, resilience, and agility of processes. Due to the pandemic, workforce availability was also constrained, unearthing a gaping hole in the supply chain calling for an urgent fix through artificial intelligence (AI) and cloud computing. The pandemic has been a reality check for the infrastructure sector, which has been historically slow in the pace of digital transformation. IndiGrid has pioneered digital transformation in the power transmission sector through its groundbreaking multiyear agreement with IBM to build an AI-enabled asset management platform. IndiGrid will deploy a hybrid cloud solution with IBM Maximo Application Suite running on the secure and open IBM Cloud to optimize the quality and utilization of its assets throughout their life cycle, increase productive uptime through preventative and predictive maintenance, drive efficiency, and reduce operating costs — ultimately ensuring access to reliable power for all.

4. **Utilize strategic and conscious capital structure planning.**

Being nimble in the asset management industry means having the organizational and capital agility to adjust to changing market dynamics and capitalize on emerging opportunities. Given the uncertainties regarding cash flows, third-party risks, and disruption of the supply chain, financial agility remains paramount. This is important not just for business continuity but also to ensure that the business model is robust enough to make the best use of the market dynamics. Through continuing focus on prudent capital management, an AAA-rated balance sheet, and timely raising of preemptive growth capital at IndiGrid, the platform was not only able to maintain steady operations but also managed to make accretive acquisitions during the pandemic. Despite a dip in collections, IndiGrid grew its quarterly rate of distribution through efficient working capital management. Apart from the optimal capital structure and cash management, COVID-19 also underscored the need for a long-term conscious business plan to proactively align the business objectives with the greater good of the community and environment. As a step in this direction, IndiGrid became the first listed InvIT to announce its foray

OUR VISION

To become the most admired yield vehicle in Asia

Focused Business Model	Value Accretive Growth	Predictable Distribution	Optimal Capital Structure
• Long term contracts • Low operating risks • Stable cash flows	• DPU accretive acquisitions Y-o-Y • Creating growth pipeline for future	• Quarterly distribution • Minimum 90% of Net cash flow distributed • Sustainable distributions	• Cap on leverage at 70% • AAA rating; prudent liability management • Well capitalized

FIGURE 10.5 The details of IndiGrid's vision.

into the solar sector with the acquisition of 135 MW of solar projects, which generates ~200 million units/year and saves 1,600,000 tons of CO2, equivalent to CO2 absorbed by 7,600,000 trees.

Armed with these learnings, IndiGrid is on track to achieve its vision to become the most admired yield vehicle in Asia, underpinned by predictable DPU and growth, best-in-class corporate governance, and delivery of superior risk-adjusted total returns to its unitholders. It continues to focus on growing our portfolio and maintaining the underlying portfolio to the highest standards of reliability, especially in this volatile period. (See Figure 10.5.)

Ready for the Future

In a short span of 3.5 years since its listing, IndiGrid has successfully transacted 11 deals that acquired assets over USD 2 billion and generated ~18% annual return (including distributions since listing until March 2021) for its investors while adhering to the highest standards of corporate and social governance. IndiGrid has provided superior risk-adjusted returns and is one of the best-returning infrastructure platforms in the country, with a beta of just 0.07 when compared to NSE 500. At a compounded annual growth rate of ~18%, it is substantially ahead of India's 10-year G-sec and other indices such as NSE Infra, BSE Capital Goods, and NSE 500. Even when compared to marquee global yield platforms, IndiGrid stands tall, with a current yield of ~9% (Source: Bloomberg, April 2021) despite ~50% capital appreciation over FY 2020–21. While the COVID-19 pandemic has temporarily derailed economic growth, we expect that the long-term focus on the need for infrastructure development to enable India's progress will remain intact. To this end, there will be a need for significant private sector participation. As a vehicle that helps free up capital for developers while offering investors participation, IndiGrid is well positioned for this massive potential opportunity in the power transmission and renewable energy sectors. Over the last three years, IndiGrid's underlying performance has been robust, and it remains well capitalized since the recent rights issue to grow faster than ever before. Backed by KKR and its investment expertise, it intends to keep the momentum of growing the underlying portfolio as well as enhancing unitholder returns.

About the Contributor

Harsh Shah, CEO and board member of IndiGrid, has been instrumental in setting up IndiGrid, India's first power sector yield platform. He brings extensive experience in the infrastructure sector across financing, operations, M&A, and regulatory policy. He serves on several committees for shaping Indian InvIT regulations and transforming infrastructure financing in India by establishing InvIT as a successful asset class. Mr. Shah holds a master's degree in business administration from the National University of Singapore and a bachelor's degree in electrical engineering from the Nirma Institute of Technology, Gujarat University.

CHAPTER 11

Julius Baer

By Toni Scheiwiller (Global Head of Corporate Services) and Andreas Zingg (COO Asia Pacific)

About Julius Baer

With origins dating back to 1890, Julius Baer is the leading Swiss wealth management group. We focus on providing personal advice to private clients around the world, powered by high-end services and expertise. We help our clients to achieve their financial aspirations through holistic solutions that take into account what truly matters to them – in their business and in their personal lives, today and for future generations. Our vision is to be the world's most personal and pioneering pure wealth manager. Our ambition for the next decade is to be the most admired global wealth manager. As entrepreneurs, we actively embrace change to be at the forefront of the private banking industry.

With headquarters in Zurich, Switzerland, Julius Baer employs 6,600 people globally with presence in over 20 countries and more than 50 locations. Asia is the bank's second home market, with both Hong Kong and Singapore being the key booking centers. At the end of 2020, the bank's assets under management in Swiss francs amounted to CHF 434 billion.

Backdrop: Wealth Management Industry and Julius Baer Before the Great Lockdown

Wealth management is one of the most attractive sectors within the financial services industry. During the last ten years, personal financial wealth has grown on average at about 6% per annum globally and more than 10% per annum in Asia. Relatively low capital requirements result in attractive returns on capital.

However, in recent years, the industry has been facing numerous challenges:

- Client needs are shifting structurally, from wealth creation to wealth preservation and from individual needs rooted in one geography to changing family settings with multinational requirements. Complexity is increasing and expectations are on the rise – factors that call for banks to provide even broader capabilities and deeper expertise in wealth management.
- Client needs are constantly changing. In particular, there is a demand for more enhanced digital channels and tools. Clients who are used to digital channels and services from their retail banking relationships are expecting wealth managers to also offer a seamless client experience across both digital and face-to-face channels.
- Generational dynamics are accelerating. In the next 20 years, huge numbers of assets will be handed from one generation to the next. This future generation is looking beyond the management of assets solely and is also interested in giving meaning and purpose to their wealth.
- New competitors are challenging the established players; for example, local banks are establishing their own private banking offering, and fintechs (financial technology organizations) are launching pure digital offerings for the mass affluent segment and also targeting higher-value segments.
- The economics of what was traditionally a high-margin business have changed. Commoditization combined with negative interest rates in many of the bank's key markets have resulted in strong margin pressure over recent years. Between 2011 and 2020, in line with the industry, the bank's return on assets (gross margin) dropped from 105 basis points to 88 basis points.
- More comprehensive regulations and changes in technology are driving up the structural costs of doing business and hence the critical mass. This has accelerated the trend of consolidation, as evidenced, for example, by the decrease in the number of banks in Switzerland from 320 in 2010 to 246 in 2019.

In response to this industry evolution, the Julius Baer CEO presented an updated and refined strategy at the start of 2020 with ambitious new medium-term targets and KPIs for 2022. The strategy in a nutshell:

- **Shift** leadership focus, from an asset-gathering strategy to sustainable profit growth.
- **Sharpen** value proposition, from historically grown individual client management to a distinctive segment value proposition.
- **Accelerate** investments in technology, from building the foundations to delivering a state-of-the-art client experience.

First Signs: When COVID-19 Hit the Wealth Management Industry and Julius Baer

The bank's Business Continuity Management (BCM) teams in Switzerland and Asia closely monitored the developments at the beginning of January 2020 and reviewed the bank's preparedness for a pandemic, including inventory checks for masks, hand sanitizers, and thermometers. The Singapore Crisis Management Team held its first meeting immediately after the Chinese New Year weekend and one week later, the Crisis Management Team (CMT) established a subteam – the Pandemic Management Team (PMT) – to manage the bank's response to the pandemic.

In a first phase, the PMT focused on swiftly providing basic protection to staff, clients, and the bank. Travel advisories were issued to staff initially traveling to China, later to selected other countries, and eventually it progressed to a global travel ban. During the Chinese New Year weekend, a call tree was triggered, and staff with travel history to China had to observe a self-quarantine away from the office for 14 days. This was initiated out of caution ahead of local health advisories. When the local authorities issued national advisories, the bank incorporated them quickly and ensured staff strictly followed those guidelines. At an early stage, the protocol to manage suspected and confirmed cases among staff was already established.

Temperature screening for all visitors, including clients and business partners, was set up at all of the bank's offices in Asia as of the end of January. Additional temperature screenings by landlords were soon implemented as a further measure. For the first time, the bank canceled its investment conferences for clients to prevent social interaction or community spread; these conferences are the bank's flagship events, held periodically to share with clients the bank's market outlook and investment insights.

After the declaration of DORSCON[1] Orange in Singapore, the bank invoked a split operations setup in Singapore and Hong Kong. Split operations enabled the bank to immediately increase the resilience substantially by physically segregating the relevant teams in two different locations. This ensured business continuity, should any infections be detected among staff. Preparing and executing split operations on short notice, without meaningful space reserves, proved to be a daunting and challenging task for the organization. However, the setup yielded a positive effect because it provided staff an opportunity to meet and interact with colleagues from other offices, instead of interacting only via emails or phone calls.

When the number of infections increased drastically, not only in Asia, but also in Europe, Julius Baer began to facilitate staff to work from home (WFH) to minimize their exposure to the potential infections during their commute and to reduce density in the office. At the same time, the bank was also getting ready for a potential lockdown by authorities.

However, the bank's WFH capabilities were not sufficient at the start of the pandemic. Similar to other private banks, Julius Baer traditionally limited remote access to its systems and client data, in order to protect and safeguard our clients' confidentiality. The default workspace for most staff was a desktop in the office with remote access to email and a few selected applications via mobile devices. Only a few employees, mostly senior management and project staff, were using bank-issued laptops plus secure tokens. During the demonstrations in Hong Kong in 2019, a full remote access solution via VPN was implemented for users of company laptops. When the bank considered rolling out this solution to a significant number of additional users, it became evident that it was not possible to procure the required equipment, whether laptops or secure tokens, within

---

[1]The Disease Outbreak Response System Condition (DORSCON) is a color-coded framework established by Singapore's Ministry of Health that shows the current disease situation.

a reasonable time frame, and that this solution would also very heavily consume bandwidth capacity. Alternative ideas centered around a BYOD (bring your own device) solution while meeting the bank's information security requirements.

The global COO gave the IT infrastructure team the following challenge: "If you can enable me to work from home in a stable and secure manner in one week's time, I invite the whole team for dinner!" Within days, the team developed a Citrix-based[2] solution, named the "Temporary Pandemic Workplace," which was rolled out successfully to all staff in Switzerland in the middle of March and one week later across Asia. All this took place just before the local authorities implemented the lockdowns.

One final challenge was slightly unexpected, though: a significant number of staff shared that they did not have a laptop or had to pass their personal laptop to their children for home schooling; therefore, 150 consumer laptops were procured from retail stores to support WFH.

During the Great Lockdown

The lockdowns imposed in most countries triggered the first "manmade recession" in history and a larger decline in GDP than during the global financial crisis (GFC) in 2008. This led to a sharp correction in equity markets from their all-time highs at the beginning of February, in fact the fastest decline in the US equity market in history from an all-time high. However, unlike during the Global Financial Crisis banks were not part of the problem; they were part of the solution, facilitating government schemes to provide liquidity to temporarily closed businesses. For Julius Baer as a wealth manager, the focus was on advising clients how to navigate this unprecedented storm in financial markets. The key recommendation for clients by our bank's Chief Investment Officer was not to panic and to stick to their strategic asset allocations while taking advantage of opportunities identified by our investment experts in the volatile markets.

Traditionally, stock market corrections have a strong negative impact on Julius Baer's profitability and share price, since a significant part of revenues is fee-based income linked to assets under management. Indeed,

---

[2]Citrix Remote PC Access enables users to access their physical office PCs remotely from their own device.

the bank's share price declined from CHF (Swiss franc) 51 in January to CHF 25 in March 2020, in line with the global market correction.

Globally, stock exchanges experienced a massive drop in March, followed by very volatile further developments. Although private banks, such as Julius Baer, do not finance business or consumer loans and are less exposed to deteriorating economic environments, they do issue secured loans that are exposed to fast and deep drops of the collateral values. Julius Baer's relationship and risk managers responded swiftly to the financial turmoil by following up with clients on their risk and credit exposures, as well as managing certain capital ratios due to heavy inflows of deposits. Jointly, solutions were developed and credit shortfalls were solved, while regulatory minimum requirements were adhered to at all times. In fact, liquidity and funding ratios as well as the classical regulatory capital ratios even strengthened during the crisis.

Furthermore, due to the highly volatile markets during this time, clients' transactions increased substantially, reaching record volumes and leading to record-high net profit for the first half of 2020 for the bank.

It is against this backdrop in financial markets that the bank sent 90% of staff to work from home in full compliance with regulatory requirements at the start of April.

Management's immediate focus was to maintain the usual service levels in a remote office setup and at the same time to systematically increase the bank's resilience. Measures implemented were grouped into five categories: (1) process workarounds and optimizations, (2) new ways to interact with clients, (3) project work, (4) employee communication and management, and (5) training.

Ensuring continuity in transaction processes and availability of the underlying IT systems was the first priority of the Pandemic Management Team (PMT) given the spike in transaction volumes, which reached 300% of the usual levels due to the market volatility experienced then. Therefore, the daily system morning checks were further enhanced. Despite a high degree of straight-through processing in the bank's operations department, a few processes were still paper-based before the pandemic. The various teams defined tactical workarounds to replace paper-based workflows with soft copies, which were then stored in shared network drives. In parallel to such tactical quick fixes, more robust solutions were implemented, such as the processing of incoming "Swift" messages for corporate actions such as dividend payments, which were automatically routed to the Operations Team's mailbox. One key change was the (temporary) acceptance of scanned or digital signatures instead of wet ink for client documents, as well as scanned copies instead of original documents.

Trust is the key element in client relationships when it comes to wealth management. Since relationship managers could not meet their clients in person, the bank enabled video conferencing via Cisco Webex, supplemented by guidelines and recommendations for relationship managers to conduct virtual meetings with their clients. Together with the use of scanned signatures and soft copies, we were able to continually open new accounts while observing safe distancing measures. In addition, investment seminars are now held "live" and "virtual" via webcasts.

It became evident that the pandemic would last longer than initially expected. Therefore, tasks that typically required a lot of physical collaboration among the employees, such as project work, had to move forward in high speed and quality. Thus, the PMT enabled staff to effectively use collaboration tools such as Webex Conference, Webex Training, and SharePoint to ensure engagement and communication. For example, in Asia, the investment management team migrated to a new portfolio management system during the lockdown. During the cut-over weekend, a project team of more than 50 employees collaborated virtually across three time zones to complete a runbook with approximately 200 activities.

To stay in touch with staff and to keep everyone abreast of any changes, a dedicated intranet hub with all related information was set up. Staff got access to useful information about the pandemic, home office guidelines, and essential help lines. The site also included recommendations for managers on how they could continue to engage staff effectively in a remote environment. One of the recommendations was for managers to hold regular check-ins with their team members. This initiative eventually improved employee engagement and communication, as some employees commented that they had more interactions with their superiors during the lockdown than before. Some managers sent weekly emails with key updates to their staff so every team member was aligned. Others contributed to intranet blogs to share their personal work from home experience with practical tips and personal pictures about maintaining a healthy work-life balance. The regional and global town halls, for the first time, were conducted fully virtually. Many questions were fielded during the virtual conferences, and there was even more active interaction between the speakers and the participants than in the traditional physical format.

JB Academy, the bank's learning and development unit, developed a comprehensive list of remote training workshops. Some of the workshops ranged from health and resilience, and mental wellness to team building. Additional training and sharing sessions were rolled out to support staff in managing substantial changes brought about by the pandemic and to build life skills on adapting to a new normal. One of the most popular workshops was on conducting effective virtual client meetings and how to improve engagement in virtual team meetings. Leadership training was carried out virtually too. During the pandemic, the average learning hour per employee increased by 37% compared to the previous year.

Future Outlook

Having established measures and guidelines to protect the health of the staff and the interests of the bank, management took the crisis as an opportunity to accelerate the implementation of its change strategy, especially the digital transformation of the bank's value proposition.

COVID-19 will continue to change the way we interact and work with clients, partners, and colleagues, thereby accelerating existing structural trends rather than creating new ones. The strategic outlook is based on a few key assumptions regarding social interaction, client needs, and work patterns. The current behavioral patterns like social distancing and remote interaction will likely remain to a certain extent. This affects not only how we collaborate internally, but also how we serve our clients. Clients are rapidly increasing their adoption of digital technologies from video conferencing with the relationship manager to online banking and the use of digital advisory tools. Workwise, staff are expecting greater flexibility and autonomy with work from home becoming more common. A well-rounded and well-functioning work-from-home solution will be more important than ever to attract top talent. These increased work-from-home patterns will not only blur the boundaries between private and work life, but also impact the way we measure productivity. The cultivation of trust, new styles of leadership, enhanced processes, and governance will become even more important for the bank.

Based on this outlook, the bank's executive board launched several strategic initiatives as early as April 2020, which were structured according to three key themes: client needs, employee needs, and organizational needs.

The first set of initiatives invested in accelerating the digital transformation of the bank's value proposition. The foundations were already in place before the pandemic struck in the form of globally harmonized mobile and e-banking platforms. In Switzerland, a secure chat feature was rolled out in September 2020 that allowed clients to interact with their relationship managers conveniently via their WhatsApp account. Clients in Asia started benefiting from this solution in May 2021. In order to support digital document flows and to facilitate administrative tasks, an electronic/digital signature solution was also rolled out during the pandemic. The digital onboarding of new clients and video identification for prospects were launched in Switzerland in October 2020. The bank has already started using advanced data analytics tools to generate personalized investment recommendations, which were distributed via digital channels.

Remote working is expected to continue in the new normal. In a recent employee engagement survey, 78% of our employees globally expressed the wish to work more than 20% of their time remotely post-pandemic. The survey yielded similar results in Asia, with 85% for Singapore and 72% for Hong Kong. Julius Baer employees will have greater flexibility in choosing their preferred work setup. This new way of working will be supported by the COO's values of Ambition, Courage, Collaboration, and Trust, values that already served us well during the pandemic.

The new flexible working arrangements will provide an opportunity for the bank to redesign our office space to enhance collaboration and engagement. Since some employees will work partially from home, "hot-desk" seating arrangements will be introduced for certain functions. This frees up space to embrace creative thinking, foster innovation, and support the "agile" transformation. An additional benefit is an expected reduction in infrastructure costs in the future.

Learnings from the Great Lockdown

While the pandemic was not expected, the bank was generally well prepared for the situation. Having been exposed to various crises before, the business continuity plans were already in place with an adequately equipped and ready team. Nevertheless, the need for staff to work from home was clearly underestimated and so the team needed to provide out-of-the box ideas. The solutions and changes that were implemented in response to COVID-19 will remain and allow the bank to operate fully remotely in the future, if required. Today, the bank has increased its resilience considerably, notably since all locations worldwide were affected simultaneously and learned "on the go." The pandemic moved business continuity management – traditionally regarded by many as a paper exercise to be ticked off once a year – to the forefront, and adding resilience in general has become a company priority.

The global crisis certainly fostered the bond between the bank and its employees. We received very positive feedback from our staff on the handling of the pandemic situation and how the bank took care of its staff. Since we lived up to our values, the staff went the extra mile to find solutions to challenges. This translated into improved collaboration, agile and faster product and project deliveries, as well as being highly adaptable while delivering continuously high-quality service. The extraordinarily high volumes of client interactions and transactions were handled promptly without errors or operational incidents. The bank will certainly emerge stronger from this crisis and apply the same sense of urgency, alignment, and commitment demonstrated during the pandemic to carry out the bank's strategy.

Bringing people back to work at the office has turned out to be more challenging than sending them to work from home. Interaction and information flow within teams was easier when everyone was working from home, compared to a scenario where half of the staff population are in the office and the rest are working from home. Some staff also got used to working from home and saved time commuting to and from the office.

It will certainly be a challenge to find the right balance going forward between work from home and work at the office, physical and virtual interaction with clients and staff, and providing flexibility to employees while ensuring high service levels.

By responding with swift and effective measures to counter the challenges brought about by the pandemic, our bank has actually emerged stronger. This experience will have a lasting impact on our organization and will motivate staff to further foster entrepreneurship, agility, and client centricity.

About the Contributors

Toni Scheiwiller (Global Head of Corporate Services) and Andreas Zingg (COO, Asia Pacific)
Toni Scheiwiller is the bank's Global Head of Corporate Services based in Zurich, and Andreas Zingg is the COO Asia Pacific, based in Singapore. They led the bank's response to the COVID-19 pandemic globally and in Asia, respectively, and were instrumental in leading the bank's changes in adherence to regulatory requirements while ensuring business continuity and sustainable growth.

CHAPTER 12

RealWear, Inc

By Andrew E. Chrostowski (Chairman and CEO), Rocky Scales
(Executive Vice President, Global Sales), and Aaron Cohen (Director
of Communications)

About RealWear

RealWear, the world's leading maker of industrial-strength, assisted-reality, hands-free devices for frontline workers, has been providing in-situ information and in-the-field training with software and hardware since 2016. We catapulted quickly into prominence by creating a wearable computer that operates flawlessly in extremely noisy industrial environments, freeing a worker to focus on the task at hand. For example, the RealWear HMT-1 assisted-reality (AR) device is designed to maintain full situational awareness while allowing communication and collaboration with the team. (See Figure 12.1)

For us, it was never just about technology. From the very beginning, our mission has been to empower, engage, and elevate people. We believe that connected workers are inherently more engaged with their business and customers; that having access to relevant and critical information, hands-free, empowers workers to do their jobs more safely and productively; and that these two things combined elevate the frontline worker's personal performance for the enterprise.

In the early years of our operation, the industry was still trying to define itself. The Gartner Hype Cycle[1] had pushed consumer expectations for augmented reality into the "trough of disillusionment" as experiments and implementations failed to deliver, leaving an opportunity for a rugged

---

[1] "5 Trends Appear on the Gartner Hype Cycle for Emerging Technologies, 2019," Gartner, https://www.gartner.com/smarterwithgartner/5-trends-appear-on-the-gartner-hype-cycle-for-emerging-technologies-2019/

FIGURE 12.1   The device can be connected to a variety of head-mounting options.
Source: RealWear

industrial solution. ABI Research now projects that smart glasses hardware unit shipments in the industrial and healthcare sectors will grow globally by a factor of 12.8 between 2020 and 2025.[2] Nevertheless, we saw several key competitors shutter due to a focus on the hype around technology rather than on driving value; in early 2019, three AR companies failed within the space of four weeks alone.[3]

In contrast, we maintained a laser focus on the safety and needs of industrial frontline workers. Our hardware was ready, as was our hands-free software platform; the solution had been proven in real-world use. From the outset, we structured the company for scale, including establishing strong relationships with resellers to support large industrial customers. We were certified in more than 60 countries[4] and a dozen languages[5] and had strong partnerships with Microsoft, Cisco, and Zoom.[6] An impressive number of global companies had embraced and deployed RealWear for their workforce, including BMW, Volkswagen Commercial Vehicles UK, Lexus, China's State Grid, Groupe PSA, and Italgas. Our products are uniquely designed to be compatible with personal protective equipment (PPE) such as hard hats, bump caps, hearing protection, and even N95 respirators and surgical masks. Hundreds of app developers have now built and optimized voice-enabled apps just for the device, creating an ecosystem that gives RealWear an appeal across diverse industries.

....
[2] ABI Research.
[3] Craig, Emory, "That Was Fast: Three AR Companies Fail in a Single Month," Digital Bodies, December 28, 2019, https://www.digitalbodies.net/augmented-reality/that-was-fast-three-ar-companies-fail-in-a-month/
[4] "Approved Countries," RealWear, https://realwear.com/approved-countries/
[5] "What Languages Does HMT-1 or HMT-1Z1 Support?" RealWear, May 2, 2020, https://realwear.com/question-answer/what-languages-does-hmt-1-or-hmt-1z1-support/
[6] "Cisco Webex Front Line Workers in Hazardous Environments," RealWear, February 25, 2021. https://realwear.com/solutions/cisco-webex-expert-on-demand/

Incredibly, the pandemic would ultimately serve to push us across the chasm of technology adoption,[7] but we thrived on "the other side" because we already had in place the structures, culture, team, and ecosystem needed to succeed.

The Early Days of the Pandemic

We gained early insight into the pandemic through our joint venture in China. RealWear China's focus as the virus spread was to help the medical and first-responder community and help ensure business continuity for organizations in the affected areas. In addition to donating a number of devices to minimize the spread of COVID-19, we partnered with Tencent, one of the world's most prominent technology companies, to launch a joint solution designed to help governments, companies, and organizations recover their operation, specifically in the areas of employee management, customer service, and plant maintenance. The innovative solution leveraged AI and big data capabilities from Tencent Cloud together with our device to enable employees to receive faster zero-contact temperature screening, self-guided training and digital workflow, and remote video support for production, service and plant maintenance. Everything was done remotely, from solution concept to release.[8]

In Wuhan, the Tongji Hospital became the first to use the system's real-time audio and video capabilities to lower the risk of infection by enabling frontline medical teams to communicate directly with senior staff members working outside the hot zone. The chief physician and specialized experts alike were able to propose a diagnosis and treatment plan, helping speed recovery, all while working remotely. With PPE in short supply, the HMT-1 assisted-reality device also allowed the hospital – and other hospitals that later adopted our technology – to minimize the number of times physicians needed to enter the isolation areas, reducing the protective gear required. It also increased their capacity to treat patients and reduced the critical constraint of physician capacity during the pandemic – something

----

[7]Moore, Geoffrey A., *Crossing the Chasm Marketing and Selling Disruptive Products to Mainstream Customers* (Harper Business, 2014).
[8]"RealWear Rapid Response to COVID-19, Including Donations of Technology," RealWear, March 23, 2021, https://realwear.com/blog/realwear-rapid-response-to-covid-19-including-donations-of-technology/

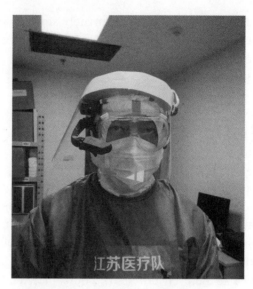

FIGURE 12.2 Medical professionals in China used HMT-1 during the pandemic.
Source: RealWear China

that has been of critical value to healthcare systems worldwide during the pandemic. (See Figure 12.2.)

All the while, we began experiencing the early effects of the pandemic on our business. There was a lot of uncertainty about how the pandemic would affect our customers' buying behaviors and whether they would freeze their discretionary and CapEx budgets. This uncertainty, plus our low cash position, caused us to tighten our budgets to ensure that we could survive and position ourselves for future growth. We immediately launched into negotiations with our manufacturer to reduce output; we needed to hold less inventory and increase turns, thereby increasing our available cash and reducing the cash tied up in inventory. These successful negotiations were a central piece of making it through this challenging period.

Navigating the Great Lockdown: The Race to Adapt

To make things even more interesting, we were already going through significant changes unrelated to the pandemic. As the company evolved from an early-stage startup to a company in full-tilt growth mode, both the leadership team and processes needed to evolve. That evolution led to the restructuring of our board of directors in March 2020. Andrew Chrostowski was named chairman and acting CEO, and RealWear cofounder Sanjay Jhawar was appointed to the board.

Entering the pandemic, our cash position was extremely low, and we were burning substantial cash from operations. The situation required a complete turnaround initiative. Our new leadership team acted decisively to protect the company. In the early months of the pandemic, we put product development on hold, eliminated paid marketing efforts and travel, and negotiated with several key vendors to reduce or defer payments significantly.

We also moved swiftly to conduct a round of layoffs, a difficult move but required, to match our burn rate to what could be uncertain economic reactions to the pandemic. The layoffs were also designed to guard against having to lay off additional workers down the road. During that painful process, we were proud to be able to preserve the jobs of all of the special needs workers we employed.

Like many in the business world, we proactively pivoted to a remote model to protect our employees and put in place key safety measures, including masks and sanitation protocols, for those workers who would still be going into the office; we were designated early on as an essential critical infrastructure company because we made products for manufacturing, healthcare, and other essential functions.

We also turned our focus inward. Just as we want our solutions to empower, elevate, and engage our customers' frontline workers, we were committed to doing the same for our employees. In the early weeks of the pandemic, we made concerted efforts to check in personally with team members across the organization to see how they were handling this unprecedented change. We held small group meetings to find out what our employees liked about their jobs, what they would change, and what they needed to be happier and more productive. As a result, we moved our "all-hands" calls from a quarterly to a weekly frequency to improve the communication that was even more important during the most critical transition period before settling into a new, monthly cadence. We also held a video contest to share life and productivity hacks to ensure that our teams could balance the new work-life challenges the pandemic created. Our focus on *people* kept our culture strong and morale high.

Beyond RealWear, the work-from-home movement globally acted as a massive catalyst to turbocharge digital transformation as companies embraced remote collaboration tools like Microsoft Teams, Cisco Webex, Slack, and Zoom.

Almost overnight, we found our solutions on the world stage. The challenges of managing the pandemic led existing and new customers alike to accelerate their adoption of telepresence and other solutions for frontline and first-line workers. We worked with Microsoft for about two years to optimize its Teams solution for our hands-free platform. The results of this effort were announced by the Microsoft chairman and CEO himself, Satya Nadella, at the 2020 Inspire Conference, where he highlighted how our combined solution was used by Honeywell to commission a plant automation system entirely remotely, with dozens of engineers collaborating and signing off on the project without ever having to travel to the site. Purchases of HMT-1 wearable computers that supported the COVID-19 battle increased to 35% of sales in six weeks.

For companies like Goodyear, the Microsoft announcement was a tipping point. Goodyear had a mature Teams deployment, and they understood its benefits and didn't want to introduce a new collaboration tool. The moment Teams became available on RealWear was the deciding factor. When they added the device to Teams meetings, like any other device, adoption of the RealWear solution moved quickly.

While RealWear already had the structures, culture, team, and ecosystem in place to support large-scale expansion, we had to figure out how to do business remotely, just as every other organization did. Our sales and customer support teams logged long hours as we all improvised, experimented, and adjusted as a long consultative sales cycle turned into the need to simply take orders and support customers in evolving use cases.

We were fortunate to have supportive investors, namely CVC, which provided a bridge loan to help us get through this difficult period. We worked quickly to put a line of credit in place to free up additional cash. As our revenue increased substantially and we continued our efforts to keep inventory low, we produced substantial cash to operate and expand the business. We opened new offices and shifted to a third-party logistics provider to support continued growth driven by new hardware products, cloud, and recurring revenue, and the expansion of our ecosystem and use cases through large software partners.

And we did it all with three transformative goals in mind – goals that guided our everyday actions, discipline, and decision-making: to reach USD 1 billion in revenue, be IPO-ready in how we operated, and become a market leader with a recognized brand name at the industrial front edge. Among the actions we took toward these goals were:

- Opening a customer experience center in Dubai
- Adding local offices in the Netherlands, Singapore, Germany, the UK, Japan, Australia, and Korea
- Adding 24/5 global, rapid-response support, including over holidays
- Rapidly growing sales staff in high-demand regions
- Broadening sales channels through global distribution and resellers
- Leveraging customers as advocates
- Making significant investments in marketing to increase awareness of the RealWear brand

The rebound was palpable. Sales in 2020 tripled over 2019, and we reached an important milestone in early 2021: that of having shipped wearable devices to more than 3,000 unique enterprise customers worldwide in a wide range of industries. And a year after Microsoft announced the deployment of Teams on the HMT-1, it again highlighted RealWear as its featured device at Hannover Messe 2021, the largest industrial manufacturing event in the world.

Success Story: How Goodyear Fueled Collaboration with the HMT-1

Goodyear depends on more than 2,500 engineers to keep its complex production processes running optimally, and with 46 facilities around the world, the company wasn't about to let travel restrictions due to COVID-19 slow it down. When its engineers could no longer travel to factories for equipment installation or troubleshooting, Goodyear turned to Microsoft Teams running on RealWear, using assisted-reality wearable computers to bring the engineering experts into the plants virtually.

Instead of sending an engineer to a local factory, they used the Microsoft Teams and RealWear solutions to collaborate remotely and instantaneously. Not only did they reduce their dependency on travel, but they can fix problems faster.

Learnings from the Great Lockdown: Going Forward to Work

Companies talk about going back to work, but at RealWear we believe that's the wrong way to think about it: We will be going *forward* to work, incorporating the lessons from the pandemic. Those learnings run the gamut from work-from-anywhere practices to sanitation and corporate culture. They've introduced some existential questions into corporate America: What does it mean to collaborate, and what's the purpose of physical office space? And how can we continue to put people ahead of technology?

There's a better way to work. We envision a brighter future where frontline workers are fully connected for their entire shift, not only during a remote call. Our technology and platform, paired with our partner solutions, have the power to make everything that person does easier, better, and safer—all day long. In the end, we can expect to see more flexible work and greater respect for the individual and his or her work-life balance. Work will be more distributed and perhaps a bit more asynchronous as we continue to leverage technology in ways that eliminate the limitations of time and distance.

There will also be more automation, and as that happens, upskilling will increase in importance—and RealWear can play a critical role in that upskilling. Workers can use assisted reality to narrate and curate a video detailing their work daily; a new or less-experienced employee can access that information, move up the skills curve, and spend more time on the higher-value activities that require a human touch. It's about connecting people—to remote experts, peers, and customers alike—and transacting with all systems of record seamlessly, so the business of business can continue to happen.

RealWear's knowledge transfer platform can do so much more than even we know; we've tapped into perhaps one-tenth of its value. Pre-pandemic, our mission focused on connecting people and fueling digital transformation by closing the knowledge gap. What the pandemic illuminated, however, is the tremendous power the RealWear devices and software wield to truly empower the two billion people[9] worldwide working

---

[9]"Empowering Firstline Workers to Gain a Competitive Edge," *Harvard Business Review,* 2020, https://www.microsoft.com/en-us/microsoft-365/blog/wp-content/uploads/sites/2/2020/01/HBR_MSFT_Retail_Final.pdf

on the front line. These workers can do and be much more. The more you can empower and enable them, the better service they can provide customers, the more accelerated their learning curve, and the higher the rate at which they can contribute value. The lockdown made this clear because we were watching it unfold at scale.

The pandemic also underscored the need for us to continue to plan for an uncertain future. We are preparing our business units for growth, which means improving people, processes, and systems to scale as the business continues to expand. At the same time, we maintain a high degree of discipline around spending and scrutinize every expenditure to ensure that it is additive to our growth. To that end, we are expanding our line of credit and our access to cash to ensure that we can withstand the speed bumps we will inevitably encounter. And regardless of our plans in the capital markets, our preparations to become IPO-ready will only make our business stronger.

Assisted reality is not just about more technology; instead, it's about better understanding the challenges faced by people doing the jobs that can't be done from home or the office and providing exactly the kind of solutions that will engage, empower, and elevate them. RealWear stands ready to make their jobs safer and more productive as we go *forward* to work together. The future of work is clearly here today.

About the Contributors

Andrew is a senior executive with deep experience in developing teams and strategies that enable innovation, growth, and profitability improvements. He also has specific experience in pandemic risk management and business continuity planning gained as the leader for Goodrich Aerospace's Avian Flu risk management team. As an NACD Certified Director, Qualified Technology Executive, and a founding executive member of the Digital Directors Network, he strives to improve board performance and digital governance excellence.

Rocky is widely recognized as a leader in scaling global sales. Most recently, Rocky led the ecommerce business unit at Vesta Corporation. Prior to that, he was SVP of Sales for SheerID, a digital verification SaaS provider for ecommerce merchants. He also served as VP of Global Sales for Ondot Systems (recently acquired by Fiserve), an international supplier of payment card management products for consumers and card issuers.

Aaron Cohen is a seasoned global communications leader with diverse technology experience raising awareness and building brands for technology pioneers. He has an MFA in creative writing from the Iowa Writer's Workshop and has spent over 20 years in communications and other strategic marketing roles.

CHAPTER 13

SAP

By Peggy Renders (SVP and Head of Customer Experience Solutions)
and Tanuj Vijay (Industry Ecosystem)

About SAP

SAP is the global leader in business applications and analytics software, a market leader in digital commerce, and the world's largest enterprise cloud company with over 200 million cloud users. We have over 440,000 customers in more than 180 countries, from small companies (80% of our customers are small and midsize enterprises) to global organizations (92% of the Forbes Global 2000 companies run SAP software). Globally, more than 77% of all business transactions worldwide touch an SAP software system.

Our unique ecosystem comprises thousands of startups, 18,000 partners, and more than three million SAP community members in 200 countries. More than 100,000 SAP team members in 140 countries, including over 27,600 research and development employees and 20,200 professional services staff, help our customers tackle complexity and guide their transformation into digital businesses.

Our core business is focused on the software and services markets. We offer end-to-end solutions across 25 industries and 12 lines of business, localized by country and for companies of any size. SAP is headquartered in Germany, with office locations in more than 78 countries across the globe.

Introduction

Like everyone else, at the start of 2020 I, Peggy, had some plans for my personal and professional life. As a Belgian living in Australia and working across Asia, I am fortunate to have a global network of friends and family. My 83-year-old mother lives in Belgium and we were looking forward to welcoming her in Melbourne in 2020. She was so excited to spend time with my boys, her grandchildren, whom she saw last in 2016, and there was an equal enthusiasm on their part to see "Moeke" again. On the professional front, while we had kickstarted the year with a bang, we were looking forward to executing our strategic plans.

However, the global pandemic transformed organizations globally and changed how we work, interact, and play. The key challenge is how to make sense of all the noise, draw meaningful insights, and dynamically allocate all resources for a positive outcome. What has become even more apparent is that everything we do is underpinned by the most critical resource: people.

This has also led us to an emotional roller-coaster ride of uncertainties and unknowns. This has been not only my story, but something that resonates with everyone. One of my colleagues, living in Singapore, lost his father at the end of 2019 and had planned to spend time with his grieving mother during 2020, but has had to go more than a year without meeting her. Families were lost, isolated, and separated in 2020.

We realized that nothing could be done by individuals other than to follow the basics of hygiene and safety, and all was not lost. I got an opportunity to spend more time with my boys, focus on personal fitness, sharpen my skillset, and get ready for a new post-pandemic world.

Reflecting back on 2020, I do feel there was a massive shift in humanity. It might be a personal projection, but I hear it all around me. People have reassessed their priorities; most have gone back to basics and a simpler life, and above all I have seen a massive shift in authenticity. When people ask how you are, "good" is often an automatic response, and that was how we responded initially during the pandemic, but it's hard to keep that up for long periods when your world has been turned upside down. I personally felt really challenged as a single parent. The weeks I was on my own were not easy, particularly for someone who gets their energy from being with others. But going deep allowed me to emerge stronger and more aligned with who I really am. I have seen people around me, mostly the people I work with – employees or customers and partners – open up a whole lot more about what is really going on in their world, and about the changing thought patterns and beliefs they and their families have, how there are reassessing their priorities and their focus. All this leads me to believe that COVID-19 has brought us to an era of freedom – the freedom to take ownership of our life, to decide what is right for us and our family, to show up authentically, and to do the right thing for our planet.

At SAP, together with our vibrant ecosystem of partners, we have continued to innovate software and technology solutions that empower our customers to become intelligent enterprises and create a better and more sustainable economy, environment, and society. The use of our innovative technologies to connect processes, automate tasks, and translate data into action has helped a lot of organizations. This leads to higher efficiency and agility, enabling them to develop new processes and business models and to focus more time and resources on strategic and higher-value activities. The insights based on different data have helped them anticipate needs, predict future opportunities, and deliver more engaging experiences.

Being a global IT company, we did have our own set of challenges to get through 2020. It has impacted our approach in managing customers, partners, and employees – three critical pillars to our business. We also had to reexamine our medium- to long-term business strategies against many challenges that affect operations, employees, customers, and our ability to innovate through technology. (See Figure 13.1.)

With these core pillars of our organization, we were able to further strengthen our processes, move ahead with strategic investments, deliver

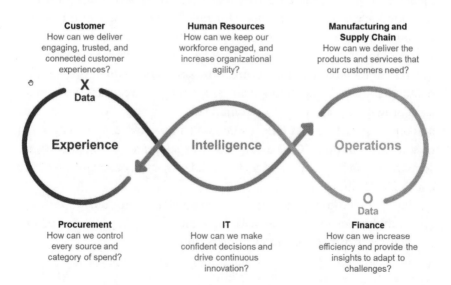

FIGURE 13.1   Considerations in moving the company forward.

economic value, and continue our commitment for growth in 2021. Later in the chapter we share our experiences to offer a glimpse of how we are on track with our strategic purpose, which is helping the world run better and improving people's lives.

Whether it serves as preparation for a new global pandemic in the future, business school literature, or lighthouse learning for startups or leadership teams, this chapter will help everyone gain something out of "How We Run Anywhere" at SAP APJ.

Backdrop: The Pre-COVID-19 Era

Before the pandemic, I traveled a lot for business planning and reviews, leadership connections, customer meetings, and events, and 2020 was supposed to be no different, and I was looking forward to a rewarding business year with meaningful connections across Asia. Our travel budget was secured for my team to take care of our customers and colleagues. Of course, I had also planned some overseas and interstate trips with my boys, who also love new experiences.

On the business front, SAP has always been a profitable growth company and the proof of our successful strategy lies in our achievements from inception to 2019. (See Figure 13.2.) We saw strong growth in our cloud and software business. Our rapidly expanding cloud business combined with solid growth in support revenue continued to drive the share of more predictable revenue. (See Figure 13.3.) We made substantial progress in transforming our company by shifting investments from non-core activities to strategic growth areas, enabling us to capture the tremendous growth opportunities in the market. We expanded our addressable market, acquired best-in-class assets, and innovated a new generation of software solutions. Our strong cloud backlog and the high software support renewal rates allowed us to confidently raise our high-level 2020 and 2023 ambitions.

Little did we know that our strategy and plans were going to shift significantly further into the year. We were all set to grow and expand our strategic goals by helping our customers transform.

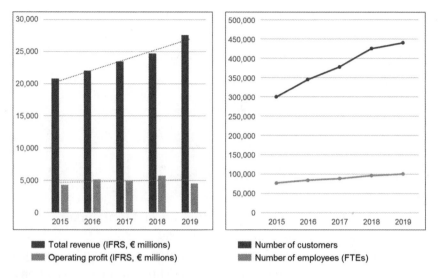

Total revenue (IFRS, € millions)
Operating profit (IFRS, € millions)

Number of customers
Number of employees (FTEs)

FIGURE 13.2   An overview of the past five years at SAP.

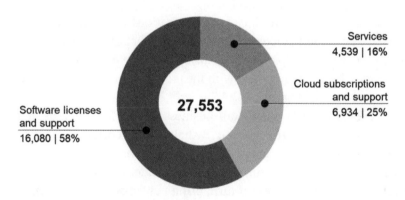

FIGURE 13.3   Sources of revenue.

Growth Strategy

Our core vision for the intelligent enterprise is an event-driven, real-time business. We want to deliver on these objectives by leveraging the power of data in SAP software with technologies such as artificial intelligence and machine learning to build powerful intelligent applications. This enables

FIGURE 13.4   SAP's strategy for connecting experience.

enterprises to get steep changes in productivity and focus on innovation, customer experience, and new business models.

We believe every digital interaction is an opportunity for an organization to positively influence a customer. Through these interactions, organizations can measure "experiences," such as customer satisfaction, employee engagement, partner collaboration, and brand impact. These interactions are also opportunities for organizations to understand how end users and customers perceive a vendor or a product. How is their brand perceived? We want to help every SAP customer thrive in today's "experience economy" by equipping them with the technologies to become intelligent enterprises. (See Figure 13.4.)

Our business model supports our business strategy and puts us in a strong position to drive future growth. By helping our customers operate better, we see enormous potential to increase our share of their overall IT spend while providing them with greater value. As our technology empowers our customers, they, in turn, bring new opportunities to their customers in areas that directly impact people's lives.

Goals for Sustained Business Success

SAP has strong ambitions for sustainable business success, both for our company and for our customers. We believe the most important indicators to measure this success comprise both financial and nonfinancial indicators: growth, profitability, customer loyalty, and employee engagement. These four goals affirm our commitment to innovation and sustainability and will help us deliver on our vision and purpose.

Growth

Looking beyond 2019, we have expected the share of more predictable revenue to reach approximately 70%, non-IFRS cloud subscriptions and support revenue to reach €8.7–9.0 billion, and total revenue to be in a range of €29.2–29.7 billion.

Profitability

We expected our non-IFRS operating profit to be in a range of €8.9–9.3 billion in 2020.

Customer Loyalty

We use the Net Promoter Score (NPS) to measure customer loyalty. In 2019, we achieved a global customer NPS of –6. With a sustained emphasis on follow-up, we are targeting an increase by 3–5 in 2020.

Employee Engagement

We use the employee engagement index to measure motivation and loyalty of our employees, how proud they are of our company, and how strongly they identify with SAP. Our score remained stable in 2019 (83%) compared to 2018 (84%) and we remain committed to achieving a score of 84–86% in 2020.

First Signs: Global Nervousness

People remember where they were when 9/11 happened because it was such a shock and triggered strong emotions. COVID-19 will be the same. I still remember it vividly. We were in Hawaii in February celebrating our results of 2019 together with colleagues from all over the world at our yearly Winner Circle event. There were more and more discussions on the topic of this virus from China and how it was spreading and impacting travel. I'm naturally a very optimistic person and didn't think too much of it. But we did have the first serious business discussions on this topic in Hawaii, because most of the business leaders and global leaders were all together, and some of them were more prudent than others.

Our global risk teams also got activated at that point, and they were actively reviewing the situation, SAP's response, and putting employee safety, welfare, and well-being as our top priority, while continuing to serve our customers and partners during this time.

We recognized that it was getting difficult for our colleagues and their families in China and other directly impacted countries. Our employees showed great resilience and flexibility in adapting to the very challenging circumstances. We ensured them that we stood together and supported them in a practical sense, and as friends and colleagues.

This unpredictable and fluid situation with COVID-19 was developing daily and we were taking recommendations from regional and local health authorities on how to best adapt to safeguard our employees' health, and our business. In the interests of all employees and our customers, we quickly updated our policies and added guidance.

Travel

SAP asked all colleagues to conduct business-critical travel only. We considered business-critical engagements to be those requiring SAP's physical attendance to ensure business continuity. This included technicians who had to travel to SAP data centers or colleagues needed to provide secure support at specific SAP locations.

All existing prebooked travel plans that were not business-critical for all of March – including internal events and meetings – were canceled immediately. My business trips to Tokyo, Mumbai, Bangalore, Seoul, Singapore, and Sydney were suddenly put on hold. I was so looking forward to meeting our customers and ensuring the team we were all set for 2020 and they were feeling energized and supported.

The well-being of our employees was our priority. Employees who did not feel comfortable traveling, even within areas of perceived low risk, were allowed to use our virtual technologies for meetings. While this was a little difficult initially, given the cultural nuances of APJ, we were confident of sailing through.

Because my team was fully customer-facing, it was quite difficult to manage customer interactions and make that true human connection. However, I must say that my team did a great job virtually.

Working from Home

Though SAP has always been flexible with working location of employees, we guided all employees with concerns about coming to the office, medical risk conditions, or COVID-19 associated risk factors to align on how they could best work from home. Through close collaboration between employees and managers, we focused on protecting health and well-being and ensuring business continuity for our customers and partners. While we started this arrangement with China, soon all countries had adopted the home-office model. I have always been a strong promoter of not taking work back home after a long day in the office, and I always encouraged my team to believe that when you are at home, be at home. Ironically, I was now asking my team to do "work from home." When I am working, I like to have full concentration to finish the task at hand. My long overhaul flights were always perfect to get that silent time where I can focus, strategize, create, and get things done. In the new normal, we had to get used to situations where we could hear infants crying, kids playing, and dogs barking during customer sessions. It was a real eye opener to see how professional and personal life was slowly merging for everyone.

Globally, SAP topped up the corporate health insurance policies for all employees and their families. In some countries, like Australia, SAP provided employees with "one-time home-office setup allowance" of up to $250. We also introduced additional "mental health leaves" to ensure that people do not get stagnant as the cycle continues, as well as periodic "detox days" and "meeting-free days" to give employees some time away from their calls and laptops.

Learning, Social and Marketing Events

SAP has amazingly smart people (we always say that SAP stands for Super Awesome People) and they are the foundation of our continued success. To make sure we continue adding value for our customers, there is a massive investment every year in continuous learning and enablement. We have a concept called Learn-2-Win (L2W), which consists of yearly weeks where all people specialized in a particular solution or industry come together to learn from development, from external thought leaders, and from each other by sharing best practices.

However important L2W is, we had to reexamine the way we made this happen in 2020. That day in Hawaii, over breakfast with the global leaders, the decision was made to make all the 2020 learning events virtual. I left Hawaii at the end of February to return to Melbourne, thinking that things would get back to "normal" fairly soon, not realizing what the rest of the year was going to look like – and thinking we were just extra prudent at SAP.

In conjunction with all of the above, SAP formed a Global Pandemic Task Force, which included representatives from security, health and well-being, travel, HR, IT, real estate and facilities, and corporate affairs. The team started working closely with international as well as local health authorities to monitor the situation closely as it unfolded.

Though it started with the L2W event, we had to follow this up with all other events, including our annual customer event, SAPPHIRE. Little did we know that virtual events were going to be the new normal.

Navigating the Lockdown and Dealing with Reality

We all had our way of dealing with the lockdown and our own personal challenges. For some, it was a blessing in disguise, while for others it was more of an opportunity to do something different. I had to juggle many business calls, homeschooling my boys, and managing household activities.

SAP, like other global companies, was operating during the pandemic with lots of uncertainty and the impact was different in every region. Although we were still seeing robust customer interest in our solutions to drive digital transformation, we too experienced a more tempered demand. Furthermore, all throughout 2020, we experienced a significant currency headwind versus our previous assumption, translating into a negative effect on revenue and operating profit.

In this context, we anticipated non-IFRS cloud revenue in a range of €8.3 billion to €8.7 billion, and cloud and software revenue in a range of €23.4 billion to €24.0 billion. We expected total revenue to range between €27.8 billion and €28.5 billion, with more predictable revenue anticipated to make up 72% of this result. Furthermore, we projected our full-year 2020 operating profit (non-IFRS) would end between €8.1 billion and €8.7 billion. In July 2020, we adjusted our outlook for the effective tax rate (IFRS) to between 28.5% and 29.5% and for the effective tax rate (non-IFRS) to between 27.5% and 28.5%.

In October 2020, we therefore adjusted our projection for cloud revenue downward to range between €8.0 billion and €8.2 billion, which represented a growth rate of 14% to 17% at constant currencies. In addition, the Company then anticipated cloud and software revenue of between €23.1 billion and €23.6 billion. This range represented a growth rate of 0% to 2%. We also expected total revenue of between €27.2 billion to €27.8 billion, which represented a growth rate of −2% to 1% at constant currencies and assumed a share of more predictable revenue of 72%. We also set a target range of €8.1 billion to €8.5 billion for our operating profit, which represented a growth rate of −1% to 4% at constant currencies. We expected a full-year 2020 effective tax rate (IFRS) of 27.0% to 28.0% and an effective tax rate (non-IFRS) of 26.5% to 27.5%.

Many companies were closed or supported by governments through various subsidies but for us, it was all about how we support our customers, partners, and employees.

Business Impact and Helping Our Customers

As early as March 2020, we saw a dramatic change in our customer base and the type of support they required from us. Add that to the fact that most of our people were faced with a completely new way of working, potential physical and emotional health challenges, as well as a significant dose of fear, and we realized that we needed to make it easier for our people. We came out with a simple and straightforward three-step approach for how to engage with our customers and have the right type of conversations.

I was part of many conversations where our deals were pushed out, businesses were struggling, and some were facing cash crunch. We even had customers who were sound enough to pay their invoices but could not do so because their checkbooks and other documents were locked in offices.

SAP was required to prepare for the concerns of our customers and prospects given COVID-19-related financial pressures. Globally, we had roughly €3B of outstanding account receivables and an equal amount from invoice pool considered high risk for collection. Additionally, we were anxious about €10B of global RoY pipeline and services bookings being impacted by the pandemic. Through the risks were spread across the region, industry, and market segments, some of these were more heavily impacted than others. We still had to look at a multifold mitigation approach focused on processes and programs.

The guidance we provided to all our customer-facing employees was pretty straightforward. First of all, as simple as it might sound, we emphasized that we should connect on a "human" level with our customers, getting a good view on how things were for them personally, for their family, and for their organization. We also used the time with them to share how SAP was reacting to the crisis, how we managed to go fully digital in one day, and the free resources we offered to help our customers getting through this. One of the great examples here is the employee pulse check, which allowed organizations to get a thorough understanding very quickly about how all of their employees were coping. We also performed in-depth industry analysis and our customers were very interested in hearing our observations and getting inspired by how other customers from different industries were managing the situation.

The second step was around assessing our customers' situations and categorizing their level of impact on their operations. This is where "Sink/Swim/Surf" came into play. Depending on the category and severity of impact, the customer would have different key concerns that we could potentially help them with. (See Figure 13.5.)

The final step was about how we could help our customers get back to surfing again, or sometimes merely help them keep their head above water. The activities here were focused around four categories:

1. Commercial actions: helping our customers with their costs.

2. Value realization: helping our customers to assess the ROI they realized thanks to our solutions and where we could refocus together with them so that they could achieve a higher ROI.

	Degree of COVID-19 Impact		
	Sinking – Trying to Survive	Swimming – Will Survive	Surfing – Will Prosper
Customer Situation	• Companies with a complete or partial stop in core business activities • Immediate challenge is to manage near-term cash flow issues	• Companies with disruptions in their supply chain/ecosystem • Immediate challenge is to find new avenues or partners to progressively resume business activities	• Companies with continuous demand or sudden surge for product/services • Immediate challenge is to fulfill demand while trying to scale operations
Key Concerns	1. Where can we cut immediate cost? 2. Can we delay payments? 3. Who are the essential employees to run our business? 4. Can we find new revenue streams (adj. industries)?	1. Is our contingency plan good for the long-term? 2. Where is our supply chain failing? 3. Have we evaluated all risks? 4. Where can we cut cost? 5. What are our options for the future?	1. What do we need to take advantage of that growth? 2. How can we ramp up the workforce in a virtual setting? 3. Can our existing supply chain and suppliers support the demand? 4. How can we grow sustainably (post COVID)?

FIGURE 13.5 "Sink/Swim/Surf" helped us determine how best to help our customers.

3. Assistance packages: quick time to value, lightweight applications, which could be deployed within three months and deliver an immediate ROI around spend management, supply chain optimization, asset management, customer experience, employee experience. The key areas where our customers urgently needed to address its impact on their businesses, ecosystem, and customers were:
   - Supply chain disruptions leading to higher costs and missed sales
   - Lost productivity due to lack of labor availability
   - Dampened sales from lower consumer sentiment and confidence
   - Global financial market shock leading to potential cash flow impediments
4. Transformation opportunities: some of our customers used the crisis as a forced opportunity to reinvent themselves and go to market with different business models.

One of the key learnings for me during this process was that every market is different, both culturally and economically. We had some countries where businesses were trying to get some benefits out of these policies and programs, while in others it is culturally insensitive to default on payments or avoid any bills. With our highly skilled team, I knew that we were going to do the right thing.

Engaging with Empathy

Amid ongoing concerns about the pandemic, SAP's top priority remained the safety, health, and well-being of everyone. There was no playbook, no manual, no step-by-step process to overcome the evolving crisis. While the uncertainty of the situation was frightening, SAP took action to help our sales teams and customers by rolling out temporary commercial changes. These programs were put in place effective immediately and through to the end of Q2 2020.

On one hand we realized that our processes must first focus on enabling our customers' requests to be captured and addressed. We had set up a global and regional task force across various lines of business and teams. New templates and systems were set in place to capture all required information and execution on contract/payment modifications.

On the other hand, we came up with some programs focused on new commercial models, refinancing, and commercial restructurings to support our customers. We had additional financing and commercial recommendations to cater to customer requests and new deal relief rolled out on an as-needed basis.

- **Cloud Start Date:** Our existing policy required the cloud term to begin Q+1 from the signature date (e.g., a deal signed March 31 must start no later than June 30 to be considered a Q1 deal). However, we extended this to ensure that cloud term can begin Q+2 for deals signed during the lockdown period (e.g., a deal closed March 31 can have a contract start date until September 30 and be considered a Q1 deal).

- **Cloud Ramping:** We required year 1 commitment from our customers to be at least 50% of total annual value in order to receive the full bookings credit for ramped deals; otherwise the maximum booking value is 2x year 1 value. Given the challenging times for our customers, we reduced the year 1 commitment to 25% of total annual value to allow for uncertainty in the deployment plans.

- **Flexible Financing Options:** SAP also introduced additional financing programs that provided flexibility with little paperwork for customers in need of extended payments. These programs allowed SAP to receive funds short term while providing customer payments over an extended period of time. We encouraged our customers and partners to leverage these finance and commercial support programs, in case they have a liquidity crisis.

Although we believed these were the right measures to drive incremental business in a tough time, they did put significant pressure on 2020 cloud revenues and overall margins for SAP.

My team was skeptical initially with such measures because we have often seen that this results in layoffs or salary cuts. Some IT companies did go for these stringent measures, but SAP clearly decided to put people first and the inclusive approach made sure no one would be left behind.

Compassion at Work

My main priority during the pandemic was to take care of employees and teams. All of us know that the pace of change in our industry is relentless, technology is evolving so quickly, and as a technology organization, advising our customers on how to transform and achieve their goals by using our technology, we have to make sure that our people are on top of the latest and greatest. People work hard, for long hours, covering more and more, sometimes putting their physical and mental health second – which in the long run is detrimental to them personally but also to us as a business. At the beginning of 2020, we already decided to drive a resilience program and we organized workshops in the different countries to inspire our people and get them on the bandwagon. Our first reaction with the pandemic was to cancel, but fortunately we didn't, and we challenged the external provider to partner with us and develop an online program. We ran the program for a couple of months across all of our Asia Pacific and Japan teams and it was designed in such a way to encourage individuals to adopt daily rituals to improve their resilience, such as exercise, connecting to others, gratitude, box breathing, healthy food, cold showers, and so on. There was also a gamification element with both team and individual leaderboards. We had a group of passionate program managers, and we established resilience ambassadors in every country.

The resilience improvements have been noteworthy, especially because most academics feel that resilience is more of a trait than a state, and therefore harder to move the needle on. I've personally received some great feedback from the participants, stories about how the quality of their life has improved, and how they are a better version of themselves. Last week, one of my team in the Philippines had a birthday, so I dropped him a note. He responded that the resilience program we have provided was one of the best gifts he has ever received. That truly moved me, because I know this causes a ripple effect; the fact that he feels better and more resilient will have a positive impact on his family and so many others around him. Based on the great results we achieved, we have kept on going and are launching the 2021 program soon.

While everyone talks about employee behavior, I personally felt that there was a big shift in the leadership style of our top management. Usually, there is a fairly big focus on results and customers. But we all dropped into our heart as leaders and opened up, and we became a whole lot more vulnerable. We had all-hands calls with all our APJ employees where our leaders spoke about not having all the answers and being OK with it. If you as a leader can be authentic and vulnerable, you are providing permission to everyone else to do the same. And this creates the magic of truly coming together as one team, one region.

We also realized that we had to revisit our company values and behaviors, and we decided to run this as a groundswell program, giving each one of our 20,000 APJ employees the opportunity to participate. Employees are the lifeblood of our business from the front line to the back office – their passion, excellence, and service impact customers every day. Today, employees are counting on their employers more than ever before – not only to maintain their standard of living, but also to keep them safe as they return to the workplace. To ensure that we make our employees work better, we developed a 10-week journey. (See Figure 13.6.)

When you bring people back to physical offices, doing so in a way that is not only safe but also keeps teams motivated and able to adapt to inevitable changes is crucial to your ability to move forward. People were adjusting to hybrid remote and on-site work environments filled with a mix of videoconferencing, social distancing, new policies, and regulatory mandates. As a result, communication was vital in keeping teams engaged and stronger than before.

One of the clear takeaways from this program has been that our people are rethinking where, when, and how they want to work, and more importantly how that fits into their life overall. The pandemic has absolutely triggered reflections on how they want to live life to the fullest, optimizing time with family and getting the most out of what they expect from the organization they work for. Rethinking our office spaces has been one of those focus areas.

We have adopted the idea "Work where you will be most productive" across our APJ region, which means that for some activities, the office will clearly be the best location (i.e., for certain meetings, idea generation sessions, client demonstrations). For other activities, working at home might be the preferred choice. Most importantly, we are giving our employees the choice to decide what works best for them. The approach we are consistently taking when it comes to big decisions like this is to give our people the opportunity to be part of the process, as well as with the redesign of some of our biggest office spaces across the region. For example, for our Singapore office, we are appointing a designer who will

FIGURE 13.6   We developed the idea for a 10-week journey to help employees.

be working with our people to co-create the environment and their future workplace at SAP.

Reflecting on all of 2020 and the effect that COVID-19 had on us, I feel that a lot of us have dropped our guards. We show up more authentic, more vulnerable, more human – in every interaction we have, and definitely, the remote meetings. It's truly a gift that people feel comfortable now letting others into their world. We had many special moments in 2020 across our APJ region, celebrating customer wins and go-lives, birthdays, anniversaries. One I will never forget is my 20-year anniversary with SAP, with colleagues and friends from all over the world dialing in to say a couple of words and reflect on my 20-year journey. (See Figure 13.7.) Before the lockdown I would have celebrated this milestone with a few colleagues and friends, but thanks to the pandemic, many more people could participate in my celebration.

We also celebrated many other company-wide employee events. Many times, employees would have to miss these events due to business travel and other commitments. But for 2020, everyone was able to get involved irrespective of their location. In some cases, they also got to celebrate with family – we provided vouchers like Uber Eats, virtual wine tastings with boxes being delivered beforehand, or Netflix for our people to enjoy with family.

FIGURE 13.7   For my 20-year anniversary with the company, my manager organized a surprise virtual get-together.

Assimilation of Knowledge

Once the pandemic was in full swing, we completely focused on remote and digital ways of working. What we were not fully aware of was that a large part of our customer-facing organization was not enabled to use the best technology to digitally connect with their customers. This was really the case for our sales teams, who are based in the same location as their customers and were relying 90% of the time on face-to-face connections.

We had to quickly come up with a plan to get our people enabled, but also take into consideration that we could not assume that everyone had the same starting point. Therefore, we began the APJ-wide enablement program "Crawl/Walk/Run," which allowed our people to pick the sessions best geared toward their needs.

The program covered the right tools for the different types of engagements, such as connecting with a customer one to one, or which tools are best suited for digital marketing campaigns, as well as which tools allow you to provide the best keynote experience when you have thousands of customers participating.

What our business leaders realized early on was that it's very possible to inform our customers on our solution capabilities and business cases, as well as inspiring them with the art of the possible. Within our APJ business, we organized some enablement sessions around creating awareness on "How to build trust in a virtual world."

We instinctively all understand that personal bonds and connections are very important to us as humans. But with the Great Lockdown, suddenly the usual rituals of human connection and bonding were no longer possible: the social rituals that require physical proximity, face-to-face meetings, handshakes, eating and drinking together, the subtle signals of facial expression and eye contact. It was all put on hold. We realized that in the realm of business relationships, this can have adverse consequences, because without personal contact we become less trusting and more fearful of others (herein lies the root of prejudice). The lack of a bond of trust (the ancient Greeks called it *ethos*) leads us to look for other things in order to become comfortable with a business decision or a choice. We noticed opportunities being delayed, as our customers sought more facts and details. The spreadsheet justifications were getting more rigorous and time consuming. What was happening was the mistaken quest for more details, facts, and logical justification when in fact what our customers really desired was the comfort of trust. In my experience, an overdose of facts is a poor substitute for a trusted connection.

The awareness sessions we organized were focused on explaining to our sales leaders the principle of trust, how to build that in a virtual world with customers. We looked at trust as a bucket to be filled. Pre-pandemic, you could perhaps fill it with a single big-meet event. You might fly to meet an important individual, entertain them with a fine dinner, and swap stories over drinks. Or maybe it would take a couple of intense face-to-face meetings to fill the trust bucket. But in a virtual world, it comes back to filling that bucket with a teacup rather than a firehose. We need to show our customers multiple signals (teacups) of intent, which replace the firehose to make a person feel special and build that trusted connection. Examples of those signals can be handwritten notes, personal video messages, calling a customer without an agenda but just to say hi. There are of course many other ways to send trust signals but creating this awareness with our teams has been a very important part of doing business in this new world.

And eventually, we also handled onboarding and offboarding processes remotely, thereby covering the entire hire-to-retire cycle. However, we could not completely replace the face-to-face connections that a new joiner needs to make – some things are better left for a connected world.

Inorganic Growth – Acquisition

During the 2020 lockdown, we observed a huge trend in online commerce and made some very strategic acquisition decisions. We were constantly keeping an eye on market trends and the needs of our customer. As customers are becoming more diverse, expectations are rising toward hyper-personalized digital experiences with brands across all channels and at any time. SAP decided to help organizations build a foundation that supports customer freedom. In doing so, we augmented our offering through the acquisition of Emarsys.

Though most companies were struggling at managing 2020, SAP started investing in the future to scale decisions, build loyalty, enrich the customer journey, and increase revenue. This inorganic growth, combined with SAP's core, will enable us to accelerate our strategy and set a new paradigm for how businesses are managed. This was not restricted to our inorganic growth strategy but also extended to people.

By the time you read this book, I will have embarked on a new and exciting journey. I will be leading the APJ Customer Experience Solutions team of SAP – an area that has been the backbone of every item added to your shopping basket or every promotional message you have received. This is an area of strong growth and where delivering the best experience for our customer's customer prevails.

Workforce, Business, and Consumer Insights While we are all adapting to different work and collaboration models, the newness and the experiences are all unique to each of us, depending on our job or industry. Understanding, acknowledging, and acting on the challenges and questions people have will help us equip them to navigate this new normal.

Whether an organization is doing good or bad, it is important for them to understand "what's next." They need to understand the mental health check of all employees, the support required by customers, and the requirements of partners. Once they come up with ways to tackle all of it, it's important to understand if this is in the expected direction.

To manage that end, **Qualtrics** has helped organizations with a wide range of **free surveys and pulse checks**, including:

• Remote Work Pulse	• Customer Confidence Pulse
• Healthcare Workforce Pulse	
• Remote Educator Pulse	• Brand Trust Pulse
• Higher Education Remote Learning Pulse	• Supply Continuity Pulse

We had multiple employee pulse check surveys to continuously learn and evolve on how we could support them better. I ensured that I went over all the comments and took necessary steps to support my people.

Digital Learning As a company we have always believed in our responsibility to support the next generation of professionals and users with our best-in-class digital learning. People lost their jobs and it was an opportunity for them to reskill or upskill themselves to be employable again. While everyone wanted to expand their horizon, they needed safe and healthy learning environments to continue their education virtually.

Therefore, we worked to broaden access and facilitate the continuity of innovation and enablement, which usually comes with small fees and access to learning platform. This included **free access** to:

- Select **learning journeys for students at one of the 3,800 member universities** of the SAP University Alliances program
- **Online courses for young learners** to explore technology
- The **massive open online courses (MOOCs)** available on the open-SAP platform

Many of my team members and acquaintances developed cross-skills to navigate through the corporate ladder and pick up activities which they could not in the past. Lack of resources was no longer an excuse for anyone.

Connected Supply Chain   One of the key challenges we recognized was the massive disruptions impacting global supply chains. There were instances where one part of a region had ventilators and another had an acute shortage. The same was true for other medical equipment, PPE kits, masks, and so on. I knew that we had the right technology to provide this visibility but some companies were not yet in the journey to adopt these solutions. So we decided to open up access to our solutions like **SAP Ariba Discovery** and **SAP Integrated Business Planning.** These solutions help connect parties through real-time management of sourcing needs and provide supply chain planning as a service to companies.

I was really proud that SAP was doing its part to help the world. Have we done everything? Possibly not. It is a long journey, but we have taken the right steps, which have laid the foundation for a better tomorrow.

Future Outlook: Beyond 2020 and COVID-19

Looking at yesterday and living in today, I am optimistic for tomorrow. I have started reexamining my personal commitments toward my family, friends, the business, and the community. I am fully embracing the era of freedom and creating my best life, which involves quality time with the people I love, doing the things that make me feel alive, and having an impact by inspiring others to create their best life.

On our business revenue side, we exceeded the outlook adjusted in October 2020, and on the operating profit side, we reached the upper end of the guidance. Our current cloud backlog (contractually committed cloud revenue we expect to recognize over the upcoming 12 months) reached €7.61 billion at constant currencies (€7.15 billion at actual currencies; 2019: €6.68 billion). This was an increase of 14% on a constant currency basis. At constant currencies, the resulting non-IFRS cloud revenue grew from €7.01 billion in 2019 to €8.24 billion in 2020 and therefore ended above our guidance range of €8.0 billion to €8.2 billion. That represented an increase of 18% at constant currencies. Cloud and software revenue (non-IFRS) grew 3% at constant currencies to €23.72 billion (2019: €23.09 billion), and thus ended above our range forecasted for 2020 of €23.1 billion to €23.6 billion. Thanks to the strong increase in cloud business described above, we were able to increase the share of more predictable revenue by 4.4pp to 72% (2019: 67%). As such, our total revenue (non-IFRS) increased slightly despite a decline in software license business as a result of the COVID-19 pandemic. Total revenue (non-IFRS) on a constant currency basis rose 1% in 2020 to €27.90 billion (2019: €27.63 billion), thus exceeding the guidance for 2020 that had been amended in October (€27.2 billion to €27.8 billion). Operating expenses (non-IFRS) in 2020 on a constant currency basis remained constant at €19.39 billion (2019: €19.43 billion). Not only did we demonstrate cost discipline in 2020 when it came to discretionary spend and employee hiring, but we also cut costs naturally through less travel, lower facility-related costs, and virtual rather than physical events. This enabled us to keep our 2020 operating expenses at the previous year's level. Our expense base in 2020 was impacted by our transformation to a fast-growing cloud business. In our outlook for 2020, we expected to see an increasing cloud gross margin, but we saw a positive development on the cloud gross margin for 2020, due to the increasing efficiency in the operation.

At SAP, our future investment outlook will coordinate and distribute development initiatives, accelerate product delivery, and drive a corporate strategy focusing on innovation and business growth. (See Figure 13.8.) First, we are reinventing how businesses run, enabling our customers' business transformation in the cloud for greater resilience. As a result,

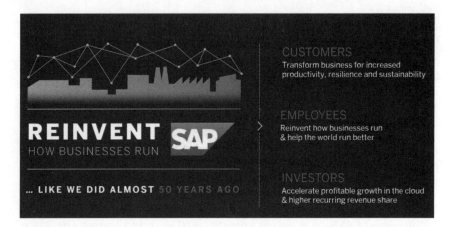

FIGURE 13.8   The corporate strategy focuses on innovation and business growth.

we intend to accelerate their transition to the cloud, which will add value over the long term but in the short term for SAP will result in a decrease in on-premises revenue, which will not be immediately made up by the increase in cloud revenue. We have also decided to speed up the modernization of our cloud delivery to enable a more resilient and scalable cloud infrastructure for our customers. This will require additional investments in the next two years but allows us to largely complete the modernization and achieve an improved cloud gross margin in the longer term.

We recognize this is a significant change compared to the previous strategy and former 2023 ambition. We are at an inflection point, where customers are asking us to help accelerate their business transformation, to gain resilience, and to position them to emerge stronger out of the crisis.

While we will be helping everyone on their way back to reaccelerating growth, SAP has identified areas of investment for the company going forward, including higher spend on research and development and on SAP's employees.

Revamping Solution Offerings and Focusing on Customer Success

We recognize that we must continuously improve our portfolio of products to maintain and build on our current position as a leader in business software.

In this regard, we have decided that going forward, we will focus on harmonization of SAP's cloud delivery infrastructure, to modernize it, to make it resilient, to make it scalable and highly automated. Financially, this has an impact on our books; it shifts upfront revenue to recurring revenue and means that for some time, there will be a margin differential between the cloud and on-premises.

However, the move makes more sense over the long term because it will drive higher customer lifetime value for customers who trust SAP with their business.

We are looking at increasing our R&D spending from 13.5% to 16% of our revenue. SAP innovation groups work jointly with our customers and partners on a wide range of initiatives focused to benefit our stakeholders and customers.

I will also have to unlearn and relearn some business tricks that I have acquired throughout my 20 years at SAP. But isn't this what the pandemic has taught us – nothing lasts forever.

People

We are looking at continued investment in our people and hiring right talent. When we looked at the bonus plans for 2020, we decided to readjust the targets and bonus plans for our people going forward. We have secured the required funding to pay out more than 110% of target achievement for our employees. Though the higher bonus will cost SAP an additional €300M, it was absolutely the right thing for us to do because it was our people's dedication and commitment that gave SAP such a successful year.

We are also addressing specific needs to recognize, develop, and retain talent through different programs. This will be reflected by an increase in our investment in targeted equity grants to nurture our high-performance winning culture.

In every step we take as a company, our key consideration is – how does it benefit our people? This has been and will continue to be our North Star.

Learnings: Preparedness for the Future

The global pandemic has exposed the vulnerabilities of highly connected supply and demand across borders, industries, and companies of all sizes. Even industries that have not been as widely impacted by shutdowns have had challenges finding ways to meet unexpected surges in demand.

I have learned a lot from this pandemic. I got more opportunity to spend time with my boys, I understand them better, and they understand me and my life better. They are a lot more aware of what I do all day, the decisions I need to make, the challenges I face, and the opportunities I receive. I also feel more closely connected with my team, I know the names of their pets, and I have also (virtually) met the extended families of my direct reports – all the beautiful simple things we had lost in the hectic lifestyle.

Similarly, when I look at companies, resilience and agility are key to an organization's survival and performance during unpredictable and volatile events. However, business continuity surveys show that very few organizations are prepared for the impact of a pandemic. While the company must ensure they have the financial stability to weather a volatile climate, investing in technology is key to help implement flexible processes and use insights that will also strengthen their ability to adjust for risks and take advantage of new opportunities as they arise.

For me, this will be my motto moving forward – resilience and agility so that you can create your best life.

Building on Business Resiliency

As the saying goes, "cash is king," and in this uncertain environment it is more important than ever for us to understand our financial position to make sound business decisions. With the help of digital technologies, we can deploy flexible processes that deliver insights that help to balance what is needed to keep the business running today and tomorrow.

- **Maintain business continuity:** Use technology to streamline tasks, such as financial close, so that we not only improve transparency across the business but also increase efficiencies.

- **Manage cash flow:** Ensure we have real-time visibility into finances to recognize potential reserves and shortages and improve financial position.

- **Plan and respond to change:** Match demand with supply using tools that can help segment, predict, and allocate orders.

- **Maintain manufacturing agility:** Understand and respond to production changes in specific plants, such as changes in labor availability, materials, and demand.

- **Deliver critical products:** Allocate product to ensure we can deliver to critical locations, while monitoring changes in access due to changing local conditions.

These are tricks that were taught to us during B-school, but over a period of time we deviated. However, the pandemic showed us the importance of these basics.

Supporting Customers

During the pandemic, we learned that conducting business in a virtual world is new territory for many companies and customers. Many behaviors will be slow to revert to the way they were, and some will likely be permanently changed. As more and more people choose to purchase through digital channels, what will not change is the need to meet customer expectations with relevant, timely, and personal experiences. It has never been more important to know customers, understand their context, and deliver on brand promise.

Memories of good and bad interactions during the pandemic will stay with consumers for a long time. Companies that invest in delivering better customer experiences – both in physical locations and online – will potentially be able to rebound faster, enjoy greater customer loyalty, and drive future growth.

Will you not support your local grocery store that provided toilet paper and eggs during the pandemic?

Reinvigorating People

When we bring people back to physical offices, doing so in a way that is not only safe but also keeps teams motivated and able to adapt to inevitable changes is crucial to move forward.

I commit to support all people around me, and definitely my teams, because they were the ones who kept me going. What about you?

To a New Chapter. . .

I am proud and blessed that, during this pandemic, I worked for SAP, a company that remains focused on uniting people and technology to make a positive change in the world. My team and I will be with you on the journey to recovery, stability, and long-term success. We are inspired as a company and as individuals to forge a new future, together.

We can help each other move forward from the COVID-19 pandemic for our people, customers, and business. SAP has all the employees here to support business recovery and future growth . . . and this is my commitment to all of you. We will move *forward together* to a better world.

About the Contributors

Peggy Renders is an executive leader in the digital space focused on business transformation and growth. She is passionate about building high-performing teams and running an end-to-end business in a fast-paced environment where you need an effective go to market strategy across multiple channels. Peggy has spent most of her professional life contributing to the growth and success of SAP, being recognized as a leader in IT space. She is one of the top Asia-Pacific and Japan leaders for SAP, and recently got nominated in the Global Top 100 Women in Technology. Peggy also focuses on mentoring women and ensuring that a diverse workforce is used to get to better results. She drives multiple programs to get more women and young girls into STEM.

Tanuj Vijay has been with IT industry for almost two decades and spent the majority of this time with SAP. He has extensive work experience in value selling, presales and sales support with leading IT companies, and handling global customers and partners. He has been instrumental in driving partner success by driving various growth programs. Tanuj has picked up different new initiatives at SAP and scaled them for long-term success. He has been recognized at multiple forums for contribution to SAP's success and growth. He is very enthusiastic about working at SAP and believes in SAP's dominance in the global IT industry. He also contributes to various community forums, primarily around supporting underprivileged children.

CHAPTER 14

SOS Children's Villages

By Siddhartha Kaul (President)

About SOS Children's Villages

SOS Children's Villages is the world's largest nongovernmental organization focused on supporting children and young people without parental care or at risk of losing it. It has been contributing for the last 70 years in 136 countries and territories to improve these indicators for children, young people, and vulnerable families. Locally led, we focus on strengthening families who are under pressure so they can stay together. When this is not in a child or young person's best interests, we provide quality alternative care according to their unique needs as advised in the UN Guidelines for the Alternative Care of Children. In 2019, with more than 2,800 programs that safeguard children, provide alternative care and education, strengthen families, promote youth employability, and advocate for child rights, we have reached 1.23 million children, young people, and their families. (See Figure 14.1.)

After the 2008 economic crisis, civil society suffered a double whammy. While on one hand the government and private actors cut their spending on social causes, on the other hand the sector was put under intense scrutiny. In addition, the world started to experience an increase in the migrant crisis, religious conflicts, and the rise of right-wing forces, not to mention the ever-present issues of gender inequality, racism, and the economic divide. The COVID-19 pandemic arrived on the scene with this backdrop. Normally, civil society looks for precedents and good practices to address such emergencies, but this time there was not much to relate to. The fear of personal safety and life became a major factor in designing the

FIGURE 14.1 SOS Children's Villages supports children and young people throughout the world.

response. Generally, "emergencies" have a starting point and a projectable end. COVID-19 had a starting point, but the end? Who knows?

The pandemic and the lockdown that followed have impacted the poorest of the poor the most. Among them, the children are the most vulnerable group. According to Joining Forces, a global alliance of six leading child rights organizations of which SOS Children's Villages is a part, before the pandemic, more than half of all children worldwide were living with daily exposure to different forms of violence. The measures to contain and respond to the pandemic have further increased the risks of physical, sexual, and emotional violence against girls, boys, and children with different gender identities.

The digital divide in the developing and underdeveloped world has also become wider since the onset of COVID-19. Even before the pandemic, an estimated 258.4 million children, adolescents, and youth weren't in schools, representing one-sixth of the global population of this age group,[1]

---

[1]UNESCO Institute for Statistics.

a number expected to rise due to the continued shutdown of schools. The mobile Internet penetration rates of 20.4% at the end of 2019 were much lower than the 62.5% for developed countries,[2] thus depriving a large number of poor children the opportunity to offset the loss of education via online schooling. Almost 267 million young people (aged 15–24) were not engaged in employment, education, or training,[3] a staggering number expected to grow further due to disruption caused by the lockdown.

While it may be difficult to estimate the income of the sector as a whole, in 2019 SOS Children's Villages and 16 of its peers internationally raised around USD 41 billion in cash and kind. A little under 60% of this came from government sources, while the rest was contributed by individuals, corporations, foundations, and other sources. More than 75% of these funds was raised in Europe and North America, while the rest came from Asia, Oceania, the Middle East, South America, and Africa, in that order. The income for these 17 organizations had been growing at a rate of less than 2% since 2017,[4] a trend that likely continued for the sector in 2020 too.

From 2018 to 2019, SOS Children's Villages' projected combined revenue of EUR 1.4 billion grew by 7%, up from a growth rate of 2% in 2018. Individuals, with donations large and small, continue to be the financial backbone of our organization, sustaining nearly half of our annual revenue (growth rate of 8% in 2019). Our other primary funding source, government subsidies, was up by 5%, driven by an expansion in domestic programming and government partnerships in the American and European regions. Funding from our institutional partners continued to rise at a rapid rate of 22% in 2019. Before the COVID-19 pandemic, we were planning to reach out in 2020 to 1.65 million children, young people, and their families and expected our combined revenue to remain at the 2019 levels.

First Signs

SOS Children's Villages' first reaction, like any other development organization of its size, was to rapidly assess the safety of children and youth under its care and its own coworkers. Very early on, an advisory was

....

[2]World Bank.
[3]International Labour Organization (ILO).
[4]International Fundraising Leadership Forum.

issued for coworkers to avoid nonurgent official travel. Additionally, each member association (generally one member association in a country) was asked to follow precautions as per the advisories or instructions issued by their local authorities.

Most of the SOS Children's Villages program locations stopped or regulated entry of visitors and started practicing hand and cough hygiene. The children and caregivers were coached on handwashing techniques and wearing cloth masks when they left homes. The program locations were also asked to evaluate the need for procuring health and hygiene essentials. At the same time every country's office was given an option to spend emergency funds up to EUR 30,000 for providing essential items to children and families under their care. (See Figure 14.2.)

It soon became apparent that the COVID-19 infections were spreading rapidly and the international public health emergency could very well become a pandemic. In order to provide a strategic and well-coordinated

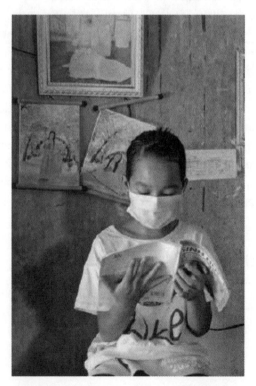

FIGURE 14.2   Children were provided with hygiene essentials and other needed items.

response, SOS Children's Villages formed a COVID-19 Consultation Group, comprising the organization's senior leadership with suitable representation from all parts of the world. In its very first meeting, the group agreed that although there might be a gap in the global revenue, SOS Children's Villages would make all possible effort to ensure there would be no premature end of care for the children and young people it supported. At the same time, it was decided to issue a Global Humanitarian Appeal to raise funds for supporting the special need arising due to COVID-19 pandemic.

It was clear that countries around the world would remain under sustained lockdown, with Asia and Europe being the first two continents to be impacted. This was also the time SOS Children's Villages experienced its first set of challenges:

- Although family homes in SOS Children's Villages by design have good social distancing, keeping scores of children safe from COVID-19 was a challenge. At the same time there was the urgent need to quickly create an infrastructure for isolating children and caregivers in case someone contracted the infection.

- The children's inability to continue education due to the closure of schools and limited availability of IT infrastructure (hardware and software) at program locations for ensuring online education posed a significant challenge. While our facilities had Internet capabilities and a few computers, the increased demand due to online education suddenly put immense pressure on the existing IT infrastructure.

- Also, ensuring the safety of children from physical and mental abuse in a pandemic had its own challenges. We witnessed an increase in psychosocial issues among children and youth due to insecurities presented by continuous lockdown.

- The young people who had become independent after receiving care from our programs were suddenly left with reduced or no income due to the lockdown. Some of them could not afford to pay rent and hence had no habitat. With meager savings and inability to pay rents, for obvious reasons, they returned home to SOS.

- Due to the lockdown, SOS social workers were not able to visit and support the vulnerable families in the communities, whose plight was worsening at the same time. A logical step in the life cycle of a welfare program is when the participants become self-supporting and move on. However, the prolonged lockdown disrupted this cycle as the participants who were ready to move on suddenly started struggling to meet their basic needs. In addition, the participants who had exited the programs also needed fresh support due to the economic impact of lockdown. This increased the pressure on programs being run by all civil society organizations.

- With an intense response required, the people under the greatest pressure were the SOS parents and caregivers. They had to work 24/7 under lots of limitations. There were additional needs for sanitizing SOS family homes and quarantining children. Many of the coworkers who live outside our facilities could not come in due to travel restrictions. This put additional load on caregivers and coworkers who lived inside the facility. Similarly, the coworkers in supporting offices had to counsel and guide these caregivers from a distance, which we all understand by now has its own limitations. The coworkers responsible for monitoring the programs had to rely a lot on technology and spend extra hours to ensure that the financial and quality parameters did not suffer.

- Fundraisers faced the inability to approach donors in person and seek funds. There was also a fear that the pandemic could bring a downturn in the giving sentiment. In all, the organization feared that its worldwide revenue would witness a 7% negative growth. As part of its alternative care program, SOS Children's Villages provides family-like care, foster care, short-term care, and youth care to various participants. A vast majority of these children and young people are with SOS Children's Villages for a long time, and ending care for them despite the expected downturn in income was not an option.

Navigating the Great Lockdown

As countries entered lockdown, there was a sudden spike in demand for food and basic hygiene items. Since more than 65,000 children and youth are cared for under the SOS Children's Villages alternative care program, locations all over the world were asked to keep adequate stocks of essential items so as to provide for the next couple of months.

However, poor and vulnerable communities who survive on their daily earnings did not have enough resources to procure the basic necessities. SOS Children's Villages supports more than 80,000 vulnerable families around the world. The vast majority of them needed help. Also, the families that were on the verge of becoming self-supporting could not exit the program due to the lockdown. On top of that there were new families who urgently needed basic amenities. Not only did we have to prevent hunger but we also had to support the upkeep of hygiene to prevent infections. All this was to be done within a highly restricted mobility in most places around the world.

Given their extensive experience with short- and long-term responses, our teams in the field immediately started providing locally relevant solutions. In many countries around the world, SOS Children's Villages distributed food items and dry rations to the needy families in our program areas. At the same time, depending on the local realities, other solutions were tried. For example, in Kenya and the Philippines, instead of distributing food items our coworkers distributed vouchers that could be redeemed at local shops for procuring essential items, thus eliminating the logistics involved. The preventive health responses, including awareness raising in the communities on personal hygiene, and distribution of soap, masks, and so on, were carried out across most program locations.

Provision of IT material (computers, mobiles), Wi-Fi connections, and IT support were a basic requirement to help children continue their education, but we could only provide these facilities mostly to children and young people in our family-like care programs. Although we strove to support development of basic IT infrastructure in our Family Strengthening programs, due to a lack of additional funds, we did not succeed to the extent that we desired.

> "Although I use social media, I was unaware about virtual meetings. Now, I can freely use Microsoft Teams and Skype to make a presentation in a virtual world. It has enhanced my digital skills. It has been a platform to express feelings and exchange ideas."
> –Pratikshya Poudel, President of the National
> Child Club of SOS Children's Villages, Nepal

There were some interesting examples of using IT platforms to deliver results during the lockdown. For example, our existing digital learning module, Text for Change, which uses short messaging service (SMS) to reach parents living in remote communities in Sri Lanka, was adapted to build awareness of the COVID-19 pandemic. In Ukraine, SOS Children's Villages psychologists conducted a special series of webinars and virtual counseling sessions for foster care families and even others in need across the country. Similarly, in Ecuador, virtual support on parenting skills helped families to stay together in tough times, while in Italy a software bot helped in providing psychosocial support to program participants. An online platform was used to deliver various services to children and caregivers in Belarus.

Our office for Latin America and the Caribbean organized a virtual photography exhibition in September 2020, "Your reality from inside your home in the time of COVID-19," giving opportunities to young participants and coworkers to express their feelings during this unprecedented health emergency. Moreover, during the pandemic, SOS Children's Villages also supported economic empowerment of communities. For example, in Rwanda we supported participants in running savings and loans groups virtually, using a group mobile wallet. With partners in Lebanon, SOS Children's Villages helped vulnerable families to produce and sell face masks.

We are happy to say that despite the travel restrictions that could have otherwise impacted the results, many of the intended actions were adapted and delivered virtually. For example, in Asia our teams were able to adapt the skill development workshops for young people in a way that these could be conducted online. At the same time, the member association in Gambia adapted its monitoring and assessment of child safeguarding to ensure children and young people under our care remained safe during these difficult times.

The short- and mid-term response was expected to put financial pressure on our program locations. Therefore, SOS Children's Villages decided to make up to EUR 30,000 available as fast-track funds in each country that was in need of providing an urgent response. This affected liquidity but also accelerated our ability to respond in most countries. At the same time, we started to work along with our offices in the industrialized world to raise more funds through a Global Humanitarian Appeal. Our initial assessment was that in all, we would need up to EUR 50 million for the short- to mid-term response. Our member associations in Europe,

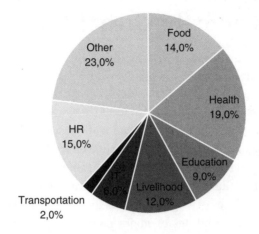

*Health includes water, sanitation, WASH activities
*HR includes hiring, training and support expenses
*Other can include evaluation costs, research, bank charges, furniture etc.

FIGURE 14.3   The funds raised through the Global Humanitarian Appeal addressed various needs.

North America, and emerging economies around the world appealed for additional funds from existing and new donors. Special campaigns were launched and received, encouraging response, especially in our German and Austrian markets. Figure 14.3 shows the breakdown of the needs that are being addressed by the funds we raised as part of the Global Humanitarian Appeal. However, many member associations used their local funds to provide the pressing needs of the communities they work with.

In order to deliver urgent results, SOS Children's Villages had to maintain its workforce at an optimal level despite an expected reduction in income. Therefore, at our international office in Austria, we implemented the Corona-Kurzarbeit (reduced working time) scheme, an offer by the Austrian Labor Market Service (AMS) to provide employers with some salary relief in the form of government subsidies. This meant reduced working hours (ranging from 10 to 80% of normal working time, adjustable across the months) and salary reductions (ranging from 10 to 20%).

As the lockdown progressed, it was clear that most of 2020 would be spent under full or partial restriction. This implied that it would impact our ability to provide the best care for children not only in the present year but also in the following years. Surely we had to look at our long-term plans too, and we had to do so fairly soon.

Learnings from the Great Lockdown

Since COVID-19 is an unparalleled incident, there are several lessons learned. The key ones for us are these:

- During this pandemic, especially in its early phase, the reach that the local community groups demonstrated while responding to this grave emergency was simply amazing. Resident welfare associations, neighborhood cultural societies, and many other informal groups were the first to feed the hungry and even ferried migrant workers who had no shelter to their places of origin. At times their ability to deliver results far outstripped the abilities of major civil society players and state machinery. In some countries, SOS Children's Villages supported the efforts of such organizations to increase its reach. Therefore, it is imperative that the civil society designs its future response in a way that empowers these community groups to implement locally relevant and needs-based solutions. Such partnerships should become one of the preferred ways of delivering responses in the future.

- The Convention on the Rights of the Child, the world's most widely ratified human rights treaty in history, states that childhood is separate from adulthood and lasts until 18. It is a special, protected time, in which children must be allowed to grow, learn, play, develop, and flourish with dignity.[5] However, even in normal times the violations of the rights of a child are abundant, and these only increase during humanitarian emergencies. A pandemic like this made it very difficult for SOS Children's Villages and other civil society players to ensure children remained safeguarded from physical, mental, and sexual abuse and trafficking. This required putting in place more robust mechanisms of prevention, reporting, and early redressal that even work when there are extended lockdowns and similar disruptions. For example, in many of our program locations, we placed boxes right outside family homes, so that children could report incidents of abuse without having to go out. At other locations we conducted monthly virtual meetings with caregivers focusing on child safeguarding issues.

---

[5]Convention on the Right of Child, UNICEF.

- For organizations like SOS Children's Villages that provide care and protection to children, there is an impending need to innovate care solutions. The COVID-19 pandemic has taught us that suddenly a large number of people could be in the hospital with no one to take care of their children. Therefore, all of us should work with governments and other partners to develop child-friendly spaces in the hospitals and also, if required, bring in children for short-term care to alternative care facilities of SOS Children's Villages.

- The existing disparities in who benefits from technology were amplified several times during the pandemic and lockdown. While the middle and the upper classes were able to provide some semblance of educational continuity for their children, the poor had to struggle and the education of their children was severely compromised. Not only did they find it challenging to provide a stable Internet connection, but they were also unable to provide dedicated computers or mobile phones to all siblings having online classes at the same time. In addition, the challenge of the digital divide is not only limited to elementary education but also holds true for the young people from disadvantaged sections pursuing higher education (see Figure 14.4). We cannot let the digital divide squander our talent and brilliance. Therefore, we need to appeal more vehemently to corporations and relevant authorities to help us in accelerating our pace in bridging this socio-technological chasm.

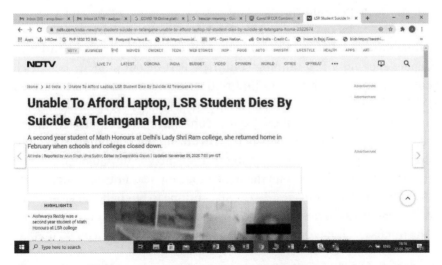

FIGURE 14.4 Without access to technology, many students struggled greatly during the pandemic.

- SOS Children's Villages and others in civil society also need to address the issues in mental health that surfaced during this unprecedented event in the lives of people. While as an adult one learns to move on, certain experiences can leave a lasting impression in the minds of children and young people. The young population has experienced disruption not only in their education or newfound jobs but also the way they interact socially. The risk that the young generation's world-view was getting confined to virtual communication has only been accentuated by this pandemic. Therefore, it is a priority for all of us to work on these issues with our participants and provide psychological first aid, long-term counseling, and even bespoke solutions.

- All said and done, finally it is the state that is accountable for delivering sustainable solutions for the needs of its citizens. The clear and present lacunae in public welfare systems and the inequity in our socioeconomic environment have come under heightened public scrutiny during the pandemic and lockdown. Learning from this experience, we need to intensify our partnership with the state so that not only is lost ground recovered but also new horizons in public welfare are reached.

Future Outlook

COVID-19 negatively affected SOS Children's Villages' fund development efforts in many countries in 2020. However, there were happy exceptions too, led by our encouraging fund development efforts in Germany. While this is a relief, it also highlights SOS Children's Villages' continued dependence on a few funding countries. Part of our strategy is that all countries must work hard to find resources within their homelands. At SOS Children's Villages, we are even more emphatic now that self-reliance and sustainability are critical for our continuity. In the sidebar you can see how the 16 leading civil society organizations, including SOS Children's Villages, have performed in terms of income development during the first half of 2020, despite the pandemic and near universal lockdown. For SOS Children's Villages, 2021 will continue to be challenging in terms of income because new donor acquisition was minimal in the year 2020. The trends as of now are not very clear and in fact remain a bit confusing.

Income for the Sector During Lockdown

According to the International Fundraising Leadership Forum, the sum of income for 16 international civil society organizations grew by half a billion US dollars in the first half of 2020 as compared to same period in 2019. The growth was led by operations in the US, Germany, Japan, and Brazil in respective continents.

It is evident that many gains of the last few years have been lost due to the pandemic, and we will have to invest more in bringing in new donors and diversifying our sources of funds.

In terms of staffing, at our international office in Austria, we had to reduce around 10% of our headcount, which also included people taking early retirement and eliminating job redundancies not related to COVID-19. We hope to maintain the optimized headcount in the year 2021. For an organization like ours that provides services to children, youth, and vulnerable communities, we would need to scale up our services substantially, and financial and human resources would have to be found for this.

SOS Children's Villages has taken the critical step of reviewing its strategy for 2030. While we remain on our strategic path, the pandemic has necessitated that we prioritize our actions and responses based on the COVID-19 reality. Going forward, we at SOS Children's Villages feel the need to focus on and empower children and young people and have identified the following top priorities:

- **Education**: Most children and young people in SOS Children's Villages care programs are in danger of losing one year of education due to school closures and the digital divide. The lack of access to online education due to nonavailability of necessary hardware or infrastructure puts the younger generation in a disadvantageous position. We have decided to prioritize our resource allocation to enable continuity of education for the children in our programs. We are in the process of getting the children and young people the necessary hardware and a fast Internet connection to enable them to connect to online education programs.

- **Youth**: The youth in SOS Children's Villages programs who were just beginning their lives in society have suffered in the last year. Many lost jobs and places of abode. The situation is further compounded in countries that have little or no social security system. Over 7,000 of our youngsters have returned to SOS Children's Villages asking for help and emotional support. It is a tough task, and we are trying to find ways to support them.

- **Child safeguarding**: This goes to the core of SOS Children's Villages work. In 2008 we adopted our formal child safeguarding policy. Since then, we have come a long way with robust reporting and responding mechanisms and being transparent in reporting incidents via our Annual Child safeguarding report. However, this is an area where more can always be done. We have developed systems that must be rigorously followed, and in addition, we are working toward continuously sensitizing our community that abuse is never acceptable. A victim-centered approach is our way, placing the needs and priorities of victims/survivors at the forefront of any response. We have resolved to continue showing to our donors and authorities how we live our zero-tolerance policy through our actions.

Due to COVID-19, the need for our services has grown tremendously. Unfortunately, SOS Children's Villages' ability to provide additional services is constrained by the amount of funds available.

However, the founder of SOS Children's Villages, Dr. Hermann Gmeiner, used to say, "When you do good work, people will trust you and give you money and demand that you do more." He had no resources except a very firm belief, and with that, he was able to create a globally relevant childcare organization.

All of us at SOS Children's Villages are appealing to more and more people and governments to support SOS Children's Villages in helping to ensure that every child grows up in a loving and caring family environment.

About the Contributor

As president of SOS Children's Villages International since 2012, **Siddhartha Kaul** provides overall leadership to the global federation of 117 member associations. Siddhartha started working with the organization in 1978 when he was appointed director of SOS Children's Villages Chennai in South India. He established SOS Children's Villages in Sri Lanka and led the rebuilding of the organization in Vietnam, Laos, and Cambodia after the conflicts in these countries. While representing Asia as deputy secretary-general from 2001 to 2012, he was a member of the senior management team and played an active part in the organization's strategy processes. His efforts to improve the lives of children across the globe have earned him numerous awards, including the highest civilian honors in Cambodia and Vietnam.

CHAPTER 15

Tapsi

By Hooman Damirchi (Cofounder and COO), Mitra Azimi (Financial Manager), Milad Dowlatnia (Chief Human Resources Officer), Mehrshid Fadaei Nejaad (Product Manager), and Negar Arab (PR and Communications Manager)

About Tapsi

With more than 15 million registered passengers and 35% market share, Tapsi is one of the two leading ride-hailing companies in Iran. Five years after its establishment, Tapsi now offers a wide range of goods-delivery and ride-hailing services, has created about 1.5 million jobs for drivers, has over 1000 employees, has won some major legislative battles paving the way for other tech start-ups, and is going to be the first tech company to go public in Iran.

The Calm Before the Storm: Industry and Company Overview Before COVID-19

By Hooman Damirchi (Cofounder and COO)

Ride-hailing is most probably the youngest and fastest-growing industry in Iran. It was brought to life in 2015 by Tapsi as an answer to the growing expectation of urban travelers to have a higher-quality and cheaper transportation option at their disposal.

In fact, Iran was much more ready for this concept when compared with developed countries where ride-hailing initially came to existence. The reason? On the demand side, inadequate investment in public transportation and consequently the slow pace of growth in this sector left a wide gap in the market. The traditional yellow cabs and their licensor companies could not fill this gap for two reasons: (1) they had a reputation for the worst customer experience on all fronts (drivers ripping off passengers, extremely low quality of the cars, drivers' impolite behavior, concerns of safety, and more), and (2) the available capacity of the cars was less than 40% utilized, resulting in a shortage of capacity and lack of consistent availability of passenger rides.

On the supply side, a subset of privately licensed cars was already in the business of moving people from point to point either as a side job to help them with their living expenses or as a full-time job. Regulators did not ban this but did not encourage it either, so there was a gray regulatory area that allowed private car owners to work in this space. This was key, not only because the number of yellow cabs was limited, but also because their behavior could not be quickly addressed because it had become commonplace for some of them to cheat passengers whenever possible. Therefore, for the industry to grow fast, a fleet of private cars was essential. A report published by the Municipality of Tehran in 2018 indicated that the total number of daily urban trips in Tehran was 19.3 million, of which only 23.8% was being handled by yellow cabs and 53.9% by private cars.

As a result of the market's readiness, the ride-hailing industry experienced an explosive growth rate soon after its debut. Tapsi started in early 2016 and reached 10,000 rides a day in one-sixth of the time that a ride-hailing giant like India-based Ola Cabs got to the same point and one-fourth of the time that Careem took to get there in Egypt. From there on, Tapsi grew another ten times in less than a year and continued the consistently upward trajectory with a compound annual growth rate (CAGR) of 63% and reached roughly 600,000 rides a day (about 15 million registered passengers and over 1.5 million drivers) with a 34% market share by the end of 2019. At this point, Tapsi already had the backing of a big local bank and the largest consumer electronics manufacturer (which joined in investment rounds C and D). The growth was so fast and the future was so promising that we decided to raise sizeable funding by taking the company public and not only to increase our transportation services (from our low-cost minibus option to a VIP chauffeur service to an end-to-end goods delivery solution) but also to expand to adjacent businesses as well in 2020, with a vision to become one of the top 10 largest tech holdings in Iran.

Fear, Shock, Depression

The state media broke the news to us on Thursday, February 20, 2020: a patient was diagnosed with COVID-19, which was the first official case in Iran. In less than a week, not only did our number of rides drop by 70%, but due to the new supply/demand imbalance in favor of demand, the market price also dropped by 30%. Overall, 80% of our daily revenue evaporated in a week, with no clear outlook of when the situation would change. We had had several financially difficult situations in the past, but this was the first time nobody had any idea when to expect our revenue to recover. Later, in a report published by the Ministry of Industry, Mining and Commerce, ride-hailing was listed among the top 10 industries negatively affected by COVID-19. Two factors drove the effect:

1. **Demand:** The majority of economic activities were halted, and the companies had moved their workforce to remote-working mode, reducing the need for transportation. Also, for most of the remaining essential needs for transportation, people started using their own vehicles to stay safe.

2. **Supply:** The majority of our part-time drivers, whose numbers were much larger than our full-time drivers, stopped accepting rides. They already had a main income source and did not want to risk contracting a deadly disease from random passengers just for the benefit of side income.

While these were the most important problems, they were not the only ones. Another major issue was that the team was shocked and extremely anxious about the risk to both their health and their job security with Tapsi; a range of well-known tech companies had started to have significant layoffs triggered by COVID-19.

In a nutshell, the once flourishing company that was a very well known brand all around Iran suddenly turned into an unstable company with low morale and no clear outlook for financial recovery. The company's senior management had to put all their expansion plans and dreams of a rosy future on hold, to manage the crisis on two very critical fronts: cash flow and team spirit.

Our Strategies to Overcome the Crisis: Being Creative and Agile While Transforming the Threats into Opportunities

Cash flow and team spirit had to be addressed quickly, for which we formed two dedicated task forces.

Cash Flow Management

By Mitra Azimi (Financial Manager)

Our revenue drastically dropped (~80%) in a week after the official announcement of COVID-19's arrival in Iran. There was more: we have a relatively seasonal business, and during the last calendar month of the Persian year (February–March) we see a natural increase in trips and consequently revenue increases by 30–40% every year. This was a key assumption in our cash flow planning for the last month, and we had even pushed a few of our mature debts to that month. So not only did our baseline revenue drop significantly, but our expected growth (which was not insignificant) was also not realized. Following is an overview of what we did to overcome the situation.

Cost Reduction

- We immediately stopped almost all of our growth-related operational expenditures and only stuck to those that were essential to maintaining our core service. This included items such as online and offline advertising, sign-up bonuses for attracting new drivers, subsidies and discounts on rides, launching new markets/cities, and loyalty club expansion. We ruthlessly dropped everything that was purposed for fueling future growth and kept only the basics.

- Second in line was our payroll. Fortunately, we managed to have no layoffs, but we sent almost half of the company on furlough (largely from the operations team, whose workload is linearly related to the scale of rides per day), temporarily cut the salaries of our executives (which was a significant chunk) to half for as long as the revenue was going to be as low, and paid no bonuses for a full quarter. It was very difficult to manage, and you'll hear more about it later, but it was the most optimal decision to make if we wanted to avoid layoffs.

Debt and Duty Postponement

- We dedicated two of our most senior government lobbyists to negotiate with the government and postpone all of our duties, including staff social security, for three to four months.
- The head of each department was appointed to negotiate with our vendors to push back the debts that were going to be due in a four-month time frame. The reason we did it at this level of seniority was the difficulty of negotiations, because all companies, including our vendors, were facing financial hardship, so asking them to give us time was quite challenging.

Capital Injection

- The CEO and COO both engaged with the government and the banking system to get short-term loans as bridge financing.

The combination of the above actions helped us immensely to navigate through our financial situation.

Human Resources

By Milad Dowlatnia (Chief Human Resources Officer)

Before the spread of COVID-19 in Iran, we had set three main goals in HR:

- Improving our brand image in the talent market and promoting Tapsi as one of the best employers in Iran
- Increasing the number of Tapsi team members by 40% to meet our growth targets
- Carrying out a series of projects within the company to promote a sense of participation and engagement among our staff

However, in the middle of preparation for these projects, the lockdown forced the human resources team to change course:

- Performing significant cost reduction in HR while maintaining the existing team intact
- Providing the staff with a safe and hygienic environment for work at Tapsi offices
- Devising and implementing a strategy for remote work

It's easy to articulate it in summary now, but back then, given the stressful context, each step was difficult and tense. Making decisions to manage this crisis was extremely difficult and complicated, even more than dealing with the cash flow, given the complex nature of people and the wide variety of everyone's concerns and conditions. Over quite a large number of meetings with board members and the managerial team of the company, the plan of action was defined, including the overall direction that we wanted to stay as safe as possible (health-wise) and ideally have no layoffs.

For that to happen, all Tapsi members had to undergo hardship and adversity to some extent, which made the execution of the plan rather difficult (but helped us avoid massive layoffs, which would have been worse for the people who would have been let go otherwise). What helped us the most to keep people motivated and committed to work was twofold: (1) over-communication about everything, especially short-term tangible goals and important medium-term milestones like the IPO, and (2) making a rather bold promise to the people on furlough that we wouldn't fire anybody and they would be back to work in three months It was a risky promise but in hindsight it was a very good decision. Based on the objectives and the devised strategy, the following measures were defined and implemented.

Cutting Expenses

- As a result of the considerable decrease in the company's operational activities, a subset of our colleagues involved in those activities had nothing to do. To keep them employed and reduce our costs, we asked them to leave for three months while receiving half of their salaries. For those on the furlough list, this was not an easy sell, and we had to do some heavy communication to justify it to the whole organization. Still, in the long run, it helped us keep jobs for everyone and avoid long-term damage to employee morale.

- Salaries of all executives were reduced to half. This was very important not only for financial reasons, but more importantly to show all the team members that the whole organization, including its most senior members, were going to fight this battle side by side and no one was an exception.

- We also had limited downsizing and releasing of staff who had performed below expectation levels in the preceding quarter.

Creating a Safe and Hygienic Environment for Our Colleagues in Our Offices

- We provided our staff members with enough space to be able to follow social distancing and other safety protocols by rearranging the existing office layout and staff presence and adding new space to our HQ, which was equipped and made ready within three weeks.

- We marked safe spaces to sit or stand in public spaces in the company (for example, in elevators and meeting rooms).

- We designed new regulations for meetings and having food at offices.

- We enforced the use of face masks.

- We opened a line of communication with disinfectant producers to ensure availability of such products all the time. (To put this in context: in the early months, there was a vast shortage of disinfectants in the country.)

- We hired more service staff to constantly sanitize the office.

- We created a health and safety committee among our colleagues to oversee and make decisions on health- and hygiene-related issues in an agile way.

Enabling Remote Working for Select Staff

- Regarding remote work, the main challenges at Tapsi were the lack of experience and the fact that there was no infrastructure to perform our duties remotely. To solve these issues, we instantly formed a technical taskforce to create an appropriate platform to enable staff members at Tapsi to work remotely. As a result, it became possible for 70% of our staff in tech and call center teams to do their job remotely from their homes.

Making Our Product Suitable for the Pandemic

By Mehrshid Fadaei Nejaad (Product Manager)

Before the pandemic hit, our product teams were in the middle of planning for massive changes in our passenger and driver apps, the most important of which was to redesign both applications from scratch to provide a much easier-to-use experience for the users. However, two weeks before launching the new apps, due to the COVID-19 lockdown, we had to cancel the launch. Then, within quite a short period, due to the newly emerging needs of our users, we had to redesign our product.

Impact of COVID-19 on Our Product and Users   The main and most important impact was the rapid drop in the frequency of usage because: (1) overall, the majority of activities in the cities were halted, resulting in a decreased need for transportation, and (2) those who still needed to move preferred their own vehicles, because they feared being in a car with a random person they didn't know.

As a result, an application that once was an essential part of urban life for people who needed to move and was an important way for others to make a living by providing this service turned into just another app on users' cell phones. The biggest risk to overcome was the possibility of the app being forgotten and ultimately uninstalled if it remained unused for too long. Therefore, we had to come up with creative solutions to keep our application useful. Here is what we came up with:

- Because people were hardly leaving their houses in the early days, there was a surging need to handle their daily routines through a third-party assistant. Time was of the essence to capture this opportunity, so we developed and deployed two services in less than two weeks for this purpose:
  - **Hamyar:** A shopping assistant through which our users could specify their shopping list and the store on the application, and Tapsi drivers would do the shopping and deliver the purchases to the users' doorstep. The main focus of this service was on groceries and medicine. Not only was it successful in meeting the newly emerged needs of our users, but it also helped our drivers to partially recover the income they lost due to the decrease in passenger trip demand.
  - **Delivery:** The need for package deliveries surged during the pandemic. There was a considerable demand for sending parcels, and the overall capacity of the country's delivery infrastructure was not

sufficient. Delivery time of e-commerce platforms had increased to two to three weeks (up from the previous time of two to three days), and people were having a hard time finding a courier to handle their deliveries. As a result, we decided to utilize our fleet – which formerly only transported passengers – for goods delivery.

- Providing transportation service with hygienic standards in compliance with COVID-19 guidelines was key as people were worrying more and more about their health and had fewer such options:

  o **Tapsi's Core Service:** For those who did not have the luxury of staying at home all the time and had to travel, most often because of their jobs, having a transportation option that complied with hygiene protocols was of the utmost importance. The same was true for drivers who did not have the option of sitting home and doing nothing. Therefore, we started enforcing a set of rules and built monitoring tools via the app to ensure they were being practiced. To begin with, we enforced wearing face masks among our drivers and then among the passengers. Second, to protect the drivers, we decreased the number of passengers allowed to sit in one car. And finally, we worked closely with the government to temporarily ban drivers for 14 days if they tested positive for COVID-19, which we checked through a real-time connection with the Ministry of Health database.

  o **Hamkhat:** This ride-sharing service was based on minibuses and vans and offered a cheap option to passengers who could not afford Tapsi Classic for their daily commutes. Given the price point, Hamkhat was a substitute for metro and public buses. Hamkhat had been newly launched right before the arrival of COVID-19, and there was an opportunity to customize it for much better hygiene, as the metro and buses at the time were struggling to meet the current hygiene protocols. We cut each vehicle's capacity in half to ensure compliance with COVID-19 social distancing guidelines and made sure everybody was wearing a mask on board.

Communication and Marketing Fields

By Negar Arab (PR and Communications Manager)
We were working around the clock to prepare for a rapid growth phase. Awareness of Tapsi as a brand was on the rise vis-à-vis our market share. However, as said before, everything turned upside down once COVID-19 hit. Nobody cared about anything but their health anymore, let alone a commercial brand and its service, and we were worried about not being actively in the forefront of our users' minds. As a result, we needed to keep our users emotionally engaged with our brand.

Our Communication Focus Before COVID-19   Before the pandemic, the majority of our communications with users were focused on the these three pillars:

1. Introducing Tapsi and its advantages to new users and encouraging them to install and make use of the application

2. Creating competitive preferences and distinctions among our users

3. Turning our users into loyal customers through emotional and social interactions

The first two pillars became irrelevant in the pandemic era; even worse, it was against the hygiene protocols to encourage people to move. So, in a sense, the core of our communications worked against the pandemic, and we needed to remove it momentarily.

Complexity of Communications: Stay Home, Do Not Travel!
People had to stay home to avoid catching the virus and spreading it to others. Schools and universities were closed. Sports centers, cultural sites, and shopping malls were shut down. Many people opted for remote working, and everyone did their best to stay home. Also, businesses were trying to encourage people to follow the protocols and stay at home, because it was their social responsibility while adapting their services to meet the newly emerged needs to continue working.

At Tapsi, we were caught in a real dilemma: Our business relied upon people traveling in cities, and now we had to advise them to do the opposite. It was such a sensitive situation that we could in no way encourage people to travel; doing so would be in conflict with the public interest and could cause considerable damage to Tapsi as a brand. Because our main communication had traditionally focused on encouraging people to move, interaction with our customers plummeted drastically as a result.

Our Solutions to Keep Interaction with Users   To be able to continue communicating with our users and mitigate the risk of being forgotten, we identified distinct categories of users and tried to communicate with each category, according to their conditions and needs, through messages on social networks, the application, and the media:

Our Passengers   Our passengers belonged to one of two categories: users who had to stay at home due to restrictions or work remotely, and users who had to commute to work or leave their homes for any other reason.

In maintaining interaction with the group of users who stayed home, we aimed to remind them of our brand and to promote it through performing our social responsibility. For instance, our communication with this group consisted of the following:

- Sharing information on hygiene protocols for them and their loved ones to stay healthy
- Providing information on the hygiene protocols of traveling with Tapsi, if the need should arise
- Informing the public about what Tapsi had done as part of its social responsibility (such as distribution of masks and disinfectant, offering free service to medical care staff, and so on)
- Introducing new services (such as Hamyar and Delivery) to help people stay at home

In interacting with the users who had to leave their homes and travel in the city, we did the following:

- Encouraging them to use Tapsi for necessary trips while assuring them of full compliance with hygiene protocols
- Raising awareness about measures taken at Tapsi to offer safe services, such as controlling the health of our drivers through access to the Ministry of Health database and barring drivers infected with the virus from work until they were completely healthy again
- Introducing our new services such as Hamkhat
- Facilitating traveling with Tapsi and offering discounts for necessary trips

Drivers   What drivers were going through was different from passengers' experience. On the one hand, due to the drop in the number of trips, driver income plummeted, and they had difficulties making ends meet. On the other hand, even if they worked, they were worried about their health. Consequently, our objectives in communicating with the drivers were defined as follows:

- Reducing their stress and worry through teaching them how to properly follow the hygienic protocols

- Informing them about support measures available to help them (such as loans, discounted necessary consumer goods for their household, schemes to guarantee their income, and so on)
- Communicating with part-time drivers who had stopped working with Tapsi and encouraging them to work again as we further tightened hygienic rules on the passenger side

Learnings and Takeaways

By Hooman Damirchi (Cofounder and COO)
As outlined in the previous sections, the impact of COVID-19 was profound on our company, and we went through four different phases:

1. Experiencing the initial shock
2. Overcoming the fear and ambiguity
3. Capturing new markets opportunities
4. Getting ready for the post-pandemic world

    ○ Rebuilding the organization
    ○ IPO

Since the inception of the company, we had been through a handful of crises, and each time the organization grew more prepared for the next one. The COVID-19 pandemic was without a doubt the most significant one. I believe that had we not gone through other prior crises, we would have been much more vulnerable to the pandemic and could have even been defeated by it, as were a range of companies in Iran and particularly a few tech companies (such as Chillivery, a food-delivery company that fully shut down its business and identified COIVD-19 as the only reason in its official statement). So this wasn't our first crisis and, in my view, it won't be our last one. The key is to learn from each one, build a stronger organization, and always be ready for the next one.

Team Integrity Is the Ultimate Asset!

As mentioned earlier, the whole organization was in deep shock and confusion when the pandemic hit. People had a range of concerns: Will I lose my job? Or should I stop worrying about it because I will die sooner or later anyway? Will the company sustain itself? Will we ever have our once bright future again?

At the top of the organization, we soon realized that if we were to survive this crisis, we needed to work together. It was about calming people down and mobilizing every single soul in the company to fight aggressively. To achieve this, one of the most important messages to send to the team (and one of the most difficult decisions we made) was to assure everybody that their job was safe and we would not release anybody who had met minimum performance expectations in the past. It was difficult because we did not know how long we would be able to sustain this situation, but there was no other option for us. Laying off people would have further decreased the morale of the team. We needed motivated warriors, not a dead army.

Cash Is King

We immediately started to cut costs and look for external sources of funding to make sure we had enough cash available should the situation be prolonged, and fortunately we were able to secure a loan in a couple of months. It may seem as if I am stating the obvious, but with all the context and ambiguities I described, it would have been very possible to act shortsightedly and optimistically, hoping that the problem would go away shortly. "Hope" can be a very dangerous trap when it comes to cash flow.

Transparency and Inclusiveness

From the get-go, we chose to be fully transparent with the team. We knew we faced difficult decisions along the way and could only navigate them if we had everyone's support and understanding. I mentioned earlier that we aggressively cut down on costs; here are two examples: (1) we furloughed 40% of the organization, and (2) we decided to pay zero bonuses in the first three months of the pandemic. Both were unpleasant news to the team – not as bad as layoffs but still a financial hardship.

We decided to be very upfront with the whole organization about the revenue situation. To maintain the team's integrity, we needed to cut down on these two items to avoid laying off employees. Once the team realized why we were doing this, not only did the majority of them support our approach, but some also volunteered to be the ones to go on leave. Without such clear communication, it would have been easy for people to mistakenly think that the board was cutting costs to avoid losing profits and the first and easiest cost to cut was people. To reinforce our message, we reduced the executive team's salary to half to show everyone that the most senior people are the first ones to sacrifice and that everyone is equal during times of crisis. This strongly helped with keeping the team integrated while cutting down on expenses.

Opportunities Are There, Even in a Crisis

From capturing new market needs to rebuilding internal infrastructure, there are always opportunities in crises that, if capitalized on, help companies emerge stronger. For us, it was the IPO, rebuilding the team, and launching new products that were needed in the pandemic era.

In fact, we were the first tech company in Iran (at the time of this writing) approved to be listed on the Tehran Stock Exchange. This development was heavily accelerated by the pandemic. For one thing, our need for investment was more real than ever before. Also, in the ambiguity that COVID-19 created, private investors were wary of investing in assets with higher risk profiles and large ticket size. Ultimately, there was no other option but to go public.

We also launched three new products and strengthened and expanded the capacity of our team. The past 12 months have been like a training camp for us to get ready for the post-COVID-19 world.

Agile and Autonomous Decision-Making

Once the pandemic hit, our established order was not functioning anymore and, at least for the first few months, it was rather replaced by chaos. So, if we were to manage the organization and cash flow, keep the team intact, and at the same time capture market opportunities, we had no other option than to increase our tolerance for failure and let people have more ownership and decide more autonomously. The top of the organization was busy with topics that normally weren't on the agenda, and for the first month, it became a bottleneck to our progress. But we soon realized we had to let go and empower all individuals to push the boundaries of their own scope further and more freely. For instance, our product team got full autonomy and authority to decide about the scope of the new services that were going to be built in response to the new needs in the market, and the previous approval processes were removed fully. And it worked! Many of our people stepped up during this period and meaningfully improved their sense of ownership. We now have more independent leaders and middle managers than we did before the pandemic.

As a result, a range of structural changes emerged in the company and in my view are here to stay even post-pandemic. For instance, we now have a more agile product development process and let product managers decide more autonomously about what to build and how to build it, as long as it supports our strategic priorities. Also, our cash flow management tools and mindset have completely changed, and we have become a much more cautious organization from this standpoint. And the most important development is that now it has become second nature for the managerial team of Tapsi that whenever business is at a low, it is time to build the growth infrastructure/processes/plans for when demand picks up again.

About the Contributor

Hooman Damirchi is COO and cofounder of Tapsi, one of Iran's two ride-hailing giants. He has an MBA from INSEAD business school and has worked in the tech and telecom sectors in companies such as MTN for most of his decade-long career. He and his two other cofounders, Milad Monshipour and Hamid Mahini, went back home in 2015 to start Tapsi with the ambition of having a major impact on Iran's economy through technology.

CHAPTER 16

Terumo

By Probir Das (Executive Officer of Terumo Corporation, Japan, and Chairman and Managing Director of Asia-Pacific operations)

About Terumo

Terumo is a global leader in medical technology and has been committed to "Contributing to Society through Healthcare" for 100 years. Based in Tokyo and operating globally, Terumo employs more than 25,000 associates worldwide to provide innovative medical solutions in more than 160 countries and regions. The company started as a Japanese thermometer manufacturer, and has been supporting healthcare ever since. Now its extensive business portfolio ranges from vascular intervention, cardiosurgical solutions, blood transfusion, and cell therapy technology, to medical products essential for daily clinical practice such as transfusion systems, diabetes care, and peritoneal dialysis treatments. Terumo will further strive to be of value to patients, medical professionals, and society at large.[1]

Context

This is an attempt to pen my views on the impact of the COVID-19 pandemic on the medical technology industry. With medical technology being immensely diverse and spanning from a simple gauze dressing or syringe to complex remote robots that perform the intricate intravascular repair of the arteries in the heart or that disinfect hospitals, it is difficult to monolithically describe the pandemic's impact on the industry, and hence I must limit this piece to that constraint of generality. Also, the views

---

[1]Corporate profile, 2021, https://www.terumo.com/about/profile/

expressed here are my own and do not necessarily reflect those of either my employer or of the several trade associations on whose boards I serve.

Healthcare has a unique dichotomy. On the one hand, it is the most "local" business (perhaps apart from food), with very uneven levels of maturity, access, service, infrastructure, skills, and financing across countries. On the other, the technology providers (both pharmaceuticals and medical devices) are rather globally consolidated, standard-driven multinationals. Healthcare has long been a global challenge; even though it is the second-largest industry globally, it still has not sufficiently served larger parts of the world's population. Functionally, it has somehow been built as "sick care," with incentives having been structured around creating a cure, rather than "health care" that promotes a healthy lifestyle and wellness. Hence, we have seen an equal measure of failure to deliver quality healthcare, both in developed and underdeveloped countries.

Medical technology serves healthcare. It is the smallest component by size, much smaller than its hospital, diagnostic laboratory, pharmaceutical, and insurance cousins, but in the last half-century, it has enabled the maximum disruption to maximize the impact of the outcomes of those cousins. Yet its contribution has been little understood and often underappreciated by the general recipients of its benefits.

Before the Pandemic

Ours is a century-old medical devices and technology corporation, founded in Japan in 1921, uniquely by a group of scientists, led by the legendary Dr. Kitasato Shibasaburo, with a mission of contributing to society through healthcare. Such was the impact of Dr. Kitasato on medical science and education that he will become the face of the 1000-yen note, perhaps the most circulated Japanese currency note. (See Figures 16.1 and 16.2.)

Terumo Corporation is recognized as a top medical devices company, primarily for its innovations and contribution to advancing newer therapies. If I split our 100-year history into three equally divided historical horizons, the first would be when the company became a bedrock of public health, almost entirely in Japan; the second would be when it diversified into infection prevention and started exploring the global markets;

FIGURE 16.1   Dr. Kitasato Shibasaburo led the group of scientists who founded the company to manufacture the most reliable clinical thermometer possible.
Image credit: Terumo Corporation.

FIGURE 16.2   Dr. Shibasaburo will be honored on the 1000-yen note in 2024.
Image credit: Ministry of Finance, Government of Japan.

and the last is when it pivoted into the intervention/minimally invasive space, where it is now a firm multinational player with globalization as its key strategic imperative. We currently have three major and distinct business areas: cardiac and vascular, general hospital, and blood and cell technologies. I have led our Asia Pacific region for the past three years.

Asia Pacific (APAC) is a relatively younger region for us. Before 2012, our many countries in the region worked directly with the headquarters in Japan. It was only in 2018 that we enabled a Singapore-based Asia Pacific headquarters to drive "business-led" management. I had spent 2018–19 envisioning this new HQ and creating board and executive management alignment on its reconstruction and scale-up. Since our erstwhile double-digit APAC growth rates had come down to early singles, we put in place a strategy to get back to double-digit growth. In the 2019–20 period, under the theme of "Reenergize," we started enabling a business unit–led management structure, created strong and fight-worthy functional capabilities in our regional office, and were raring to unleash this growth strategy on our Asia Pacific focus markets. We aspired to start a reclaim journey to double-digit growth with an 8% goal for 2020–21. This is precisely when COVID-19 hit us smack in our face.

Early Signs

We had started hearing about this virus that was affecting Wuhan, China, at the beginning of 2020. At the time, it was a bit of a faraway problem and not entirely well understood. Right after the Christmas and New Year holidays in 2020 I read that the government of Singapore was to screen all incoming travelers from Wuhan for the virus. By the end of January, we had the first confirmed COVID-19 case in Singapore, and we were already urging our associates to be careful and check their fever status frequently. I started taking it very seriously when I heard that Singapore's DORSCON (Disease Outbreak Response System Condition) was likely to be raised from yellow to orange. I remember that late in January, I assembled my Singapore administration leaders and began putting together a business continuity planning (BCP) team, just in case DORSCON hit orange.

It was a shaky start. There were few references on what should or should not be done. We could not ask for guidance from global HQ; they were still far away from the problem. The government guidance was very helpful. Our BCP members frequently called them and got excellent advice. We cut all cross-border travel, and we instructed our subsidiary entities to stop cross-border travel too. We influenced every single one of our nine APAC-based entities to start BCP teams. Together we started putting in place several policies designing contact-free office entry-exit protocols, split team operations, daily temperature logs, and work-from-home support systems such as more virtual private network lines, cost reimbursements, and many others. Therefore, when the Singapore government declared the circuit breaker stay-at-home preventive measures in April 2020, we were ready. By that time, many of our regional offices were starting to see COVID-19 flare up in their countries, but they too were well prepared for lockdowns from an infrastructure standpoint. Besides, through our intense discussions, regular consulting with various external specialists, and implementing the Singapore government's advice, our young APAC HQ had unknowingly also set a global COVID-19 BCP benchmark.

Early Impact on Business and Mitigation

At the beginning of our fiscal 2020 (April), we had identified that COVID-19 would affect how we worked and performed for quite some time to come. Therefore, to articulate what was required to navigate it well, we focused on commensurate themes in our APAC and India regions. (See Figures 16.3 and 16.4.)

We saw a myriad of challenges, the most impactful ones being:

- The flow of products (supply chain)
- The flow of clinical information (medical promotion/communication between the serving and served)
- The flow of patients (we saw massive shifts in patient behavior; plus policies drastically reduced elective procedure caseloads)
- The flow of money (since COVID-19 created many current and future challenges in healthcare funding)

FIGURE 16.3 We knew that encouragement was required as we began to face the challenges of the pandemic.
Image credit: Terumo Asia Holdings Pte. Ltd

FIGURE 16.4 We focused on themes appropriate to the region.
Image credit: Terumo India Private Ltd

Complex Supply Chain

Manufacturing and distribution of medical devices comprise a very complex global supply chain, for which almost 70% of global revenue is concentrated within some top 50–60 players. This is primarily due to a few distinguishing factors. First of all, no single country or region is wholly contained and self-sufficient with the research and development, component manufacturing, and assembly of its consumption of medical devices. Second, due to the often lifesaving criticality of medical supplies, the supply chain needs to be fast and flexible. Third, given the massive component-level complexities, with components often sourced from other industries such as electronics, the manufacturing of medical devices involves (in most cases) a large ecosystem approach. For most products, most companies generally do not have entirely in-house, end-to-end, component-level manufacturing systems. Finally, healthcare delivery across the world is not as integrated as it ought to be. The complex myriad of public and private health systems, primary, secondary, tertiary, and quaternary care hospitals, laboratories, radiology centers, blood centers, clinics, rural location sites, and many others, are hardly connected or communicating to each other. This burdens the supply chain with tons of duplication.

Indeed, with these complexities, most medical device manufacturers have always put great importance on integrated business planning (IBP) and business continuity planning (BCP). However, none were prepared for a global shutdown of the extent that COVID-19 enforced! The concurrent lockdowns in virtually every country forced most factories of components and finished goods to suffer capacity loss. Government orders that limited movement kept labor away from their worksites. The shortage of aircraft, ocean freighters, containers, and even space in ports and airports due to congestion, severely attacked the supply chain of medical supplies. I have personally witnessed situations where employees of medical technology manufacturing plants could not access transportation to factories, were threatened with eviction from their rented homes since they were going out to work on lockdown days, and were even mistreated by law enforcement due to early-stage confusion about travel restrictions. Everyone (myself included) has greatly appreciated the selfless dedication of doctors and nurses and has recognized the need to allow their movement and work. Unfortunately, it has taken longer to similarly acknowledge the importance of the manufacturing workers, warehousing and logistic workers, clinical support specialists, and installation and service engineers who comprise the backbone of medical technology and devices. Even as I write this (in April 2021), there is unequal access to vaccination among the core medical technology workers who create the uninterrupted flow of supplies to the doctors and nurses. It is frustrating to see airline workers, delivery workers, taxi drivers, and so many other undoubtedly important frontline roles being vaccinated while the workers who relentlessly risk themselves to keep healthcare technology going are given a lower priority.

Change from a Highly Specialized, One-on-One Communication Legacy

Medical devices see their application mostly in medical settings, directly via the hands of a specialist. This is different from pharmaceuticals, which most often are self-administered by patients. Additionally, as mechanical or electrical engineering devices that draw from user experience, medical devices have a high dependence on incremental innovation; many devices thus have short life cycles of some 18 to 24 months! Finally, devices from two different companies with the same outcome objectives can often have very different engineering and feature elements.

These factors make the continuous and open communication between the user (medical specialist) and the supplier (medical device technical specialists) mission-critical for good patient outcomes. This communication has traditionally been physical, mostly one-on-one, and relatively frequent. While meetings in a group setting (such as symposiums and group training workshops) are common, they never took away from the more personalized forms of hands-on, experience-building sessions (often on simulators), direct interactions while a product was in use, or deep discussions about clinical evidence and data.

This paradigm has seen sudden and complete disruption by the COVID-19 pandemic lockdowns and in-person contact restrictions. Starting with the lockdowns in March and April 2020, industry representatives had to suddenly (mostly) give up their time-tested model of face-to-face meetings with medical professionals, even though the need to launch newer variants or support procedures remained. This meant a scramble to build or adopt digital engagement, content, and related tools at incredible speed. Just building these tools was not enough; they had to quickly be supplemented by technology to deploy them even from home settings. At the same time, technical specialists who weren't remote-savvy needed to develop skills rapidly for effective remotely work.

This communication complexity and information flow are not limited to users. Many medical devices are part of a "consignment" model, which necessitates regular communication between hospital administrators and medtech's supply chain teams. Besides, the workstyle of the industry was primarily office-based, unlike such industries as consulting or IT-enabled services. On one hand, the need for communication across the spectrum increased manyfold to manage the vast pandemic uncertainties, but on the other hand, organizations quickly had to pivot to being almost 100% remote-based.

Procedure Caseloads and Patient Behavior Vicissitudes

This is an area where the industry has seen orbital shifts in the pandemic period. Elective procedures for dental, ophthalmic, cardiovascular, aesthetics, and several other streams have seen massive declines. The blood-center supply chains are decimated due to massive drops in donor numbers, creating acute blood shortages. Several routine screening programs in cancer, diabetes, cardiovascular, and general health checkups have been hugely affected, creating an alarming future worry that overall health indicators will become uncontrollable due to the late presentations of such diseases.

To better illustrate the overall situation, let us dive into two specialties: cardiovascular and blood centers. When the COVID-19 cases increased alarmingly during the lockdown period, many hospitals were assigned dedicated COVID-19 treatment center status, and ICU beds were reserved for acute COVID-19 patients. Beyond that, many treatment protocols were also altered. High throughput cath labs and cardiac surgery centers reduced their cases to only acute myocardial infarctions, and they spaced the time between procedures to allow for aggressive disinfection of procedure rooms and for the medical teams to don personal protective equipment (PPE). Patients were discouraged from attending outpatient departments in large numbers, screenings were abandoned, and, for the most part, patients were too scared to come into a hospital setting. Most areas of the world saw a 50–70% drop in procedure volumes. (The *British Medical Journal* reported a 50% drop in patients attending cardiovascular services in the UK, with a 40% reduction in heart attack diagnoses in a hospital in Scotland.) The expectation was that when the lockdowns are lifted, the patients would come back in more significant numbers, but this is yet to happen, partly because intermittent lockdowns continue and partly due to the slow rate of patient reengagement. In the blood center domain, donor collections are depressed 50–80% (depending on geography), and the return is seen in a trickle.

However, for acute respiratory cases, needless to say, the numbers rose to often unmanageable proportions. Hospitals were flooded with COVID-19 patients, and all hands were on deck supporting them. In the initial stages of the pandemic, there were global shortages of PPE, ventilators, infusion pumps, and so on. However, the industry has been able to quickly address these issues, ramp up production, set up new capacity, and even support stockpiling of these critical items to prevent future shortages. The pharmaceutical industry's response in developing the fastest vaccine ever is now known to most.

These changes in the distribution of cases across domains and the cost of response have created a substantial financial depression in many health systems, the extent and impact of which I shall touch upon in the next section.

Financial Complexities Arising Due to the Pandemic

Healthcare providers are severely impacted due to lockdown-induced patient flow reductions and increased operating costs due to PPE, additional testing, and the need to acquire additional equipment such as ventilators, extracorporeal membrane oxygenation (ECMO) equipment, plasma therapy equipment, and so on. In many countries, some hospitals were designated COVID-19 treatment centers and others were non-COVID-19 hospitals. The latter felt a greater financial impact, especially in highly capital-intensive departments like cath labs, cancer centers, renal care centers, and blood banks, where they are still servicing recent investments. A financial sustainability/sentiments survey conducted in India points to the existential risks that small to mid-sized hospitals express. A recent Frost & Sullivan 2021 prediction foresees a 70% reduction in hospital capital purchases. Health sector CFOs are tightrope-walking to balance immediate viability with long-term growth.

For the medical technology industry, major revenue and income depression come from the heavy reduction of all forms of elective procedures. In the Q2–Q3 calendar 2020 period, many organizations saw an almost 60–70% reduction in these areas. The high startup investment into several digital initiatives (enabling work from home, physical distancing, and other measures) has also added to this pressure. In channel-dependent markets, especially in emerging markets in Asia, where the distributors are rather small-sized, receivables had shot up to high-risk levels. Finally, logistics costs increased due to reduced consumption of goods, write-offs of expired short-shelf-life goods, and a four-to-five times increase in shipping costs.

Closer to Home, Some Business Challenges We Faced

We directly experienced the impact of the pandemic in a range of areas:

- We saw a significant (40–80%) drop in elective cardiovascular procedures (like angioplasties, open-heart surgeries, and vascular grafting). In some high-growth countries, this business contributed 30%–75% of our portfolio. Especially in India, which saw one of the world's most stringent lockdowns during the first wave, the procedures were reduced to some 20% of the original volumes.

- Blood donations were reduced to a trickle due to government orders that limited people's movement, especially among college and university youth. Our Southeast Asia business is heavily dependent on blood bag tenders, which were suddenly not forthcoming.

- We saw a very high surge in demand for syringes and needles, where several governments were stockpiling inventory for COVID-19 management and, eventually, vaccination. But our main supply was from our plant in the Philippines, which was heavily affected by the lockdown and movement controls, so we had to quickly find a supply from alternate plants/sources.

- Some markets, especially the Philippines and India, saw a significant drop in channel collection. This, in turn, created Accounts Receivables (AR) issues that we had to focus on and especially resolve.

- We have always physically met with our customers to conduct business with them, run training sessions, manage consignment quality, and provide case support. Now, for the most part, we could not visit our customers in person.

Navigating Through the Complexity

Early in the first quarter of 2020, our company rolled out a global directive to manage the COVID-19 crisis, founded on three simple guidelines:

1. All leaders were to keep their employees safe. That was our first and foremost responsibility.

2. We needed to do our absolute best to ensure that our supply chain, so critical for patients across the world, was open and protected.

3. Our technologies, unique skills, and capabilities were to be totally deployed in alignment with other stakeholders in fighting the pandemic.

Based on these, at Asia Pacific, we quickly did two pivots.

We migrated our twice-a-year performance management system to an agile monthly dashboard-based crisis management system. Starting in April 2020, we migrated all APAC countries, business units, and functions to a standard, common, 20 KPI-based, engaged dashboard. Now all of us were connected via common KPIs, and we were adjusting them as we went through the crisis.

We also morphed our Singapore HQ-based COVID-19 BCP committee to a wider-purpose, multi-geography, multifunctional, cross-hierarchical COVID-19 rebound team. (See Figures 16.5 and 16.6.) Representatives of this team intensely engaged with external specialists, peers, and our entire diverse employee base across the region through spot surveys and focus groups to design a five-point charter that proved very effective for us through the year:

- **Customer Intimacy Revival:** In the contactless world, this encompassed hearing key opinion leaders (KOLs) and chief experience officers (CXOs), developing new COVID-19 consensus standards with them, migrating our customer training and workshops to electronic formats, and evaluating novel tools such as camera glasses to remotely support critical cases.

- **Strengthen Associate Experience:** So that our associates remained relentless and energized, despite the hardships and ambiguity thrust upon them by the pandemic, this workgroup enhanced communication by driving new engagement platforms (Workplace by Facebook,

TAP Rebound Project

Region-wide initiative with Diversity

- 14 members from 5 countries
- Selected / Co-opted BU / Functional / Country leaders regularly studied external benchmarks, and resolved a variety of issues both at APAC & Entity level

Specific counter to COVID-19 crisis

- To find the best way forward amidst unprecedented COVID-19 crisis ... 'No playbook' to 'Create playbook'
- Fast and timely solutions catered to specifically address COVID-19 challenges

Holistic engagement of all stakeholders

Focus Areas

Customer Intimacy
- How to maintain and increase 'touchpoints' in 'contactless' form?
- How to re-start product demo, HCP education, multi-level meetings?
- Decode their 'Next Normal & How to become their "COVID Partner'?

Associate Experience
- Policies to ensure their Physical and Mental wellbeing
- Upskilling them to fit 'Virtual' business & communication effectiveness
- Protect their income and thus retain talented Assocs. for future

Define New Normal Workplace
- Flexible work policies
- Safer offices and field work
- Infrastructure support in case of home based work

Ensure Financial Prudence
- COVID Adjusted FY20 P&L, and FY21 Budget Plan
- Tight Cash Management & minimizing inventory and write-offs
- TC and other BU Executive alignments on these financial goals

Simplify Processes to fit 'Virtual' or 'Split team' working
- Automate internal approvals, banking, S&OP, measurement dashboard
- Harmonize inter-entity processes so that cost reduction technology and Col's can be considered

- Customer, Associate, Finance, systems, processes...
  Comprehensively cover all stakeholders and business aspects
- 5 small teams drive projects in unique, enabled and creative ways ... AGILE

1/000

Proactive and open mindset for new workplace norms

- Pulse Surveys and Focus Groups used to 'sense' stakeholder feedback
- Implementation of flexible work policies suited to each entity/ country
- Virtual tools enablement, platforms to enhance "One TAP" mindset

TERUMO

253

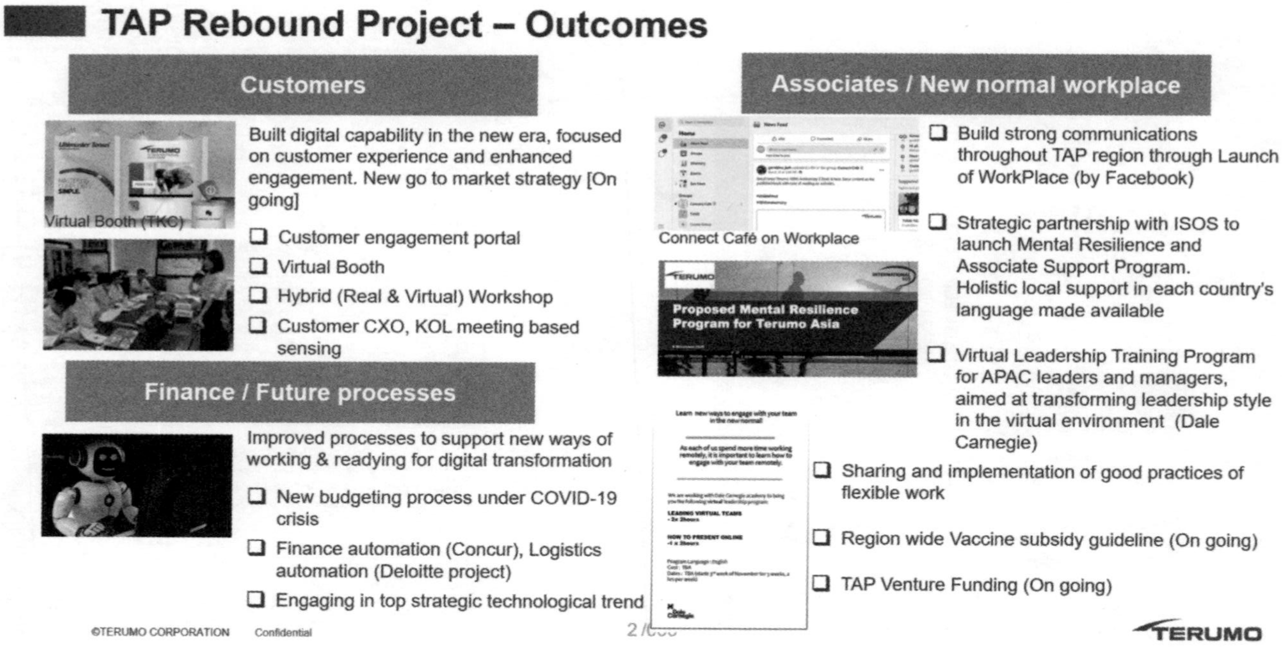

TAP Rebound Project – Outcomes

Customers

Built digital capability in the new era, focused on customer experience and enhanced engagement. New go to market strategy [On going]

- Customer engagement portal
- Virtual Booth
- Hybrid (Real & Virtual) Workshop
- Customer CXO, KOL meeting based sensing

Virtual Booth (FIKO)

Finance / Future processes

Improved processes to support new ways of working & readying for digital transformation

- New budgeting process under COVID-19 crisis
- Finance automation (Concur), Logistics automation (Deloitte project)
- Engaging in top strategic technological trend

Associates / New normal workplace

- Build strong communications throughout TAP region through Launch of WorkPlace (by Facebook)
- Strategic partnership with ISOS to launch Mental Resilience and Associate Support Program. Holistic local support in each country's language made available
- Virtual Leadership Training Program for APAC leaders and managers, aimed at transforming leadership style in the virtual environment (Dale Carnegie)
- Sharing and implementation of good practices of flexible work
- Region wide Vaccine subsidy guideline (On going)
- TAP Venture Funding (On going)

Connect Café on Workplace

Proposed Mental Resilience Program for Terumo Asia

©TERUMO CORPORATION   Confidential

2/555

TERUMO

FIGURES 16.5 AND 16.6   Representatives of our COVID-19 rebound team engaged with external specialists, peers, and our diverse employee base to design a five-point charter.
Image credits: Terumo Asia Holdings Pte. Ltd.

Town Halls, and so on). To prepare them for both resilience and skills, we rolled out a Mental Resilience Program (powered by International SOS) and a Virtual Effectiveness – Manager Training Program (powered by Dale Carnegie).

- **Define and Enable New Normal Workplaces:** This team worked to advance flexible work policies, create work-from-home support infrastructure/subsidies, and add contactless/safety features to our offices to ensure that we were taking the best care possible of ourselves.

- **Drive Balance Sheet–Based Financial Prudence:** We significantly improved our cash management, trained business unit leaders on the balance sheet/asset management approach (they were previously more focused on P&Ls), and rolled out channel financing schemes and aggressive AR collection programs in target countries. Additionally, this team worked to align all country and business unit operations and global headquarters to roll out quarterly adjusted forecasts that became our performance standard for 2020.

- **Simplify Processes:** Our former systems were very office-based. Hence, we quickly needed to dismantle many of them, convert others to be fit for remote work and split teams, and reduce decision-making time.

Quickly Mitigating Revenue and Profit Risks

The rapid drop and very slow recovery of cardiovascular cases and blood supply in Southeast and South Asian markets posed a considerable risk to our financials. Yet, at the same time, we sensed some unplanned opportunities with our syringe and infusion pumps, emergency bypass systems, blood component collection systems, and disinfection robots (from a partner company). If swiftly adopted, these products could potentially strengthen our customers' ability to scale their fight against COVID-19. Most of these efforts were complex, with global supply chains, long lead times, and forecast-based manufacturing capacities.

But our mission helped. Distant and diverse teams came together, rallied with each other, found unique and unprecedented methods, and ultimately successfully executed these projects. Just as an illustrative example, we supplied 45 machines to help a country's government set up its plasma therapy program within three months. Historically, we had deployed only two or three machines in a year. Sourcing, manufacturing, and the supply chain were scaled rapidly; we conducted application workshops across more than 30 far-flung sites through a hybrid tool consisting of videos, remote training, and 24/7 troubleshooting.

The rapid response not only helped us proudly live our mission, but also to a good extent helped us mitigate shortfalls from other therapy areas.

Future Outlook

Some significant trends have been identified. A disruption of this magnitude brings with it some significant shifts in habits. Plenty of changes are happening, but the more significant ones that I have experienced include these:

- **Healthusiasm:** Not only do we see increased use of masks and hand sanitizers (masks are authority mandated anyway), but I see people biking, running, walking, exercising, and meditating more. Perhaps quarantined living, the slipping sense of security, the realization that such huge health risks exist, and the recognition that life is so fickle has driven us to care for our bodies and minds more.

- **Online Shopping Is the New Normal:** With the massive rise of electronic shopping that allows far greater browsing than visits to physical stores, the habit is gradually permeating beyond personal or household purchases even to organized buying. Once the shopper learns how to check options, solid decision-making processes are suddenly fluid.

- **From "Just in Time" to "Just in Case":** Again, this started at home with everyone buying an extra box of masks, a few more bottles of sanitizer, and even a pulse oximeter, but it suddenly became a massive phenomenon of institutional pandemic stockpiling of syringes, needles, life support equipment, and many other items.

- **Rise of Compassion:** Beautiful to see, compassion is suddenly mainstream. Everyone began ending a conversation with "stay well," households cooked for stranded dormitory workers, and bosses were suddenly less bothered about what time a person started work. People managed through empathy what they could not manage through a plan. Louis Vuitton made sanitizer! "Compassionate" brands are everywhere now. Compassion is also a key determinant of employee "trust" currency. I foresee organization-wide compassion measuring metrics that will eventually determine both leadership capability and share prices.

- **Telehealth:** The future just fast-forwarded a few decades. Man landed on the moon in 1969 with health vitals of the famous moonwalkers monitored remotely from Houston, Texas. Unfortunately, half a century later, even Johns Hopkins was doing some 90 teleconsultations in a month. This went up beyond 10,000 in 2020. No traveling to the clinic, no needing someone to come along, no parking, no running around – the doctor just saw you in a jiffy, albeit virtually. I bet a lot of this will continue even beyond COVID-19.

There will never be a time when patients will not need to be supported through Terumo's technologies; hence our job in the future is cut out for us. However, models are likely to change, digital is expected to determine how success will look, and COVID-19 will likely stay with us for much longer than we had envisioned even six months ago. As I wrote this piece, we saw huge resurgence waves of the pandemic around Asia. We have moved from a "fight COVID-19" stage to a "live with COVID-19" stage.

Our fight will continue. Yes, when the pandemic hit, I had thought I should overcome it with enthusiasm – the enthusiasm to fight on, to try new things, experiment, and energize myself so that I could egg others to move on. That sprint quietly turned into a marathon, and a long one at that. But I realize that at some point during my run, I developed the marathon muscles. Not that I have lost the enthusiasm streak completely, but I am now more than enthusiasm driven; I am charged by the endurance to see this race through to the end. And, with countless unsung heroes pushing me a bit more every day, I know I am not alone.

About the Contributor

Probir Das is an executive officer of Terumo Corporation, Japan, and the chairman and managing director of Terumo's Asia Pacific operations. He has over three decades of medical technology experience and has worked extensively across Asian markets. Given his keen interest in policy-shaping, he is actively engaged in advocacy as director of the board for APAC Med and Medical Technology Association of India (MTaI). He held past senior roles with NATHEALTH, FICCI, and AdvaMed. Probir also has over a decade's teaching experience, specifically around strategy, leadership development, coaching, and performance management. His passion for med tech sees him mentor startups and entrepreneurs. Probir currently resides in Singapore.

CHAPTER 17

Conclusion

By Shivaji Das, Aroop Zutshi, and Janesh Janardhanan

Through the stories shared in these chapters, we have seen the similarities, differences, and variations of organizations' experiences throughout the pandemic across geographies and industries. How these organizations responded to the crisis provides insight about what can be done at various stages of a rapidly developing disruption. (See Figure 17.1.)

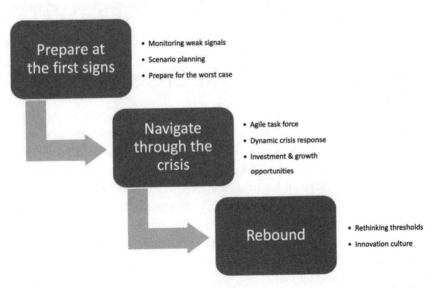

FIGURE 17.1 The ways that various organizations have responded to the pandemic provide a number of insights.

Prepare at the First Signs

Organizations that were able to prepare and react well in the early days of the pandemic generally had better outcomes. Many of the organizations that contributed to this book leveraged their overseas presence to inform their global decision-making. Many, like Terumo, SAP, Julius Baer, and Bangalore International Airport, set up a global task force, war group, or risk assessment team early to collect, analyze, and disseminate information throughout their organization, as well as to suppliers and customers. Besides closely observing government guidelines, these task forces planned ahead, verified organizational preparedness, developed business continuity and contingency plans, and shared best practices.

As more details emerged on the spread of the virus around the world, companies reassessed their ability to manage their business through an extended period of suppressed economic activity. They also studied supplier and customer trends and assessed impacts to business operations. Organizations took a hard look at liquidity positions, staffing, investment plans, and more, and they developed a range of response plans and worst-case scenario plans.

Navigate Through the Crisis

As the pandemic spread around the world, many countries witnessed first, second, and third waves of infection. They went in and out of lockdowns. Under such circumstances, local on-the-ground intelligence that fed into a central task force and enabled coordinated local responses became the key to managing large global organizations.

With a general sense of uncertainty and confusion, many organizations communicated frequently and transparently with employees.

CEOs of organizations that are emerging stronger from the pandemic used this phase not only to manage the disruption but also to identify new opportunities. Globalization Partners, for instance, doubled down on their investments in their core technology platform during the pandemic. In India, IndiGrid made several acquisitions during the pandemic. Hornet added senior engineers and accelerated product rollout during the pandemic.

Rebound

While COVID-19 is far from over, organizations around the world are already adapting to and functioning in "the new normal." Many are certain that we will never fully go back to the 2019 way of managing operations. Organizations are responding to lockdowns and movement restrictions on extremely short notice. "Digital" and "virtual" for supplier, employee, and customer engagement are deeply embedded in the new normal. Investments in automation for production resilience and logistics are growing.

Reeling from factory shutdowns and port congestion, supply chains are discovering the need to rethink the time-tested "just-in-time" strategy and are now incorporating a "just-in-case" strategy and maintaining higher inventory thresholds closer to consumers. Organizations are also paying more attention to cash and liquidity in the new normal and think differently about investment in physical office spaces and showrooms.

The pandemic has made organizations flex their agility and rapid-response muscles, and many of the hard-learned lessons will better prepare them for future such disruptions.

Perhaps the most important change in the new normal is the impact of COVID-19 on organizational culture. Organizations are rediscovering the need for higher transparency, empathy, and compassion while communicating with their employees and dealing with the broader ecosystem.

Developing a Moat of Defense Against Future Disruptions

As we finish writing this book in May 2021, the level of infection is surging again in places like South and Southeast Asia. It is clear that the pandemic is far from running its full course. Variants keep emerging and the data on the effectiveness of vaccines against them is yet to be fully analyzed. Whether the complete containment of the virus at a global level will take another one year or seven years is anyone's guess. And while we may very well overcome the pandemic, there is a growing consensus that with climate change, the erosion of natural habitats, the increase in population, rapid urbanization, and an increasingly connected world, there could be many future disruptions. These could be in the form of cyber-outages, wars, terrorist attacks, natural disasters, or new pandemics. The current pandemic has also shown how better-prepared organizations, even while not being specifically prepared for a disruption of this nature, had much better chances of survival and rebound. With that in mind, it is strongly recommended that organizations create a "moat of defense" against future disruptions, the key elements of which are detailed in Figure 17.2.

Scenario-Based Planning: As is evident from the various chapters, organizations with even a basic level of a risk management system in place found themselves better equipped to deal with the impact of the pandemic. It is therefore recommended that organizations, large or small, conduct periodic scenario forecasting exercises and form and update their risk management plans with risk mitigation plans and

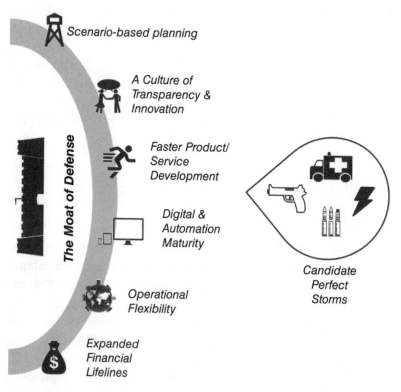

FIGURE 17.2 The key elements of the "moat of defense."

teams duly identified. Top management in all organizations should undergo basic risk training and periodically challenge each other in forecasting worst-case scenarios to develop action plans. In the process, organizations need to strike a judicious balance, being mindful of excessive preparation and the involved costs.

A Culture of Transparency and Innovation: The pandemic has clearly demonstrated how a culture of transparency and innovation proved invaluable in pushing through tough but necessary measures such as implementing furloughs, devising decentralized local solutions for localized problems, and having streamlined decision-making power to effectively solve customer and internal problems. Employees in many successful organizations have actually come closer to each other, the management, the customers, and other stakeholders as part of a shared camaraderie.

Faster Product/Service Development: In the event of any similar future disruption, organizations will need to quickly develop products/services to compensate for their disrupted operations and maintain revenues at a sufficient level. To allow for this speed, organizations should learn and adopt agile techniques as part of their usual new product development process. Maintaining a database of rejected ideas could also be invaluable because what previously might not have seemed a good idea could become a viable option at the time of disruption.

Digital and Automation Maturity: Organizations with a high level of digitalization and automation have coped much better with the pandemic. Although digital and automation elements can be disrupted in future calamities such as during cyberattacks, terrorist attacks, or natural disasters, they both allow for working remotely, managing with reduced staffing, minimizing unsafe interactions in the physical workplace, faster upscaling, and a higher level of redundancy.

Operational Flexibility: Integral with scenario-based planning is the need for provisioning for greater operational flexibility. This can amount to provisioning hybrid workplaces, automation, diversified supply chains, distributed locations, and so on. This can very well increase costs, but if a proper balance is struck, it will ensure survival and success. The pandemic has even shown the value of striving for a diversified customer base as the situation became coupled with a conflict between US and China that resulted in consumer-driven or government-driven blockade of certain organizations. Similar situations may likewise evolve during future such crises.

Expanded Financial Lifelines: For any future disruption of any nature, having a war chest of financial resources will come in handy when activating risk mitigation measures. This calls for reviewing working capital policies and receivables characteristics, provisioning for adequate insurance and lines of credit, equipping the organization for financial scenario forecasting, and providing basic training for relevant staff on tracking and leveraging government support schemes.

We hope that the current pandemic is contained as soon as possible and no such future disruptions occur in our lifetime. Regardless, it is important to note that in many ways the capabilities that are required to survive and rebound in the context of such disruptions are not that different from running a good organization during normal times. This awareness should provide a sufficient imperative for organizations to prepare themselves accordingly.

As David Frigstad, chairman of consultancy firm Frost & Sullivan, says, "Only a small percentage of organizations survive major transformations. COVID-19 provided many organizations, including Frost & Sullivan, an opportunity to do something remarkable. It gave us a unique opportunity to pull completely out of our chaotic lives of meetings, events, and business travel, and forced us to be stuck at home, working together as a team, to diagnose, analyze, design, and plan the most significant transformation in Frost & Sullivan's history, while preparing us for future similar disruptions. Organizations should take the lessons from the pandemic and embrace simplicity, invest in the future, integrate a digital experience, and accelerate adoption of technologies like data analytics and AI. In a nutshell, organizations should plan for the panic, if not the pandemic."

About the Authors

Shivaji Das is the managing director – Asia Pacific and Partner with Frost & Sullivan. He has over 17 years of experience in strategy consulting with specialization in areas such as new business models, emerging technologies, and innovation and has provided strategic direction to a diverse set of clients across the US, Latin America, Africa, and Asia. Shivaji is the author of four travel memoirs and photography books. His other books include the Amazon number one best-seller *The Other Shangri-La* by Konark Publishers (India, US). Shivaji's work has been featured in *Time*, the *Economist*, the BBC, *Asian Geographic*, and more. He is the conceptualizer and director of the biennial Global Migrant Festival, a cultural festival showcasing issues related to refugees and low-wage migrant workers. He is currently based in Singapore.

http://www.shivajidas.com

Aroop Zutshi is the global managing partner and executive board member at Frost & Sullivan. Over his management consulting career spanning 30 years, Aroop has been instrumental in Frost & Sullivan's global expansion across 38 countries. He is a thought leader in the industrial automation and mobility industries and is regularly featured in the global media, including CNBC, the BBC, Bloomberg, and TV Asia, to name a few. He has spoken at various industry forums such as WEF, SPS Show, Growth Innovation Leadership Council, and more. Aroop works with Fortune 500 companies in designing their growth strategies. He is passionate about leadership skills and has recently developed a one-of-a-kind leadership coaching program. An avid traveler, having visited more than 80 countries worldwide, Aroop has learned the art of working in different subcultures and has tried over 100 types of cuisines.

Janesh Janardhanan is a senior director with Frost & Sullivan. Over the last 17 years, Janesh has advised clients in the Asia Pacific region, the Middle East, South Asia, and Europe on best-in-class growth strategies in industries including the environment, energy, aerospace, defense, security, transportation, and logistics. He also advises government agencies on policy formulation and roadmaps. Janesh has been featured on the BBC, CNBC, NHK, *Straits Times* Singapore, *Business Times* Singapore, *Economic Times* India, *Khaleej Times* Middle East, and more. Janesh is an alumnus of the Harvard Business School and the National University of Singapore. He is currently based in Singapore.

Index